JANE
FONDA
Michael Freedland

A BIOGRAPHY

JANE FONDA

Michael Freedland

WEIDENFELD AND NICOLSON LIMITED · LONDON

For Fiona, Dani and Jonathan, the apples of a father's eye.

Published in Great Britain by
George Weidenfeld & Nicolson Limited
91 Clapham High Street
London SW4 7TA

ISBN 0 297 79102 8

Printed in Great Britain by
Butler & Tanner Ltd
Frome and London

ILLUSTRATIONS

ACKNOWLEDGEMENTS

As always, this book is a combined effort. It could not have been written without the considerable help of a great many people, particularly those who over a considerable time allowed me to discuss with them the career of an artist whose worth is perhaps only now being properly assessed.

Some did not want to be named. But among the others who granted me interviews, I would particularly like to thank: Nicholas Coster; the late George Cukor; Peter Donat; Robert Dunlap; Julius Epstein; Mike Gray; Johnny Green; the late Laurence Harvey; Jacqueline Hyde; John Philip Law; Winnie Long; Joseph Losey; Penelope Milford; Rosemary Murphy; Ida Nudel; Patricia Resnick; Rod Taylor; Mark Rydell; Daniel Taradash; and Roger Vadim (in the course of a long interview originally for the BBC).

More thanks than I can possibly express are due to Mira Broder for simply magnificent research help in Los Angeles. I also have reason to thank, in particular, Linda Wayne, Stacey Silver and my son Jonathan Freedland, as well as to the librarians of the Academy of Motion Picture Arts and Sciences in Beverly Hills and of the British Film Institute and the British Library in London, and highly significantly the officials of the FBI, Washington, who made available the copious Jane Fonda file.

Finally, to my wife Sara, as always, my appreciation for her simply being there to advise and comfort.

Michael Freedland
Elstree, 1987

J ane Fonda was a poor little rich girl who didn't realize how poor she had been until she was rich in her own right – and who had no idea how rich that was until other people started resenting her money.

So she became a left-winger involved in causes that seemed to scare the life out of even the sort of people Senator Joe McCarthy not long before had sent to jail for being Communists. Such is the power of an upbringing denied to most mere human beings. Her main poverty came from having very rich parents – so rich that she thought that was the only way people were. She lived in a rich neighbourhood, went to school with other rich children and had no idea that everyone else couldn't get precisely what they wanted simply by making a telephone call to the neighbourhood grocery store or the butcher or the . . .

What she also had no idea about was that there were some people whose parents were home all the time, who didn't shout and scream and who didn't vent their frustrations in ways that would have psychiatrists rushing to their desks to pen articles for their learned journals.

She also couldn't contemplate that other children who did go out with their daddies on a Sunday afternoon were not swamped by hundreds of strangers at every step they took.

Henry Fonda was a star. Nobody called him a superstar but that was because no one was ever called that in 1937. He was *almost* as super as stars could be – not as handsome to some women as Ronald Colman and certainly without his magnetic English accent; not as romantic as Clark Gable; not as frightening as James Cagney. But there you said it. Stars did not come much bigger than Henry Fonda.

By the time he sailed for England in 1936 to make a picture called *Wings of the Morning*, he already had what years later would be called a fair track record behind him, all of it achieved in a year. His first picture, *The Farmer Takes a Wife*, had been released in 1935 and immediately set people talking. In the next twelve months, he made *Way Down East, I Dream Too Much, The Trail of the Lonesome Pine, The Moon's Our Home* and *Spendthrift*.

The Trail of the Lonesome Pine had been filmed in Technicolor, which made it sufficiently a novelty to set Fonda apart from most of his contemporaries. Neither it nor its predecessors may have been particularly good as movies, but Twentieth Century-Fox, who had made his first picture, already knew they had a valuable commodity on their hands. Henry had signed a two-pictures-a-year deal with Walter Wanger, that then rare breed in Hollywood, an independent producer; and Wanger had lent him to Paramount for a couple of movies, including *The Trail of the Lonesome Pine*. Wanger was paying him $1,000 a week. Judging by what the studios were paying Wanger for Fonda's services, it was a very good deal indeed that the producer had.

By the time Fonda went to London, he was already fixed in many people's minds as everything they admired in Hollywood, a thirty-one-year-old, dark-haired, intense-looking actor to whom many of the young girls in Hollywood had already been delighted to offer themselves – offers that had been accepted.

He had a two-year marriage to Margaret Sullavan behind him, but that only made him more enticing to the young women who found ways of enveigling him to their bedrooms, usually without much resistance.

The studio would allow none of this to get out, but they were happy to promote the name Henry Fonda as the vital new male sex symbol they had at their command which meant that the green and blue tinted pages of the fan magazines were replete with images of those penetrating dark blue Fonda eyes staring at women who swooned under the hair dryers.

What the studio did not know then was that he would do more than merely make a film in Britain. It was there that he met an American heiress named Frances Seymour Brokaw, who had just been left widowed after an unhappy marriage to an alcoholic. The marriage had produced one child, a five-year-old daughter whom Frances had named after herself – Frances.

Frances was a member of what was loosely known as New York society. She was very conscious of her ancestry – with apparent good reason. She was directly descended from Edward Seymour, whose sister, Jane Seymour, was the third of Henry VIII's six wives and mother of his only son, the sickly boy who became Edward VI.

When Frances met *her* Henry she was on a whirlwind 'forget all the troubles' tour of Europe. They immediately began an equally whirlwind courtship, travelling the Continent. Three months later, in September 1936, they were married at an Episcopalian church in New York.

She had one real particular ambition – to have a daughter whom she could name Jane. That child was born on 21 December 1937. It was a girl – so Jane the child became. Not just Jane but Jane Seymour Fonda. For the first years of her life she was to be called by her mother 'Lady Jane' – Frances was clearly hotter on more recent history than she was on the Elizabethan period and had confused her ancestor with the nine-day queen of England, Lady Jane Grey.

When she was old enough to complain about such things, Jane did, but for the first few years of her life she answered to 'Lady Jane', quite oblivious of the fact that it was a mere affectation on her mother's part. Indeed, when she started school at Brentwood, along the road westward from Hollywood to the Pacific coast, all her clothes were marked 'Lady Jane' or 'Lady Fonda'. Such were things to boast about in Hollywood.

So, it may have been thought, was having James Stewart as a godfather – another was Joshua Logan, the eminent stage director – but that was much more common in the film town.

The family had moved to California in Jane's first weeks. Living in New York may have suited Frances's social standing and ambitions, but it was impractical for the work that Henry – or Hank, as all his intimates called him – did. Also, even in 1938, Hollywood with its swaying palm trees and sunshine so constant it was positively boring, seemed a much more pleasant place in which to bring up children.

Frances would go back to New York occasionally, taking Jane with her. When the child was two she went back again – to give birth to their second baby, Peter Henry.

The home in which the children learned to toddle – and to suffer the company of their half-sister, whom they learned to call 'Pan' (two Franceses in the same family were too much for Henry, who treated them all alike) – was a farm house high in the Brentwood Hills in a street called Tigertail Road. It was a highly prestigious road and her neighbours were accordingly of a stratum to match – children of other actors, of lawyers, corporation chiefs, other people who worked in town but could afford the indulgence of pretending to be country folks when the mood took them.

At this stage of their family life, it seemed as though – to use a phrase then current in popular parlance – Frances wore the pants in the Fonda household. She was fussy about the way Henry left his jeans draped around banisters or shirts lying on the floor in the morning. That was not the way ladies and gentlemen lived. Henry was happy to humour her – and to accept that that was the way their children would be brought up.

As she got a little older, Jane would be happiest of all when dressed as though she were about to ride a tractor at harvesting time, but Frances insisted on her looking crisp and clean and on her keeping her rooms equally tidily.

Fonda himself was a dab hand at the little farm, growing organic crops and he liked nothing better than sitting on the tractor pulling a plough. His children never seemed happier than when surrounded by rabbits, dogs or even the wildlife that inevitably crept through their fences. Later, they would have horses to ride.

Their father was an important man. By the time, Jane was old enough to enjoy what she later realized were all-too-rare family outings, he was already the star of *Jezebel, Jesse James, The Story of Alexander Graham Bell, The Young Mr. Lincoln* and, most significantly of all, *The Grapes of Wrath.*

His gentleman-farming exploits of that time made him doubly appreciate both his own good fortune and the torments of the share-cropper he played. It didn't make Jane and Peter appreciate how lucky they themselves were. Henry was nearly always away either at the studio or on location and they saw him too infrequently.

Hollywood was a factory and its employees were all cogs in the various machines it used to turn out its principal product. Henry and his fellow stars may have been cosseted cogs, pampered by the studio, made to feel exceedingly important, paid exceptionally well by any other factory worker's standard – or factory executive's, for that matter – but they were part of the machine nevertheless. The factory owners, the moguls; saw to it that their equipment was well-oiled and ready for action at all times. If that required using the equipment to its full potential, then that was what had to be done.

Fonda no sooner finished one picture than he was off on the next.

Between 1937 and 1939, Henry Fonda also made *You Only Live Once, Slim, That Certain Woman, I Met My Love Again, Blockade, Spawn of the North, The Mad Miss Manton, Let Us Live, Young Mr. Lincoln* and *Drums Along the Mohawk*.

No wonder Jane has very few memories of spending a great deal of time with her father. Perhaps no wonder, too, that the memories she has are of a crusty, bad-tempered man who allowed few of the indulgences young fathers were expected to offer to their children.

Neighbours reported seeing Jane crying a lot. Others said they heard Henry shouting at both her and her younger brother. Working for a big studio made of lot of adrenalin flow but allowed little opportunity for the kind of loving most children regard as their right.

What spare time Henry Fonda did have he seemed to devote to politics. Plainly, more than the Fonda looks were inherited by his children. Henry was never quite as left-wing as either Jane or Peter would be, but to friends like James Stewart or John Wayne, who remained Henry's firm friends despite their firm Republican Party commitments, he was pinker than a bullfighter's cloak. They never suggested that he was a Communist, but there were an awful lot of frowns from people living round Tigertail Road about some of the causes he espoused.

He worked for President Roosevelt at a time when the man with leg callipers in the White House was regarded by some as a Soviet stooge. He campaigned against General Franco during the Spanish Civil War – McCarthy would worry about that – and was what would later be called a 'liberal' in practically every issue that raised its head. If Frances had been a political animal, she wouldn't have approved at all, but that was not her concern.

She was much more interested in her social friends, with whom she corresponded regularly (and, very unusually for those days, she veritably burnt up the long-distance telephone lines between California and New York), and her home and her children. The house and the land on which it stood was something they could agree upon totally.

But there were few people around who thought that Frances was ever very happy. It is not something which, in the long years that have since passed, either Jane or Peter has talked very much about. There are plainly scars which they keep to themselves.

One of Jane's childhood friends, a neighbour in Tigertail Road, remembered for me: 'Jane was a pretty little girl, very shy, strangely enough. Her mother was talked of in the neighbourhood as being a little eccentric. The poor woman changed the colour of her hair every two weeks. And in those days it was very difficult to dye your hair. That seems to be pretty symptomatic to me of something that indicated great insecurity and probably unhappiness.

'Looking back on her now, I think she must have been trying all the time to be a different woman to Henry. I remember not recognizing Mrs Fonda half the time, because she always looked different. One day she had red hair, the next it was brunette, then she was blonde. But she was a very dear and sweet woman, who I knew was very tortured. My mother used to say Frances was madly in love with Henry.'

Fonda liked the rural life a great deal more than he liked Hollywood. His children swam in a pool that was designed as a rustic lake. They played in hills and fields, had bobcats as close neighbours.

Henry used to give the impression that he would have been happiest had he spent *all* his time with the bobcats and various forms of animal life. He would say that getting on to his tractor or working with a saw in his hands, a carpenter's bench in front of him, was a form of therapy. Maybe that is fairly close to the truth – certainly closer than his frequent statements that this was the only kind of life he wanted.

Nobody told him he had to work in a movie studio. He was by now rich enough not to worry about his next cheque from the studios – who didn't as yet have him on any long-term contract, in any case – and he could have happily spent his time (and Frances's inherited wealth) doing the things he really enjoyed doing.

And he did enjoy the fame and the money his acting brought him. It also seems difficult to accept that he could have done quite so well and been quite so impressive working in a field he professed to hate so much (to say nothing of carrying on acting into old age and when he was very sick, a time of life when he certainly could have afforded changing his lifestyle for good).

Jane for her part was not able to understand why she didn't see more of her father. She couldn't accept that Henry Fonda's job made him any different from all the other fathers she knew. There *were* people living in Tigertail Road who did fairly ordinary jobs. To Henry's credit, perhaps – and possibly to Frances's, too, because she appears not to have made too much of it either – Jane never considered her own daddy's occupation to be particularly special.

But this was the film-star belt, just the same. You drove into Tigertail Road – it wound round and round, just like a tiger's tail – via Crown Drive, where Lana Turner lived. Jane's friend recalled: 'Van Heflin lived two doors down, and *I* was very close to his daughter. We went to the same tea parties. You'd see movie stars walk in and out of the house and you wouldn't even think about it. Things were very normal. You would know that husbands would get upset with wives and wives would shout at husbands and they happened to be movie stars. But it was just normal behaviour. Everybody was like that. Only we were rich kids. Everybody was rich. And you'd go out walking the dog and see Henry Fonda and the other people driving to the studio at five in the morning.'

If a much older Jane Fonda is to be believed, the artificial world of film-stardom struck her even at this stage in her life. It made her, she was to say, decide to keep well away from the domestic world of the movie actors and actresses when she was old enough to be one herself – although she never said that she didn't want to *be* one herself; just not to live near them.

The vow was taken at this terribly early time in the existence of Jane Fonda, she maintains, that when she grew up she wouldn't live in Brentwood. And certainly not, she decided a little later on (when she found out the place existed), in Beverly Hills.

As she said: 'I'll never go back there to live. For every swimming pool you can count a psychiatrist and a kid alienated from its parents. If you grow up with privilege and on top of that you're a movie star – there are some cancers that work their way into your soul.'

She was, as they say, speaking a book. No one can now be sure whether she was also speaking with the advantage of 20/20 hindsight or simply recalling all that she felt at that time. Some people go back to childhood memories with spectacles that have been coated in distinct hues of rose and violet. Jane has allowed herself the privilege of remembering her childhood with varying degrees of hatred.

Her brother Peter shares those memories with even more – much more – bitterness. He once said: 'We wanted the intimacy that [Henry] had with his pals, Richard Rodgers, Oscar Hammerstein, John Wayne, John Ford, Ward Bond, whose pictures hang in his New York house. But it never happened.

'He had an image of us as nice, clean kids, just like those stupid photographs.'

Those 'stupid photographs' were the one that the studios liked to rush out for the fan magazines. It wasn't only the stars themselves whose images would burst forth from those publications over which girls and older women would drool. Their families were virtually created over again, as much as the stars themselves were built up in the make-up departments.

Photographers came to the house to take pictures of the Fondas at leisure – sometimes with Jane allowed to be something resembling herself on the farm, but more usually with sashes and bows which she positively hated. Sometimes they were made to smile and laugh and chase each other for 'home movies' released by the studios as the best way they knew to get over the kind of public relations they thought important.

Children are the best actors and actresses in the world and the Fonda kids were scared enough of their father to play the game. It did not mean that they had to enjoy it, however. Or again, it did not mean that they had to remember that they enjoyed it. As Peter said: 'We wondered, what did we two innocent kids do to get so screwed up?'

Jane has always been *slightly* less forthright about this 'problem'. But she said: 'I've always been ashamed of privilege. I've never understood why the people who have a lot are the ones other people are trying to give things to.'

At other moments, she has been far more charitable, following a party line more to the liking of the Establishment. As far back as 1962, she said: 'I had marvellous parents. They gave me a great deal of love. But the circumstances were a little strange. In fact, they were very abnormal.'

It was perhaps polite language for saying much the same thing. In 1962, people were on the whole a great deal kinder in the sort of memories they allowed themselves than they would be a quarter of a century later. They hadn't yet discovered how to kiss and tell – fully, at least. And certainly Jane was herself on the threshold of a career that promised to be exciting.

There were other theatrical families who had done well without a great deal of scandal attaching to themselves and she was to look at them with a considerable degree of envy. As she said: 'A firm foundation as a child is what counts. I see the Mills family and think, "How marvellous!" They have this fabulous family unit to work from. If you do not get something you need in your own childhood, you may try more than anyone else to establish it as an adult. But the *need* for something doesn't mean you have the ability for it. If you have a stable pattern in your parents, you are more likely to be stable yourself.

'I'm well aware of the fact that there is a pattern I might follow,' she said in a statement that was particularly revealing.

According to Jane's childhood friend, there was little then to indicate that she had something she intended to rebel against in years to come. At the very top of the road, where the street ended, was the Fondas' sprawling great ranch.

'Today,' remembers this friend, who is in the real estate business, 'it would be a six- or seven million dollar home. It was the sort of place where movie stars lived. We played with the children of Hollywood people, other stars, directors and producers. The whole place was infiltrated by people in the movie business. Not that we ever thought much about it. My father was an attorney. We both had friends whose fathers were accountants. Jane was just one of those kids whose fathers were movie stars.'

And indeed, nobody told Jane that her father *was* a film star. She later said that she couldn't understand why Henry so frequently grew a beard or what would today be called 'designer stubble' and then shaved it off again. She just took it for granted that fathers were surrounded by a lot of people their children didn't know.

If she had been privy to all the details, she might also have concluded that it was equally usual for the first wives of fathers to be close neighbours. Margaret Sullavan had by now married the biggest agent in Hollywood, Leland Hayward, and lived near them. The Hayward children played with the Fondas.

Whether Frances secretly feared that her husband was carrying on an affair with his first wife cannot be known for certain, but the coolness between the two women at times seemed close to being paranoid. They were both highly strung and their behaviour was seen by other mutual neighbours as unusually protective of their own children.

Nor did Jane know anything about the chic world that surrounded Hollywood and its neighbouring suburb of Beverly Hills. Blue jeans were still more her favourite and regular clothes than the kind of frilly young dresses that Shirley Temple had made most young mothers want for their daughters.

Jane certainly wanted things that way. In fact, what she really wanted to be was a boy. When a stranger to the neighbourhood pointedly asked her if she were a boy or a girl, she was so excited she could hardly sleep that night. It was precisely what she wanted people to ask.

In fact, she would later say that she wanted to be a boy until she was twelve years old – an age when she discovered that perhaps it was 'all right' being a girl.

There is not the slightest doubt that for all the difficulties in their relationship, Henry was much more of an influence on Jane and Peter than Frances was. There was something mysterious about this man who came and went without their knowing anything about him; who one day would be dressed like a business executive or a politician and the next gave the impression that he was more likely to be lining up for a bus – if he could raise the fare – then to travel in the family sedan.

When they were thought sufficiently mature, the children would be allowed to see some of his films, the more suitable ones, of course.

Years later, Jane would say: 'The way I was affected by the movies was that my father brought it home with him – not the business talk, not the movie-star bit, not the glamour, none of that, because he separated it very well.

'But he did look the way he looked in the movies. And he brought home the people that he was in pictures with. John Wayne, John Ford, Ward Bond, Jimmy Stewart – they were company at the house.'

She remembered their playing a game called 'pitch'. If that didn't bring the movies and the part Henry played in them back to the house in Tigertail Road, then Jane's memories were for a time somewhat distorted. As she explained, 'pitch' involved their sitting around a big card table, wearing cowboy hats – they were all in their thirties and forties – and with gun holsters around their waists. Then they'd take the guns out and put them on the table in front of them – and play cards.

Frances was not a part of any of this, which could account, too, for the changes of hair style and the seeking for a new identity to tempt her husband. She would say that her main concern was looking after her children – which she appears to have done to excess. Many of the things said about Joan Crawford in *Mommie Dearest* seem to apply to Frances Fonda. She may not have complained about wire coat-hangers, but she certainly did insist on all clothes being folded neatly. In fact, neatness practically *was* godliness.

Both Jane and Peter seemed to have accepted this as part of life. As much, in fact, as Jane accepted being called 'Lady Jane'. By the time she was five, however, Jane was a little less acquiescent. Sometimes she would forget to fold her clothes at the end of a busy day and sometimes she would earn her mother's wrath for so doing. Even worse, though, she hated being called 'Lady'. Before Jane was entertaining guests to her own sixth birthday party, she had buried the name completely. No more would anyone call her 'Lady'. Or, more precisely, no more would anyone *dare* to call her that.

'I just stood up in class,' she later recalled, 'and announced that I was to be known as Jane from then on.'

It was the style of statement that in later years would make the Nixon administration quake.

If Jane felt deprived of a normal family life at this very early stage in her life as the daughter of a top film star, it was nothing compared with what was to come when she was five years old.

The Japanese bombed Pearl Harbor and thirty-seven-year-old Henry Fonda was among the first to be called up. He was a lieutenant, junior grade, in the United States Navy, serving as an assistant operations officer. The Navy had wanted him to make recruitment films, the task of most of the wartime intake of troops from Hollywood, but Fonda opted for sea duty.

Henry was to be somewhat miffed, not by being away from his children but by their reaction to his going away. They seemed to resent their father the sailor much more than Daddy the actor.

The senior Fonda reacted toughly: 'It gets boring to hear them say they missed Daddy when they were young. So I should apologize because a world war came along and I had to go away or because I had to work while the kids were in a beautiful farmhouse out in Brentwood with their friends and horses?'

'That's all a crock,' Henry was quoted as saying, although no one explained what a 'crock' was and he could be a more frequent user of what he would now probably call 'wardroom' language than before.

Jane, of course, never heard any of it. By now she wore a pink ribbon in her hair, and Henry and Frances did their best to make her feel like a young lady. She didn't terribly enjoy that role; even less did she like the comparisons with the Margaret O'Brien types who were the 1940s equivalent of curly-haired Miss Temple.

But there were other problems – all of them connected with Henry's return from when the war ended in 1945.

Jane was not just a stranger to her father – and he to her – but an alienated stranger, too. Whether she was old enough to realise that there was something special about a man and a woman sharing a bed cannot and should not be a subject for speculation, but there was now an unfamiliar face sitting down for the occasional – and because he was anxious to get back to work, family meals were mere occasions – breakfast or dinner. What right had he to do that? What right had he, furthermore, to give instructions to her or to Peter? This was their home this man was in, not his. The fact that he had paid the money for that house had nothing to do with it. It was an alienation that it would take virtually the rest of Henry's life to really get over.

Getting back to family life in late 1945 was as hard for Henry Fonda as it was for literally millions of other war veterans. In a way, though, it was worse for someone in public life, who was expected to pose for all those publicity pictures that studios insisted on taking of a smiling Henry cuddling his newly-found children.

And newly-found was precisely how they felt. Their father was practically a stranger to Jane and Peter.

It has been said that Henry felt a stranger in his own house – it was not the house he had left. In the old regime, he had been content to be bossed by Frances, putting up with her mores which were never his, playing the delicate, elegant Eastern gentleman he had never wanted to be. Now, though, his Navy experience had told him that he could be boss and he was determined to be so.

He and Frances rowed constantly and even when they were not shouting, the coolness between them seemed to come straight out of the spanking new white refrigerator in the Fonda kitchen. That, too, as we shall see, was characteristic of the man who now liked to consider himself master of the house. The fights were rare demonstrations of human emotion.

It has been suggested that Jane was totally oblivious of the way her parents felt. If she was, she was a very strange young child indeed. Eight-year-olds have antennae that pick up signals of marital discord much in the way that dogs can hear whistles inaudible to the human ear. She may not have given any outward signs of being aware of what was going on, but aware she certainly was.

If she accepted the norm of the life she was supposed to live on the outside, inside she was being torn apart by what was happening at home. But she may have given little indication of the way she really felt.

To the Hollywood set, children's parties were as much social occasions as those to which their parents went. Neither generation enjoyed these functions very much. Jane liked them less than most. These weren't parties where children ate cream cakes and went home with balloons. They ate the most expensive food – with lots of ice cream and cakes – that the Beverly Hills emporiums could provide, had entertainers straight from the studio books, and wore clothes that were made to delight their mothers. A child who spent most of her time with horses and jack rabbits wasn't likely to look upon such events kindly.

In fact, she hated going to gatherings with dozens of other children. She was expected to conform at these occasions which she saw as something like an afternoon in the county jail. In fact, if truth be told, she would probably have much preferred the jail.

She saw no reason to be polite to a gang of strangers with whom she had nothing in common. The boys were obnoxious to the girls, and the girls, who were dressed in the kind of pink frilly ensembles that 'ordinary' children's parents would have to work a year to pay for, looked as though they wore them every day of the year. To Jane, wearing a ribbon in her hair and a sash around her waist still wasn't far removed from having electric shock treatment.

These kids were frivolous, and if her concern in those days was much more for the welfare of horses or the behaviour of human beings to smaller creatures than it was for any political causes of the day, the seeds were being sown for the social conscience that would become evident a few years later.

But then as she grew older and got to understand both her surroundings and the people who helped comprise them, she was liking the Hollywood life a lot less than her contemporaries. It wasn't a case of social conscience yet, but it was a feeling of unreality.

Being the daughter of a man who played (the terminology was significant, she might one day reflect) a whole lot of different people was one thing, but allowing one's whole life to be overtaken by it all was another.

She wasn't taught how strange it was at school, but it was an instinct and somehow even at seven or eight that instinct came to the surface. She already knew that she would rather live in a small house with perhaps smaller people. But she wasn't beyond being taken in by much of it. Could she really be anything but?

Jane later said that she faced the problems of having a star for a father with a degree of equanimity. As she commented: 'You have to live a special way if you have glamorous parents.'

The only thing wrong with that demonstration of hindsight was that really there was little that was glamorous about life with the Fondas. Henry was certainly stricter than most fathers. They did very little laughing and romping with him and, whether they knew it or not, their mother was very definitely not part of the social set – which Frances regretted more than they could possibly have appreciated.

Almost two generations later, in her film *California Suite*, Jane played a mother fighting for the custody of her daughter. Her own parents were, it seemed, staying together, but she didn't have the secret satisfaction that, should they part, they would be fighting over either her or Peter.

In the way of children like her, she could detect that Henry and Frances were not exactly living in the full blush of marital bliss. Henry's ultra-cool Tom Joad in *The Grapes of Wrath* or his Abraham Lincoln in

Young Mr. Lincoln was very much like the Henry Fonda of Brentwood. Nothing appeared to ruffle him, but most people like to feel they are being ruffled sometimes, that, occasionally, there is an emotional outburst which reflects an emotional kind of love.

But it was a rarefied atmosphere in which the Fonda children lived. When they met neighbours – which may not have been often – they saw the offspring of Gary Cooper or of Laurence Olivier at the height of his brief but significant Hollywood career.

Another friend remembered: 'We were all afraid of Jane's father in those days. We always felt he was a time bomb ready to explode. But it was years later when we actually saw him lose his temper over some forgotten trivia. He was booming, purple-faced, with veins sticking out on his temples. It was the only time I was ever privileged to see what may have been a constant for Lady Jane.'

But like other children of showbiz families, Jane had to learn that things were not going to be nearly as simple as those for 'ordinary' kids, those whose parents had settled jobs in offices or factories. Other children moved from street to street – just occasionally business executives were shifted from one city to another, but rarely. Henry decided that he had had enough of the goose that had laid him a very large, very shiny golden egg.

One day, Jane and Peter discovered they were moving from California. In 1948, Henry was busy establishing a big new career for himself as a Broadway actor. He had landed the title role in *Mister Roberts*, playing the executive officer on an old bathtub of a ship run by a martinet captain who quite plainly laboured under an inferiority complex bigger than anything Arthur Miller in one of his plays might have conceived possible. The show was a huge hit, huge enough for Fonda to decide to move the family out East.

After Brentwood and the Californian open spaces, it would not have been anything like satisfactory to consider simply upping sticks and taking a Manhattan penthouse, but he had to be reasonably 'local' for his work, within commuting distance. So he bought a home for the family in Connecticut, in the highly fashionable town of Greenwich, near where his wife's family lived. That was not a clever move for Henry. If he had wanted his marriage to last, subjecting Frances to precisely the kind of influences that were so totally different from his own was plainly not the way to do it.

The problem was one of communication between Henry and Frances. Their friends noticed it. Josh Logan once told *Time* magazine: 'Frances was not really interested in the theatre so she was always embarrassed to talk about it. She'd talk of children, operations, jewell-ery, the stock market. I often wondered what she and Henry talked about because these are the only subjects Henry couldn't talk about.'

But Frances had other reasons to worry. The Hayward children and their newly divorced mother had moved to Greenwich, too. The old paranoia surfaced once more. Jane and Peter were happy at having their old friends on hand again, but Margaret Sullavan was developing even worse mental problems than Mrs Fonda and it was plainly no atmosphere in which to bring up either set of children. She was highly strung, shouted a lot and set, to most people's way of thinking, a very dangerous example to the young people. She once said, in fact: 'If only I had been Jane's and Peter's mother and Frances had been the mother of my kids, everything would have been all right.'

Ironically, Jane and Peter saw their father more now than they ever had in Hollywood. He worked at night, but during the day – apart from matinées – he was mostly at home. In truth, they could never be sure whether or not that was a good thing. He was no more emotional in Connecticut than he had been in California.

There was, though, one exception to this generalization. He gave them a baptism of fire in what may now be considered to be their introduction to politics – and the kind of 'liberal' issues that would one day occupy them both so much.

When Jane came home mouthing the kind of statement that in Hollywood would have brought the entire film community out on strike, Henry put her right in a way for which she would always be grateful.

The trouble with the community in which the Fondas now lived, Jane pontificated one day after school, was the Jews. 'Since the Jews arrived,' she declared as though reciting details of one of the episodes leading up to the Declaration of Independence in 1776, 'the whole neighbourhood has gone down. Nobody will want to come to live here.'

Henry was visibly shocked. Like a parent deciding that his children would benefit from a certain amount of instruction in the facts of life, he took her aside. 'We don't say that sort of thing in our family,' he told her. What he was also telling her was that they did not believe that sort of thing either.

It was perhaps the first time that he had said anything to his daughter for which she would be able to respect him. It was a good day for the Fonda family. Peter learnt to feel much the same thing – the first flowering of the Fonda political consciousness.

But there was another point to this awakening, too. Good works and good thoughts should, like charity, begin at home. And neither of the Fonda kids really thought that it either began or ended at home – or did anything of the kind in the middle.

Jane went to the Greenwich Academy. In the sixth grade, she was already learning the art of holding an audience entranced. From some source that has never been particularly evident, Jane had developed a good supply of dirty jokes. It was an unusual craft for a little girl, but perhaps Jane's tomboy past had something to do with it. Nevertheless and for whatever reason, she kept the rest of the class enthralled as she went into the anatomical detail of these tales in a shed on the school grounds. She didn't do it merely at school. If there had been badges for such abilities in the Girl Scouts, she would have had an armful of them. As things were, she was thrown out of her troop.

Peter Fonda once said: 'I enjoyed having been born with a platinum spoon up my ass. But I remember being very down on my father for not speaking to me. He was a busy man and I was a hypersensitive kid who needed somebody to talk to, so I reacted quite bitter to him.'

Jane may not have felt quite the same degree of bitterness and perhaps was not hypersensitive to the same extent, but she would have liked more of her father's political beliefs to be related to life in their luxury mansion at Greenwich.

And Frances was coming very closely to the same conclusion. She was finding less and less in common with her husband and the rows were the only times when Henry's emotions were allowed to get the better of his super-cool exterior. They were formidable exchanges that former members of the Fonda staff still recall with a certain excitement.

Greenwich was very much more Frances's milieu than ever Brentwood had been. In a town worried about the influx of Jews into their midst, the chance to have people like the Fondas joining their clubs and bridge championships was enough to make a matron straight out of the Social Register salivate. Henry, however, was not of them and didn't feel as though he wanted to become so. Frances, on the other hand, grabbed every invitation as though it were a call to the Court of St James's. The social butterfly of 1936 had now found a whole crop of 1948 flowers on which to alight at will. If it weren't for the rows with Henry she would have seemed to be in her element, with nothing to cloud it.

But the rows were getting horrendous. Worse, as far as their children were concerned, was the swing in their fortunes with their father. What had not long before been seen as the opening of opportunities that they never had in Brentwood to be with Henry was now quite the opposite. Henry was finding every possible excuse – and sometimes, it has to be said, he didn't bother with excuses at all – to stay in a New York hotel or an apartment he kept rather than make the journey across the state line into Connecticut. The Fonda children once more felt like orphans put out to some very expensive grass with a mother who was the grass widow personified.

None of them seemed to like the life of the Easterner – how could they when in their new home there weren't the bobcats and the other creatures who had become their best friends?

Jane was a Californian girl who resented her transplantation into the other end of the country. She wrote 'I hate the East' on the walls of the house to which they had moved. (Later, when they took a new home, she wrote the same message.)

Worse than this was the fact of *who* Jane was – or rather who her father was.

Californians may have been close to country hicks to the sophisticates of the East, but they certainly had their attitudes to film stars in perspective. Movie people were just folks who worked in the local industry. To those in Connecticut they were close to gods. Jane was treated as though she had carried her schoolbooks all the way down the trail from Mount Olympus.

She was not used to that. Frances, who believed that the nicest young children were seen through a fine gauze rather than heard like the sound of trumpets, thought that was all somewhat unseemly and definitely unladylike. She might herself fancy being part of the social set, but that was definitely not for her daughter. Jane realized this and there was another mental conflict to add to all those she had been accumulating the way her so-called friends were collecting new dolls.

Frances, meanwhile, was accumulating a few notions of her own – mainly that Henry was going to go back to Margaret Sullavan, and all that that entailed. She saw the way Miss Sullavan treated her own children – enforcing a kind of discipline that had previously appeared foreign to her – and concluded that all she was doing was trying to emulate the way the Fonda kids were being brought up. She was right in this. Rivalries between women frequently involve various degrees of inferiority complex. Both Frances and Margaret Sullavan had enough of these to keep the psychiatrists of America in business for a year. And they did. But first Frances was made to wallow in an unhappiness that all amounted to one thing: she was more of a grass widow every day that dawned.

In 1949, that grass looked browner than ever. Henry's East 64th Street apartment was no longer merely a refuge to which he would take when he didn't fancy the longish journey to Greenwich. Much more, it was the 'pad' in which he could indulge his taste for other women. Now he was having a string of affairs that had varying degrees of seriousness, including one with a young woman named Susan Blanchard who seemed to haunt him.

Frances was particularly troubled by her and by what she seemed to represent. She announced that she was suing for divorce, but before it was obvious that she would be happier removed from any ties with Henry Fonda, happiness was clearly the emotion that she felt less than any other.

She was advised to take psychiatric help – which she did.

The rumour over the years has been that she feigned mental illness to bring Henry back to her. This has been compounded by other stories that she was, in fact, seriously ill – possibly suffering from a painful and particularly virulent form of terminal cancer.

Looking back now, these all seem quite fanciful. Frances's behaviour in Tigertail Road and her flirtations with the 'society' life that she believed was her just due *do* appear to indicate a form of mental instability that should have been recognized a great deal earlier. Certainly, Henry should have taken advice and not treated her behaviour as merely a means of 'getting' at him and a reason to seek extramarital pleasures.

The fact is that Frances was recommended to go into a very expensive nursing home at Stockbridge, Massachusetts, that specialized in treating the mental disorders of the rich and otherwise privileged.

She used her presence at this establishment to make the one symbolic gesture that would indicate to everyone around that she wanted to finalize the end of her marriage – which was exactly the opposite of what she really intended – by throwing her wedding ring out of the window of her room.

On 14 April 1950, she went into the bathroom of the nursing home, and pasted two envelopes to the door. One was addressed to her night nurse, a Mrs Amy Gray. It said simply 'Do not enter the bathroom. Call Dr Bennett.' Dr Bennett was the recipient of the second note. 'This,' said the note she sent Bennett, 'is the only way.'

'This' became apparent when the door to the bathroom was opened. Frances was lying in more of a pond than a pool of blood. She had cut her throat.

2

J ane didn't know at first how her mother had died. She was told
that she had had a heart attack – although Jane had little idea
at that age what a heart attack really meant. The New York
papers merely recorded at first that Mrs Henry Fonda had been
found dead. Later they told the truth and those that did were
kept away from the children.

Relatives, friends, schoolchildren – anyone who was likely to come
into contact with them – were all warned to say nothing. Henry's big
fear was that somehow the beans would be spilled – and everyone
knows how cruel children can be to other children.

It is said that her grandparents were principally responsible for
breaking the news and keeping both Jane and Peter on something of
an even keel. Another story has it that Jane discovered the truth while
browsing through a fan magazine. Whatever the precise facts of the
matter, Jane's grandparents were there to help things along.

All sorts of people read all sorts of things into the events that followed
the tragedy. When Frances's will was published, there was plenty to
keep the tongues of friends, and others who were not so friendly,
wagging. The children were the principal beneficiaries of her millions.
Henry got nothing – not that he would have really expected anything
more. She had blamed him for putting her away.

A new home was bought and her Seymour grandparents took over
most of the parental roles, once they moved in with the children.

They were perfect grandparents. Perfect enough anyway to allow the children to carry on being children; not children who had become motherless; not children who had a prominent superstar for a father.

Indeed, Henry was once more a stranger to his children – living his own life, starring in *Mister Roberts*, and with his newer romantic attachments. He was, though, a stranger who visited on occasional weekends. There are children of divorced parents who find paternal visits the hardest part of being from a broken home; they never feel totally attached to the 'visiting' parent and the occasional get-togethers only provide a disruption from routine. Jane suffered all that. She also suffered, as millions of other children have suffered, the news that her father planned to marry again.

He and Susan Blanchard decided to marry just as Jane was about to celebrate her thirteenth birthday. One friend of the time told me that she behaved as though a second tragedy was about to affect her immediate family circle. Other reports say that she treated the whole thing with a degree of incomprehension – her stepmother-to-be was only ten years older than she was herself – and a sense of fascination. She probably judged, rightly, that it would not affect her very much. Henry Fonda was hardly part of her intimate life. If he had been a peripheral figure before, he was to be much more of one now.

It all affected Peter a great deal more. He and Jane were on holiday at the time. Peter heard the news and reacted in a way even he wasn't totally able to understand afterwards.

No one has ever satisfactorily explained how it happened, but the fact is Peter found a .22 calibre pistol and shot himself – through the liver. He later said that he had no intention to do himself irrevocable harm, simply to punish Henry for all he had done and scare the living daylights out of him. In fact, he almost forced the life out of himself. Doctors battled for hours to save him – after the boy had had to beg the family chauffeur to drive him to hospital at Ossining, which was fortunately close to Sing Sing prison where such things were not unknown.

His action provided a great deal more thought and consideration in the family than Peter might have thought possible at the time.

Certainly decisions had to be made – and one of those made jointly by Henry and his parents-in-law was that Jane should go away to school, to an establishment for young ladies whose mothers generally did not commit suicide and whose younger brothers rarely took .22 pistols to shoot themselves. Many of them, however, did come from broken homes, and they were all from families whose financial situations were a greal deal more secure than their emotional states. Jane, it was thought, would have a great deal in common with the other students at the Emma Willard School for Girls at Troy, New York.

Some people may have concluded that a wooden horse would be the only way of getting into this Troy, for it was a very exclusive place indeed. But the daughter of Henry Fonda, star of *Mister Roberts*, to which everyone who was anyone in the community and the school had gone – and, more importantly, had talked about going to until the neighbourhood cows all came home to their farms – passed all the tests which could possibly be imposed.

She didn't at first – although that would come – find herself admitted to the 'Trojan Women', the elite society at the school. Nor did she find that she fitted into the atmosphere of a place that seemed to be contrary to all the principles this very young girl already had for herself.

Jane reported later that she hated her time at the school. It was all so unhealthy, being locked away in a female-only environment; but Mrs Seymour took the view that that was precisely what was needed for a girl in the midst of puberty. She was not able to look after the child herself properly and she didn't fancy a mixed-sex environment for Jane at this delicate time of her life.

Jane herself would have loved to have gone straight to ballet school. That was the life she envisaged for herself – a slight resemblance to what Henry did, but only slight.

Jane stayed something of an outsider at Troy. She didn't make friends easily and she was afraid that those who did approach her were the kind who liked to go home and boast that they were spending their time with the daughter of Henry Fonda.

That experience, as much as all that had happened at Brentwood, fashioned what would happen thereafter.

In the cushioned state of a starlet of 24, Jane was to say: 'I guess everyone has a certain vision of how they want to grow old. I want to be what I never knew when I was young. I want to live in a peaceful place and have marvellous grandchildren who come to see me and think I am a character.'

That was revealing, too – and probably reflected her views on her own grandparents, of whom she was able to think more kindly than she was of her mother and father.

Even more revealing was the statement she made on another occasion – when she said that she wanted to be a boy so that she could be more like her father. That *is* interesting. So many complexes develop because for years people pretend to revolt against the one thing they admire most. Did Jane admire Henry above all else, and show that admiration by pretending to dislike all that he stood for?

That is more than possible, and also possibly why she disliked her boarding school so much. She was away from Henry and could no longer tell him how much she hated him.

In fact, she for a time became quite happy in his company – and in that of Susan. The new Mrs Fonda was a woman to whom she could relate – vitally attractive with a superb figure, a beautiful face and the kind of joyous personality a gawky schoolgirl would love to have herself and just knows she would never be able to achieve.

She once admitted that she had a crush on Susan – at just about the time that she herself knew that she no longer wanted to be a boy. Both were important and significant stages in growing up.

Her relationship with Susan seemed only to get better. Her visits on vacations and on the occasional weekend gradually got easier. Her father was happier now than he had been when he lived with Frances and that happiness radiated itself to his daughter. His home was a pleasant place to be at this time. His play was a huge success and so was his marriage.

It was helped, too, by the way Jane took to Susan. She not only admired the way her stepmother behaved as a woman, she also accepted that her position at the side of her father was a quite natural one. She didn't hate her for taking her mother's place. On the contrary, she began to think of her as an attractive, appealing second mother.

Peter found it less easy to adapt. He lived in his own world – and in Jane's, too. They used to make up their own plays and act in them. Some would see this as a prelude to the acting careers they would both before long adopt. More likely it was a chance to escape from a world they knew, in varying degrees, was not quite theirs.

Jane was certainly more comfortable with Peter than she was with any of the other students of the Emma Willard school. And far, far happier than with the boys whom she faced at the various social functions to which girls at fashionable boarding schools were subjected. She was not sexually precocious and she regarded these occasions with no more delight than she had the tea parties she had been made to attend when she lived with Frances and Henry at Brentwood.

There were those who instinctively decided that young Miss Fonda was a prissy little thing too big for the sensible buckled shoes that the school prescribed. Being the daughter of a movie star and of the man who caused such a sensation on Broadway was quite clearly a reason for superiority. Jane, they decided, was a snob – but then wasn't everyone else at Emma Willard? Probably not, and Jane wasn't either. It was just that she was intensely shy and her shyness and reticence was to be suffered, not enjoyed.

She was quite good at her schoolwork. Not brilliant, but she worked hard at getting it done. She wanted to please and to her teachers she did just that. They saw the problems with which she lived and seemed to understand. For that reason, Emma Willard was a good investment.

Susan took her own duties as stepmother exceedingly seriously, perhaps much more so than Henry had ever had a right to expect. She would not only talk to Jane the way girls need a woman to talk to them and play and go walking with her, but she went to see Jane at school and followed her progress with the enthusiasm of a woman who might have given her birth. On parents' day, she was there in the fashionable dresses and hats of the period catching everyone's eye – not least Jane's.

She once said: 'I remember Susan – twenty-five and a ravishing beauty – at a parents' day at school. I was so proud of her I almost flipped.'

If Susan appreciated the psychological benefits she was bringing to Jane, she was a very clever young lady indeed. More likely, she was simply very kind, very anxious to make her marriage to Henry Fonda work and as fond of her stepdaughter as the girl was of her. Mutual admiration societies have the most enthusiastic of memberships and rightly so.

It is said that the Seymour family didn't take too kindly to this relationship – particularly when both Jane and Peter started calling her 'mother'. It was possibly an insensitive thing to do – perhaps most insensitive of all on Susan's part for allowing it to happen – except that it made the children happy and that should have been the first consideration. It should also have been understood that these two had been deprived of enough as it was and if they were given an opportunity merely to play at being 'normal', it should not be denied them.

Psychiatrists could have found something in that additional problem to indicate some of the things that would later happen.

For a time, Jane toyed with the idea of moving from Emma Willard. Henry and Susan would surely be pleased to have her at home. Why couldn't she move to a school in New York?

Henry decided he liked his child to be an occasional 'treat' and besides he and Susan were planning to have a baby of their own – it wasn't happening easily and they were contemplating adopting. Jane stayed at Emma Willard and joined the school dramatic society –

playing a boy. She might have preferred to make her debut as a girl. Instead she looked like a fat boy – she was still 'puppy' plump, she had a rounded, almost unisex face and her bosom was a well-kept secret that brought no problems to either the actress, who would have had to find a way to hide anything more substantial, or to the teachers who became producers for the event. She was dressed all in green – tights, hat and feather. The play, Christopher Fry's *The Boy With a Cart*, was put on in the school chapel as a Thanksgiving Day production, one of the high spots of the Emma Willard year.

It turned into an equally high spot in Jane Fonda's life. Everyone told her she would be dreadfully nervous, would hate the pressures it would bring, and would constantly be compared – even then, even in that production – with her father. Yes, she was compared with her father. When the parents and other relatives gathered in the chapel for the play, one glance at the programme told them that the lead was being performed by Henry Fonda's daughter. But she was not deterred by all this.

She loved performing, standing on the stage, acting the role. She didn't want to be a boy in real life any more, but she did thoroughly enjoy playing one on stage. Nevertheless, that of itself did not make her decide to make a career of acting.

It was simply something to do for fun. It made a tremendous change from the other things on the school curriculum. No matter how hard she worked, she was not all that impressed by geography or mathematics or even English. She wasn't particularly sporty either – and sport was not something that nice young ladies were expected to do terribly enthusiastically – but acting was a relaxation, of a kind she might not up to that moment have realized that she needed.

She and the school switched to an older classic for their next production. At the age of sixteen, she was Lydia Languish in Sheridan's *The Rivals*, a play which had figured in the school examination courses on both sides of the Atlantic.

It led more speedily than she could have predicted to her first semi-professional part – playing with her father in Clifford Odets's *The Country Girl* about an ageing actor who takes to drink. Jane would play a small part in the play.

Now that gives the instant impression that she got the role through nepotism – almost correct – because her father wanted it – which was not correct at all. In fact, Henry was firmly against the idea of not only Jane taking to the stage at sixteen but of her being in the same play as he – and, more important, at the same time as he.

The idea came from Henry's sister Harriet, who was on the fund-raising committee of the Omaha Community Playhouse. Harriet had been an actress at the playhouse in her time but had settled down to the idea of letting Henry do the acting in the family. At that time, she didn't think of the two children he was going to have.

When she did know that Jane was not only around but beginning to take up acting herself, Harriet suggested that she might like to join the summer season in which Henry was taking part. Jane loved the notion. Henry, on the other hand, did not. He didn't want his daughter to go into the profession. Certainly, he did not want to have people enjoy the curiosity of seeing father and daughter in the same production. He said 'No, no, no.' And Harriet said 'Yes, yes, yes.'

Eventually, he weakened. But only, he said, on condition that she got in on her own merits. She would have to be auditioned. Harriet agreed. The only problem, however, was how such an audition could be organized. Finally she came to the conclusion that she would do it on the phone.

Needless to say, Jane passed.

Henry was to recall their first talks together about the family craft. It was on the plane to Omaha. It was more revealing than mere chat about the theatre and the way to work on the stage and perhaps eventually on a movie set. Somehow or other, he got carried away. As he said, he found that she was giving him her full attention and was 'listening as one adult listens to another'. She got him 'talking about myself and the rough time I'd had getting started in the theatre. I'd never talked to her just that way.'

In fact, that was the truth. Jane might have said that they had really never talked to each other – *really* talked before. She seemed to have enjoyed the flight immensely.

Henry enjoyed her performance on stage at Omaha just as much. He didn't know that he would. Actually, he had been distinctly fright-ened of the experience. There were two temptations open to him – one, to 'pull rank', as he put it, on her and show her and the rest of the cast (perhaps much more an issue) that he was the big star and she was just another 'bit' player. The other was to turn his back on her performance and just not watch because it was too painful for him.

He might have done that had Jane's role not called for a crying scene. She cried so well, so believably that he almost wanted to go to comfort her, to find out what was concerning his daughter so much.

'She didn't understand,' he said, 'that she'd done what many professionals could not do in a lifetime.'

Afterwards, she smiled as she sidled up to him, as he sweated under his make-up: 'How did I do?' Unfortunately, Henry was never demonstrative enough to really tell her.

What they could talk about was Jane's next step. He decided, with Susan's backing, that the best college for his daughter was Vassar. Young ladies could not possibly have a better university education than this exclusive girls' institution which ranked, or so it seemed, with Yale and Harvard.

Henry told her she was going to Vassar. Almost to their great surprise, Jane agreed. She wanted to go to Vassar. Once there, however, she would have other ideas.

3

For all that was said about it, Vassar was a seat of privilege
and snobbery as much as of education. It gave its girls a first-
rate education in a semi-sheltered atmosphere. In the dorms,
they still talked sex and the other things other girls talked
about. Outside, it was not unknown for certain of their numbers to be
sent home when they got themselves pregnant.

Jane saw the situation at Vassar the moment in 1955 that she was
driven there for the first time, through the gate that was the only
breach in an iron-railings fence at least eight feet high – the college
believed greatly in protecting the girls, from themselves as much as
from any apparently unfortunate outside influences.

None of this indicated that Vassar was intended to be a nunnery.
The professors and teachers didn't think so. Certainly, the students
didn't.

The current adage was that girls from the fashionable East went to
Vassar to be schooled in the Three M's – marriage, motherhood and
the menopause.

And if the last was the least of the subjects under discussion, the
others certainly were of much greater priority. As Jane once said: 'If
you didn't have a ring on your finger by the end of your junior [third]
year, forget it.'

She and her friend Brooke Hayward, who was also sent to Vassar
at the same time, discussed such matters seemingly around the clock.
They were not sure whether they shared the enthusiasm for early

wedded bliss or wanted to rebel against it. This obsessive concern was not unique to young ladies of supposedly fine and definitely expensive breeding.

On the other hand, many of them were allowed to think that they were not a little superior to the poorer young women who were less privileged. Certainly, the word 'Vassar' held considerable charms for not a few society matrons searching for suitable daughters-in-law.

Jane knew all that and didn't care too much for what it represented. When she also saw all that, she cared for it even less.

To be fair, Jane quite enjoyed the social part of life at Vassar. She was popular and once she had satisfied herself that the crowd weren't enjoying her company simply because of her name – and that of her father – she settled down to accepting that there were worse things than privilege. The idea of going into the theatre professionally was eating into her more and more now. But it was more an intriguing idea than an all-abiding passion. Nevertheless, it seemed a great deal more sensible than wasting time on books, classes and the kind of study that in these mid years of the 1950s she was expected to do.

During the vacations from Vassar she wanted to talk to Henry about her future, but all he wanted to do was to discuss her poor grades at college. She had to admit that she wasn't putting all she could into her studies, but she saw no reason to do so. It was all such a *waste*, a word she would use quite frequently now.

Henry did, however, allow that she might benefit from a certain amount of holiday work. When he took a summer house at Cape Cod, he agreed that Jane might qualify for a job as an apprentice at the Dennis Playhouse nearby.

The American Theatre Wing operated its summer workshops there, and Jane was immediately pressed into service for their production of Sheridan's *The School for Scandal*. In this she played two small alternate parts. She was either Maria or the maid, sharing each with an actress named Marianna Courtney. Reading the cast list today seems like one of those revealing moments treasured by collectors of theatre programmes – 'Maid ... Marianna Courtney; Jane Fonda.'

Henry had had some of his own early theatrical experience at the playhouse, which then and now is an American institution – one that answers the question, 'What do actors do in the summer time?' The summer stock companies perform the joint function of entertaining people on vacation and giving professionals a chance to 'fill in' between seasons on Broadway at times of the year when a number of theatres are 'dark'. Henry thought that Jane could benefit by this playhouse, too. Besides which, he was starring there that summer in James Thurber's and Elliott Nugent's *The Male Animal* and he wanted to find a small part for her in the play – one of the strange contradictions in a relationship that was constantly fraught, not least by his unwillingness to see her enter his own profession.

In one scene his cue was a young girl, angrily rushing down a winding staircase and through a door. That was the one he earmarked for his daughter. On opening night, he stood in the wings waiting for her. As she did her storming scene, he just stood and stared. 'His face was shining,' Jane later remembered. Shining with pride. 'It was beautiful,' she said. And she added: 'He stood there in the wings with that wonderful, silly grin he gets, simply enjoying the fact that I was enjoying his profession.' If only all her memories of her father were of 'wonderful silly things'.

Henry remembered the event equally excitedly: 'When she came on, the audience reacted in an almost physical, audible way – a straightening up and intake of breath. What a position to be in, trying to remind yourself that you were her father! If you were any other SOB you'd say, "Get that girl into the theatre," and you'd use a ship to get her there. But of course I never let her know that.'

Which was a considerable pity. She would have benefited both professionally and simply as his daughter if he had let on there was a degree of pride in what she did. Instead, she had to surmise and judge the reasons for the expressions on his face. Part of the time, however, they were enough. She was to say that because those expressions were there, however occasionally, it was the happiest time of her life to date.

If that was really what happened – and not long afterwards she would be reluctant to say anything at all that reflected well on the way she and her father got on together – it was beautiful indeed. But beautiful things didn't happen very often to this pair, at least together. In fact, it was not a good time for the Fondas. Henry and Susan had split up and divorce was only a formality away. To Peter, and to Jane even more so, it was the second time their family had come unstuck. The tragedy of their mother's suicide had come when they were children and they learnt to cope with it the way resilient children do. Now they were teenagers who thought they were wise in the way of the world's emotions, and found it difficult to accept. They knew all the factors involved in human relations and were as disgusted as they were disappointed.

Her father's emotional problems didn't help Jane's professional ambitions either. The story at this stage is somewhat confused once more between what really happened and the sort of stories told afterwards in an endeavour to try to make both sides seem that little bit nicer.

What is certain is that Jane wasn't 100 per-cent sure that she wanted a theatrical career. She has said with the mellowness of time that doors opened much wider to her because she was, in fact, Henry's daughter. Henry has denied it. He said he could have got her an important role on Broadway even then. Undoubtedly he could have won her a Hollywood contract – the phenomenon of being Henry Fonda's daughter alone was enough. But he wanted to do none of these things because ... well, he didn't think it was a very good idea. Generation gap? More likely, it was a generation chasm.

It wasn't any reason to be emotional. Henry Fonda was never emotional and saw no more reason to be so now than at any other time. If Jane wanted a job, she'd have to work for it. And, as far as he was concerned, it was far better that the work she did was at Vassar. She did her time at the Playhouse, not just acting in the plays, but doing her share as a stage manager, learning about make-up and lighting and watching actors and actresses go through their lines in a mechanical way which she knew full well she could improve on herself. But do it full time? She wasn't sure. What she was sure of was that this was a much better way of living than what had for her been the norm until then.

When the time came for her to go back to Vassar, it was like being sent on a return trip to the Siberian salt mines after a temporary reprieve. She hated it, and showed it. This was one of the most undisciplined parts of what was to prove a fairly undisciplined life.

And it gave her a reputation. In the somewhat subdued and even old-fashioned language of 1950s Vassar, Jane was dubbed 'The Anything-Goes Girl'.

She has never denied it. 'When I discovered that boys liked me,' she once said, 'I went wild. I was out all the time. I never studied.' She didn't realise that the sort of boys she herself liked would have preferred it if she offered them more of a challenge. Instead, visitors from Harvard or Yale or one of the other smart colleges not a thousand miles from New York knew that Henry Fonda's daughter was a pushover. And what stories to take back with them!

Her college friends liked to give the impression that they were shocked at some of the things they heard in the sorority rooms. Some of them admired her and secretly wished they could follow her example. Others were worried for her.

At weekends, she would sneak out. Her fellow students giggled about it and on the whole kept her secret. They knew she was already living a fairly active sex life for a well-brought-up girl of 1956.

When Henry married an Italian baroness named Afdera Franchetti, twenty-eight years his junior (he was fifty-two), Jane saw no reason to hold back. She didn't care what her father thought about anything she did. What she did do was as much to spite Henry as to be fun for herself.

Did she really hate her father? It is very unlikely. It is also equally unlikely that she behaved as she did simply because she loved him so very much. She was angry with him. She thought that every time he pleased his own ego, he was letting down Peter and herself.

Just as Peter had shot himself as a cry for help, she was shouting: 'Hey, I'm here, too.' But she was also in a mood to enjoy herself and saw no obligation to do things her father told her to, simply because he did tell her.

The one thing he had not given his children was a sense of responsibility. He preached a great deal but there was not a lot of self-practising in what he said whenever his den at home was used as a pulpit. Ostensibly, he was a Catholic, but religious morals never came into the conversation and indeed he thought about them or his official faith very little.

'What's he done for me?' Jane could be heard to say. And in truth, looking back, there wasn't a very great deal. Jettisoning Susan – Jane's one link with normality and a vague kind of reality, too – was merely the most recent proof that her father was selfish and uncaring. Marrying Afdera confirmed everything she had feared. She no longer had to pretend to love a strange woman who occupied her father's bed. She was old enough to say what she felt and to act accordingly. Afdera asked no more for herself. She wasn't in the least bit interested in Henry's children and would have hated to have any responsibilities towards them.

Henry had met her while in Rome to film *War and Peace*. He played Pierre in this massive Hollywood-extravaganza version of Tolstoy's story, opposite Audrey Hepburn and Mel Ferrer. The film was not a success. Nor was the trip to Rome, as far as Jane and Peter, who accompanied their father, were concerned. Henry had little time for them and when they realized that he had Afdera in tow, they knew why.

Things were even harder because it was in Rome that Peter came across a magazine which told how his mother had ended her life. He not only blamed Henry for keeping this from him, but Jane, too. She was seventeen and was convinced she knew enough of the problems of the world without having this one thrust on her, too. Peter was morose and for a time hated his two closest relatives.

It is said that he got wildly drunk and staggered around the city until 'rescued' by a couple who took the boy home and then involved him in the kind of sexual practices most fifteen-year-olds never know exist, let alone participate in. It was another cause for distrust and further hate.

Jane was doing her own share of hating, too. Once back in America, Afdera had no hold on her. Jane was not about to call *her* 'mother'. Neither did she see any reason to break off the perfectly good and loving relationship she had with Susan.

One weekend while at Vassar, she skipped off with a boy and found one of her professors waiting for her on her return. Many a soldier absent without leave had experienced much the same sort of thing when he crept back to barracks only to find a sergeant waiting. The professor, however, was more understanding than any khaki-clad figure with three stripes on his sleeve.

She had an inkling of what his attitude would be when she rang up the college to say that she was going to be late. She got out those words but nothing else. Somehow, the emotion of it all got to her and she broke down, weeping.

Her monologue to the professor was drowned in tears and sobs. 'Before I got a chance to say I was sorry,' she later recalled, 'he said he understood my father had just remarried for the fourth time and that I was emotionally upset.'

None of that was new for teachers working in girls' colleges. But Jane claims she was nothing like as disturbed as the professor thought she was. 'I wasn't really emotionally upset. I'd just gone away with a boy for the weekend.' The tears were out of fear for what was going to happen to her – and soon.

The talk around Vassar was that Jane was a very exciting young woman indeed, undoubtedly the kind any young red-blooded all-American man would want to be with. But many of them found that she was more than they could deal with. She called the shots sexually and mentally. She needed to control her men, and she did – all of the many who came her way. A girl who considered she was being deprived of her emotional needs at home had to find them elsewhere.

After two years at Vassar, she decided to leave. Henry was none too pleased, but she felt she was simply wasting his money, and that the college wasn't all that pleased about having her either: 'I guess they thought I was a misfit.'

She was a misfit in other regards too. This was before what is generally believed to be the start of the drug culture. In fact, it wasn't. Perhaps not so many youngsters were experimenting with drugs, but it was happening – and Jane was one of those it was happening to. She was regularly using Dexedrine. At the time it was decribed as a 'pep pill'. It was a convenient euphemism for the beginning of an addiction from which it would take her years to escape.

She also had another problem which again was not unfamiliar to Vassar or a great many less fashionable establishments for young females. Jane suffered from bulimia. Ever since school, she had worried about her puppy fat becoming a permanent feature in her life. So she tried to find ways of bringing her weight down. Merely dieting was not the answer, so she found more drastic ways – eating and then vomiting all she had consumed. It was an addiction as strong as any drug – bingeing followed by purging.

This had now been developed into a fine art. Weird mixtures like sandwiches of bacon and peanut butter washed down by as much coffee as her bladder could take were perfect methods of bringing up the entire contents of her stomach. Of course it was unhealthy. She probably knew it was. But it certainly didn't increase the amount of fat on her body.

Little of what Henry was doing was a parental example for his children to follow. Both the wives he had taken after Frances's death were themselves much younger than he was. Now Peter and Jane – they were on friendly terms again – spent odd moments speculating on the age of the next Mrs Fonda and the one who would follow her. Sometimes they would take bets on whether or not a future stepmother would, in fact, be younger than they were themselves.

These were rare moments of levity, however. Once Peter took a mass of drugs and realized in time he was likely to be in trouble. He was at the family's Connecticut home. He was seventeen years old and had enough sense to know that he needed help. He called Jane, who was in the process of finalizing her plans to leave Vassar. She borrowed a car, drove to Connecticut and found Peter hiding in bushes engrossed in a detailed conversation – with himself. She was so worried that she called her Aunt Harriet in Omaha. Harriet then decided to call Henry – who was having a belated European honeymoon. Henry rushed back, but was still unable or unwilling to discuss the matter with either his son or his daughter. The taciturn personality he continually played on the screen was Fonda in reality. Life was not for flapping.

The closest he got to moving out of character was when Jane told him she was going to Paris to study. He hated the idea of her going. But he relented. He seems to have been talked into the notion that it would be fairly close to her going to a Swiss finishing school – the kind of institution Frances would have wanted for her daughter whose objective in life should have been to reach the top of the social ladder.

Conceivably, if life had been simpler for her, Jane might not have been unhappy with that sort of existence either. She was consumed by ambitions – the most significant of which, although she would never admit it, was to make her father proud of her. She was not sure, though, which way to go. 'I wanted,' she recalled, 'to jump in and start playing concertos instead of studying the scales. I wanted to paint masterpieces, but painting became steadily less enjoyable and more difficult to do.' But she was going to Paris to study painting, at the Académie Grande Chaumière.

She had tried painting at home and found that she was quite good at it. Henry, too, had taken up art quite seriously; and even if only subconsciously, she was trying to emulate him in this field, too, although she didn't like what she produced. Nor did she like the way she looked. 'I'm not pretty enough,' she kept telling herself – which was probably another reason why she was always so available to men. Her feelings for Paris, though, represented a different kind of relationship.

It turned out to be the beginning of an on-off love affair with the French capital which would before very long play such an important part in her life.

Vassar was full of rumours about this expedition. The story in its simplest form was that Jane was pregnant and was going over to France to have the baby. In its more lurid guise, she was there to have an abortion. There is no evidence to support either story.

With Henry's blessing, she lived in a world of artists, but without any of their financial constraints. She was never short of the price of a meal at a bistro or comfortable, clean lodgings. When she sat in the Left Bank cafés, she lingered over a single cup of coffee, not because she could afford no more, but because it was the thing to do. She wouldn't have wanted to stay at the Hotel George V.

Jane remembered that she was in Paris to study painting. 'I didn't,' she said a few years later, 'I had a good time.'

Even this, however, has been subject to the revisionist treatment. In another interview – and possibly a more accurate assessment – she said: 'I didn't like it one bit. It's lonely if you don't know a language – you feel they're all enemies. It's just the opposite when Europeans come here. Here we shake their hands all the way to the electric chair.' The sentiment was probably there in the late 1950s, although the bitterness certainly was not.

She was not having the 'fun' she claimed. 'I was nineteen, an age when you know you are not happy but you don't know why, and you think a geographical change will change your life.'

Henry might have concluded that living in Paris – in a Sixteenth Arrondissement apartment that specialized in giving a temporary home to American girls of financial good standing and virtually impeccable pedigree – would change that life for the good. It certainly did not. She might have said that she was just doing the sort of thing her father did himself. But that was not why he arranged for her to live in that particular apartment. It was run by a countess who had fallen on hard times and Henry assumed that his money and Jane's enthusiasm would combine to make sure that the woman looked after his daughter. She did, but not perhaps in the way he might have wished.

To Jane the most abiding memory of the establishment was the fact that practically every piece of furniture there was covered in transparent polythene. But you could see the Eiffel Tower from the living-room window and the girls were able to come and go more or less as they pleased. Which, considering the way Jane's social and sex life was proceeding – Vassar was tame, tame, tame in comparison – was fortunate for her.

It was a time for a whole string of on-off affairs with a horde of men. Jane Fonda was not only eligible, she was extraordinarily beautiful, too. She still took drugs, still was inclined to overeat and over drink and then vomit it all up, but she was startlingly attractive. She did not have much of a bust, but her figure was trim and betrayed no signs of that old puppy fat. Not, though, because of all the work she was doing. 'After a month, I was sleeping more and studying less.' But not everything was entirely negative.

If, as Jane said, she didn't even take out her paints during her time in Paris, it wasn't all just a search for the good time. She thought about learning French, although she didn't get terribly far with the language and was hardly able to forgive herself for the neglect. And through the friends she made – and because her name was Jane Fonda – she had opportunities to meet people in the French artistic world, painters, writers, actors and film directors. Among them was the man who had recently divorced Brigitte Bardot. His name was Roger Vadim. Bardot had starred in Vadim's first movie, *And God Created Woman*, the picture that convinced him he was more a director than an actor or a journalist, two occupations he had tried before. Other people said that his real profession was that of womanizer. When he was introduced to Jane at a party at Maxim's, the general consensus of opinion among those around her was an earnest warning to 'keep away from him'.

The evening was to be firmly and indelibly imprinted on the minds of them both. As Jane said, 'He was with Annette Stroyberg [then his wife], who was very pregnant with – well, my stepdaughter, and I'd only heard the bad things about him. How he was a cynical, vicious, immoral, Svengali-type character. I was very aggressive because I'd only heard the legend.' The legend was at work that night.

Not many words passed between them, but gestures there were a-plenty – and they were obvious to everyone around them. Vadim made it clear that he found her intriguing, but since he was with his wife decided to do nothing about it – for the time being, at least. Meanwhile, Jane was never without company – mostly the kind of people who made Henry quake when he heard about them.

Those who met her for the first time now were struck by the undeniable resemblance she bore to her father. It was almost uncanny that not only a father and daughter could look so much alike but that male and female relatives could have such similar voices. Henry's was, of course, much lower in register than hers, but the timbre was so similar it would have been picked up by sophisticated voice-print machines.

Perhaps the most important part of her time in Paris was that it enabled her to assess her future. She had gone to France not really knowing what she was going to make of life. Certainly, she had no ambitions to be a painter – it was simply a means to an escape and she took it no more seriously than the way she had, in her heart, taken her early theatrical experiences. Now, though, she gave it all another thought. The theatre? This could be the means of making use of the similarities with Henry.

The resemblance was not enough. She may have disliked much of what he seemed to stand for. They may have been on different wavelengths and the chasm no nearer bridging than before, but she was now determined to follow his profession. Back in the United States after her six months in Paris, she told him she was going to learn acting.

It was a summer in California that persuaded her to take acting seriously. She worked as a script girl for Warner LeRoy, son of the eminent director producer Mervyn LeRoy and grandson of Jack L. Warner of Warner Bros. – who liked to talk of his efforts to get Henry Fonda on his rosta of performers almost as much as he told everyone he had 'invented' talking pictures by getting Al Jolson to star in *The Jazz Singer*. Jane was offered a small part in *The FBI Story*, as James Stewart's daughter. But she turned it down when Henry treated the offer disparagingly. 'You don't want to start your acting career as Jimmy Stewart's daughter,' he told her, and for once she took his advice.

It was the first proof that he accepted that she was going to have an acting career after all. And she was sure that she was going to be an actress. First, though, she had to find ways of learning what she was determined would be her craft. She enrolled for a course in acting with the man who ran the most prestigious workshop in the United States – the Actors Studio.

4

The Actors Studio, run by Lee Strasberg, had a hallowed name among a certain clique of theatrical performers. Marlon Brando was one of its most celebrated alumni. Marilyn Monroe once started to study there. Based on the teachings of Stanislavsky, it was the temple of what was then known as 'The Method'. Briefly, this was the belief that if an actor played, say, an alcoholic, he had to draw on his personal life-experience to *feel* as though he were an alcoholic. An early exercise in some Method-type establishments was for a student to bend an arm in the shape of a triangle, move his trunk to one side and let the left arm hang at a forty-five degree angle, pointing to the ground. 'I am a teapot,' he would declare joyously – and as he 'poured', supposedly, a teapot he felt.

It is no secret that Henry Fonda thought the whole Method business not a little potty – whereas, for example, his near-contemporary Gregory Peck was a great admirer of the technique – and he tried to discourage any association that his family might develop with it.

Acting, he believed, was learnt in the 'doing' – on stage or by apprenticeships in playhouses such as he himself had had. The rest was merely playing – even it were playing at 'playing'.

It took all the efforts of Strasberg and his wife Paula – who ran the place much as Golda Meir was eventually to run Israel – to persuade Henry that having his daughter take lessons was a good idea after all.

Not in the studio itself, to which admission was restricted, but private lessons with Strasberg.

Henry was, however, partly won over by the fact that he himself was playing with the Strasbergs' daughter, Susan, in the film *Stage Struck*, at the same time as he was acting on the Broadway stage in *Two for the Seesaw*. It gives some idea of how much of a seesaw was his own life; acting in a film during the day and a play at night. His new wife was not greatly happy.

It has been said that Jane fought not to become an actress. That is totally untrue. What is more to the point is that she wasn't *sure* she could do it. When she contemplated a career 'on the boards' she was gripped by a fear many another actor or actress would easily recognize; it was not dissimilar to that of being prepared for open-heart surgery.

So she thought it was not a bad idea to try something totally different.

Go back to painting? The thought of failure – an occupational hazard in all actors, whether relating to their craft or not – was too overpowering. But when she reflected on her attempts with the easel in Paris, she realized that one thing her stay in France had taught her was that her ineptitude with the language hindered her intellectual progress – and that *was* important. So while she waited for a decision on entering Mr Strasberg's premises, she enrolled for courses at one of New York's Berlitz schools. She determined to study French and Italian. She willed herself to do well and she did. Then she began her studies with Strasberg.

Strasberg offered some of the paternal guidance she sought but usually failed to get from Henry. 'He talked as if he were interested in *me*,' she said in one revealing statement. It was 'not because I was Henry Fonda's daughter. He could sense that I wanted to act but was afraid to.' His task was to persuade her not to be afraid.

Jane loved working with Lee – who said he took her because of 'her marvellous eyes'. He denied that her being a Fonda had anything to do with it. But even the most reticent outfit would recognize the tremendous publicity value in having the child of an outstanding superstar studying with them – learning from their own teachers and not from her father, who it might be thought, would teach her all that he himself knew. Strasberg's classes, in the Actors Studio and outside it, found out what his pupils really offered. Jane offered a great deal, he came to agree.

Predictably, Henry did not want to know anything about either the Method or the Actors Studio. When Jane tried to talk to him about what she had learned, he would either feign boredom or change the subject. At other times her studies got him more annoyed than almost anything else – practically as much as at Jane's less than enthusiastic comments on his latest marriage; *those* statements virtually set his hair alight.

In the rare moments when they could actually sit down and talk, his lack of enthusiasm was daunting. 'I used to come home from Lee's classes,' Jane later recalled, 'so full of what I was doing and my father would say, "Shut up. I don't want to hear about it."'

Jane, on the other hand, *did* want to hear about it. She wanted to know about everything her teacher could tell her. She would claim that everything for her altered as a result of being with Strasberg. 'Night-and-day difference,' she called it. Walking into the room for the first sessions with Strasberg was like switching on an electric light bulb.

The problem was to keep it glowing and lighting up her surroundings. It did. In a way, it was the most satisfactory part of her life. She revelled in the classes and Strasberg was equally excited about her and the way she responded to what he said.

But Henry continued to show boredom at what she was doing – or at least she thought that he did. In one interview she claimed that talking to him about her lessons brought 'his curtain' down.

Henry was disturbed to hear that she said so. In an interview with Alfred Aronowitz in the *Saturday Evening Post*, he said, 'I don't understand this. Maybe I'm ... maybe I do things that I'm not aware of that mean something to other people. I don't know what she means by a curtain coming down. It may be that I'm trying to hide my own emotions, and to her it's a curtain coming down.'

That was revealing in itself – an admission by Henry Fonda that, yes, he did try to hide his own emotions, as though an actor's craft meant that he had to sublimate all his own feelings so that he could really feel the part he was playing. Wasn't that what 'Method' acting was all about? And he proceeded to tell a story which he said explained a lot – about an event before she decided to become an actress.

'She was with a young beau of hers who was just getting started in the theatre, and he and I were talking about using an emotion, having to feel an emotion on the stage. I told him about the process I go through, likening it to a seaplane taking off.'

At first it is a slow, sluggish procedure, but eventually, it gets ready to soar. That, he said, was how acting should be. He said that several years later, Jane told him that she had been through that process herself. But suddenly, she had started to soar.

He told Aronowitz: 'I can get emotional right now remembering Jane tell it, and probably the curtain came down to hide that emotion. Because for my daughter to be telling me about it – she knew what it was like! Well, I wasn't going to let her see me go on like this.' As he said, Jane might be demonstrative, but he wasn't.

Until that moment, when she felt that she was starting to 'soar', acting continued to be something that would never come easily. Now she believed there was hope.

'I was terrified of acting,' she recalled a couple of years afterwards, in 1960. 'I was afraid of making a fool of myself . . . But once out there, it became vital to me.' Apart from the nerves she suffered, there was another problem. She knew that she was inherently lazy. Strasberg got that out of her system. He didn't just teach acting and the Method. He taught discipline. It was perhaps the most important thing that he did teach.

In the plays in which she took part, she was as promising as she was keen. If one sought a single word to describe what this young woman was offering it could only be 'talent'.

The problem was one of financing her classes. Certainly, Henry wasn't going to help her. Even if he didn't physically stop her from going, he became more and more opposed to the school and was not likely to do anything that would make it easier for her. So she had to look for work. She was a model and photographed so well that before long she was adorning practically every magazine cover in the nation.

And she worked – taking her cue, although he didn't yet know it, and possibly neither did she, from her father.

In one of their rare moments of conversation, she had asked him how he knew when a part was really right for him. He told her 'Reading a script should be like meeting an old friend.' When she came across one particular play in 1958, she knew that she was not only meeting an old friend, but, as she put it, herself.

The play was *Invitation to a March* by Arthur Laurents, whose biggest success, *West Side Story*, with music by Leonard Bernstein and lyrics by Stephen Sondheim, was still ringing in people's ears. But it wasn't any quasi-Romeo and Juliet story that intrigued her now.

This play had a role for a girl called Norma, supposedly from a good home, who after a couple of college years and a difficult romance, decides to find out something about the world.

Her agent had warned her not to even try for the part, but she insisted, read for it and was offered the role.

She knew she was good. But she also couldn't avoid the thought that yet again it was because of her name that the part came to her. Was even a man of Laurents's standing going for her simply because she was Henry Fonda's daughter? After all, the intriguing publicity alone wouldn't hurt and could bring in some wavering, inquisitive theatregoers who might otherwise have stayed at home.

One can never be sure whether or not this really did happen. She herself was to say in 1960 that having the Fonda name couldn't really have been any hindrance. 'Hindrance? If I weren't his daughter, it would have taken me years to push through the doors. Just his example helps. I watch him and see why I should do something in a certain way. It's a professionalism he has you just can't define. His stage presence, it's never excessive or unnecessary; it's a complete use of himself without whipped cream.'

Reading this, the cream seemed decidedly whipped in her relationship with her father. It wasn't any more so now than it had been before. But it wouldn't have made good publicity to tell the truth about the way they got on – or rather, failed to get on – together. In any case, at this stage in her life, it was really no one else's business.

What she had to try to do was to convince people that it would be their business to see her acting on stage. She knew it would happen before long, but how long? *Invitation to a March* looked as if it were going to be a good start, but it was not stardom and no one with a name like Fonda would really be content with anything less. But it would take some time to gel and there were other things to do meanwhile.

There was an intenseness about her, a sense of dedication that certainly the staff at Vassar could not have imagined. Teachers there had known other girls before who failed to shine in class, but they usually left the lingering feeling that they were dumb at everything they did. Could it be possible that *any* of them had *anything* at all to offer?

She was going to be the one who did. She looked for work – not, at first, in the theatre, but as a general dogsbody in the New York office of a literary magazine, the *Paris Review*. But it was not the sort of discipline she was looking for. She knew she could be disciplined.

On the whole she was. It did not, however, occupy every moment of her day. She was twenty-one years old and she liked the things other twenty-one-year-olds have. Her relationships with men continued and she fell in and out of love with the speed of Broadway openings and closings.

But she was tormented. She was at the beginning of what would turn out to be years of psychiatric analysis. Henry thought she was mad – and constantly said so – but she would say it helped her.

Her torments were both conscious and unconscious. She had dreams that she thought would drive her mad, nightmares that horrified her when she awoke in cold sweats; like the constantly recurring one of being left alone in a vast, ice-cold house from which she can find no escape. There was another one that came to her night after night – of seeing a dog being run over. Perhaps the most disturbing of all was the continuing one of being insane – and then as a result of that insanity being arrested for a crime she did not know whether she had committed or not.

One night, she was found by a servant sleepwalking – in the nude; she hated being encumbered by nightgowns or pyjamas.

She was also experimenting with other kinds of drugs. For a time both she and Peter tried LSD. She was to say – a statement to be regretted before very long – that she found the LSD experiment 'very beautiful ... the more we can look into ourselves, the more we can see outside ourselves.'

The more Jane could see outside the more she was determined to be a serious actress. And there were opportunities available to her that would make all those girls who hopefully lined up outside agents' offices – and took part in those mass auditions so beloved of the backstage film musical – drool. She was now ready to take them. Jane Fonda was going into films.

5

Anyone knowing the later militant Jane Fonda would perhaps find surprising the way she had financed her drama classes' fees.

Not only was she modelling for magazine photographers, she was doing so with an amazing degree of success. Within weeks, four national magazines featured her on their covers – culminating with the July 1959 issue of *Vogue*. In the $50-an-hour area in which she was working, success did not come much higher.

She never considered that she was in any way demeaning herself; it was simply a job of work, honest toil that she hoped would provide the means for more studies. It also provided the opening to Jane's movie career.

Joshua Logan, one of Henry Fonda's closest long-time friends, saw the *Vogue* issue and decided that Jane ought to be in pictures – his pictures. She was his goddaughter and the possibility offered him an opportunity to exercise his godparental responsibilities.

That is the bare outline of his involvement in her career and like most bare outlines tells only a fraction of the real story.

Actually, his wife Nedda had long thought that Jane was the really talented one in her family. When Joshua heard about her progress with Strasberg, he asked her to come to Hollywood. He never pretended to think that her surname would be of no help to her career. Nedda, however, had different views. She was convinced that Jane would be an asset for much more fundamental reasons – the best of which was that her friend Lee Strasberg had told her about the girl's inherent talent.

Since Henry certainly wouldn't have given him any such message, Joshua Logan was content to take his wife's opinion, especially since he could couple it with the most important recommendation of all: his own instinct that the girl on the magazine cover would look good in his kind of movies.

There was nothing about her then that gave him any indication of the controversy that was later to surround her. 'Nowhere to be seen in those days,' he commented on this aspect of her in his own auto-biography twenty years later. 'The Jane I knew never gave a glimpse of her opinions on public affairs; she simply dedicated herself to being a good actress.'

But first she had to convince herself totally that 'being a good actress' was precisely what she wanted to be dedicated to. The Logans, Joshua and Nedda, convinced her at a dinner they gave for her one Sunday. 'Jane just sat there,' Logan wrote, 'tossing her lovely head about and making long pronouncements about how she would never go on stage or have anything to do with the theatre.'

Nedda took it all with a pinch of the salt so delicately placed in a silver cellar on the dinner table. Changes were about to happen in Jane's ambitions. The 'heavenly' girl she could see in front of her was not to be 'wasted' on anything but acting and the audiences who would watch her. If Nedda had never had any other plan in her life, she was determined that her husband would work at inveigling the girl into his office and there sign a contract with her. Jane would be good for Logan, but she would also be very good for herself. So Joshua set about the task of persuasion and succeeded much more effortlessly than seemed possible. He charmed her into accepting that failing to let the world see the talent that he knew lay beneath that 'heavenly' exterior would be unjust and unfair.

If this was a demonstration of just how clever he was at spotting talent and putting it on the right track, he could not have been more wrong. Discreet enquiries with Strasberg would have revealed that by now Jane had no other thought in mind. If she was not as yet completely married to the idea of becoming an actress – and secretly she probably was – the other students knew that she was definitely engaged to it. Nothing else had a chance. Not modelling. Not leading an idle life of leisure. The lady was playing hard to get – and Logan was prepared to work hard at getting her.

It should also be stressed that he had a particular picture in view for her. His Warner Bros. contract specified that he was to make three films for the studio, one of which, suggested by Warner themselves, was from a novel by Mildred Savage called *Parrish*. It told the story of a family of tobacco planters in Connecticut. The tale was essentially a love story larded with a considerable amount of sentiment. Logan also already had a male star pencilled in – a young actor called Warren Beatty who had achieved a modicum of success on Broadway. The fact that Beatty was also Shirley MacLaine's brother may have had a little to do with Logan's enthusiasm. Young Miss MacLaine was beginning to make herself felt in Hollywood.

Jane took to the idea of working at Warners with all the excitement of a filly given its first outing on a racetrack. There was a brand-new world out there and she was avidly breathing in its air.

Logan signed Jane to a five-year contract, but almost before the ballpoint ink had had a chance to smudge, he changed his mind about the vehicle he had in mind for her.

Instead of *Parrish*, he thought she would be ideal for his version of a successful New York play by Howard Lindsay and Russel Crouse, *Tall Story*, which was based on the bestseller *The Homecoming Game*. This novel by Howard Nemerov was about the moral dilemmas of teenagers, particularly the members of a college basketball team who were being 'encouraged' to throw a game with offers they might find difficult to refuse. Jane's role was a cheerleader, who plays on the right side – which obviously was against the gangsters trying to 'fix' the game.

The main male lead went to Antony Perkins, who had yet to make *Psycho* – it would be his next film – but had already carved a certain niche for himself with pictures like *The Actress*, *Desire Under the Elms*, *The Matchmaker* and *This Angry Age*.

Warners, probably rightly, were anxious to encourage new exciting talents like Jane – particularly because they too planned to milk the Fonda connection like a healthy cow – but they felt they needed the insurance policy of having a strong male lead to back them up.

As Logan for one should have known, Perkins was hardly strong and his skinny frame looked faintly ludicrous on a basketball court.

Jane, meanwhile, went about the business of testing for the part – one that Logan was going to give her even if, for some unaccountable reason, she photographed like an Eskimo with freckles.

She herself wasn't all that thrilled with the tests and everything they involved. The make-up department decided to make her look like *their* idea of a cheerleader, which may not have been Jane's own notion of the part. The way she dressed when she went to her drama classes made her look more as if she had stepped out of the pages of *Harper's Bazaar* than like the traditional idea of a black-leotard-wearing drama student. Certainly, she had never come close to resembling a cheerleader at Vassar.

After one session in the make-up room, she said: 'I look like a squirrel with nuts packed into its cheeks.'

Logan later revealed that for weeks afterwards she went on a diet to make sure that the squirrel no longer had nuts in its cheeks. A squirrel earning $10,000 a year – which, since squirrels liked peanuts, may not have been considered unreasonable.

Logan and his publicity people were convinced that they had a worthwhile investment in old Hank Fonda's daughter. 'I haven't the slightest doubt about Jane becoming a popular star,' the producer said. 'She has the acting ability, the beauty, the instinct for comedy, plus the desire to work.'

And she was not restricted to merely sitting and waiting to earn that money. While the plans for the film went ahead, she played for two weeks in a summer-stock presentation of *The Moon Is Blue* in New Jersey. There she learned one of the facts of American theatrical life: summer stock – the repertory shows set up as 'breathing space' between Broadway seasons – were not just national and professional institutions; in their way they were as demanding as productions on the New York stage. The actors were expected to work on them as though they were top-flight productions and the audiences expected nothing less.

The Moon Is Blue was not a great success either for the theatre or for Jane, but it was a significant governor to a young girl who now had reason to believe that she was going to be a great success at everything she handled.

She handled *Tall Story* well enough, yet it was no great hit either artistically or at the box office. But she did learn a thing or two. Making films was an entirely different technique from anything she had done on the stage and she was anxious to know more about it.

It had been fashionable to deride the movie industry as simply that – an industry in which actors played a substantial role, but usually because they believed that if the medium of films was there to be exploited, they were entitled to take the money and run. 'It's what I call retirement acting,' Walter Matthau once told me. 'I go in for a day and recite one sentence. The next day I say a line I was supposed to have delivered two hours before. That's not really acting.'

Like most former Strasberg students (of which Mr Matthau was never one), Jane felt much the same way. *Tall Story*, she was to say, disabused her of many prejudices. She learned to respect the medium. 'You have to play to the camera when you act.... You learn such fascinating things – like the fact that the audience's eyes tend to go to the right side of the screen, so you try to get over to the right side of the set. That's a subtle form of scene stealing.'

The film turned into an act of theft from the people who were generous enough to spend money on tickets.

Even Joshua Logan would later admit that it wasn't one of his proudest boasts to talk about *Tall Story*, although he felt differently about the credit he was given for 'discovering' Jane Fonda. And rightly so, too.

None of that, however, seemed to matter. The publicity department at Warners had a ball – and loved all the reviews with headlines like: 'New Fonda – Henry's Daughter, Jane, 21, Gets First Movie Role.'

Time magazine thought it worthwhile to devote a long feature to her and so did the magazine's highly prestigious stablemate, *Life*.

One reporter wrote about her: 'I have a hunch that Jane Fonda will do OK in pictures for about four years. Then as soon as she gets Hollywood out of her system she'll settle down with a nice, handsome husband, make babies and that will be it. By 1965, I think she'll be more often on the society pages than the entertainment pages.' So much for soothsaying journalists.

Jane told everyone how much she enjoyed working with Tony Perkins and Henry confided to an equal number of writers how proud he was of his daughter. 'Jane has made much more progress in one year than I have in thirty,' he told one reporter. He didn't really believe anything of the kind, but he could afford to be generous and he was impressed with what Jane was doing.

Writing for the UPI syndicate, Jack Gaver enthused like a circus barker outside the big tent: 'Attention, Hollywood! Another Fonda is headed your way.

'Next Tuesday, a moderately tall, slim 21-year-old-girl, with large compelling, dark-blue eyes and a shock of shoulder-length golden hair, will step off a plane in the movie capital to seek a screen career as her father did almost 25 years ago....'

Two interesting facts emerge from that excited statement: Jane was inevitably going to have to spend much of the rest of her professional life not just in her father Henry's shadow, but as a virtual appendage of his. It was as if Henry and not Frances had given her birth and that the placenta was still firmly in place. The other interesting fact was that, then and later, Jane – no matter how difficult her relationship with Henry had been – raised no objection to this.

There were those who wondered why she didn't change her name – that way the scale of influence would be considerably reduced. Her answer was clear and unequivocal: 'I kept my name because I'm proud of it and I'm not afraid of being my father's daughter.'

It was good to read that, especially for people who knew the tautness of the true relationship between father and daughter. Much more significant was what she added in either the innocence and unsophistication of youth or the sheer honesty that she thought her new status in the new profession demanded: 'If my name weren't Fonda, it would have taken years longer. Contacts can get you there, but they won't keep you there. I'm planning to stay on my own.' In another interview she added: 'I hope people are honest enough to admit that after walking through the opened door, I had to do the job.' For the moment, that wasn't completely the way the press saw it, and no one can blame them.

She recognized that people not only compared her career with that of her father, but that their looks, too, were constantly a subject for conversation. 'Dad has great features for a man. But there the resemblance ends. My word!'

A further point to note is that Mr Gaver referred not to *Tall Story* but to a motion picture called *The Way the Ball Bounces*. Just a fortnight before the film's going on the production floor, it had a totally different title. Wisdom of sorts plainly triumphed.

The questions were inevitable – mainly what did her father think of it all? 'Dad never tried to encourage or discourage me,' she said again and again. That was wisdom, too – and diplomacy. Also, if one analysed it, it didn't say a great deal. She plainly was not going to embarrass Henry by being too effusive.

Louella Parsons gave her the full treatment – which meant that Jane was one of the last Hollywood products to face the *grand dame* of filmtown gossip, who, like her rival Hedda Hopper, was quite capable of making or destroying a career with a scratch of her acid pen.

Ms Parsons was amazingly – one should also say unusually – prescient in her summation of this new figure on the scene, a pretty one who appeared in a photograph attached to her newspaper column wearing a straw hat at a rakish angle, with a tiny caricature of a girl with petal lips in the bottom left-hand corner.

'The second generation is often a disappointment,' she wrote and in so doing was stating no more than the complete truth. Her reasons: 'Because it's so difficult to follow in the footsteps of a celebrated father or mother. But I am willing to make a sizable wager that Jane Fonda is going to be an exception.'

If she had made that wager in September 1959, she could have collected handsomely from bookmakers who would have been in a strong position to dismiss her words as the kind of speculation they had heard a hundred times before.

But in this case she was near enough on the nose: 'Jane didn't trade on Henry's fame or success to get herself into motion pictures. She went to Josh Logan, whom she had known all her life, and said the one thing she had always wanted to do was to play in a movie.'

As was often the case with a celebrity, truth frequently gave way to fantasy, but, on the other hand, there seemed no reason to allow the facts to spoil a good story. And the fact that Logan *did* think that Jane's relationship to Henry might sell a few tickets was not her fault. She certainly did not trade on it herself.

But the plaudits came just the same. As the British magazine *Films and Filming* said, 'With her talent and a few years of experience she could easily become as famous as her father. Hollywood could certainly do with a few more of her calibre.'

It is true – and it needs to be repeated – that this sort of thing *was* said about other starlets. The difference was that only rarely was the prophecy in the least likely to come true.

She was pleased to accept it all as a challenge. 'I used to say I wouldn't go into acting because in it you must be the best or nothing. I had no confidence. Now I'm going to fight.'

It was the kind of spirit that encouraged directors; and warned, them, too. Joshua Logan was more delighted with her spirit than he was with his film. *Tall Story*, if it hadn't earned a modicum of interest as Jane's first picture, would hardly be remembered at all today. Almost everyone involved would have been much happier to see it buried in one of those film library cemeteries where rolls of film stock used to be allowed to turn to dust.

That did not go for Jane, who saw it as her opening shot in Hollywood and was not entitled to despise it. Although she later admitted that while making the picture she had been totally unable to concentrate. 'To me,' she said, 'films were just walking through doors.' When she realized that was the way she thought she decided to take a drama coach on to the set of her next picture. And she did. There were others who were more complimentary to both Jane and her acting in *Tall*

Story – including a young actor whom Jane admitted to 'mothering'. His name was Timmy Everett and his feelings towards Jane were anything but filial.

In fact, he would later say that he tried to take his life because of her.

He had met Jane on the set of *Tall Story*, where he had gone to visit his friend Tony Perkins. Everett had achieved considerable critical acclaim for a number of Broadway roles, notably in *The Dark at the Top of the Stairs*. Perkins introduced him to Jane and if most accounts are to be taken seriously, he fell in love with her on sight. Madly in love with her.

He went to Jane's apartment and, he has said, they became so sexually infatuated with each other that they tore their clothes off and then spent three days in bed together.

Everett was around her for most of the next two years, advising Jane on the sort of roles she should take; she was telling him what was good for his career and all the time they were living a life that was like a sexual thunderstorm.

Henry was the first to spot the storm warnings and resented the way the young man – he was about Jane's own age – dominated his daughter and gave her the kind of advice he believed should have come from him; except that what Timmy Everett told Jane to do was precisely what Henry would have advised against.

He wanted her to get 'earthy', to put her Method training into making a career as the sort of actress few cheerleader types aspired to being. It should also be emphasized that this was precisely the way she herself felt. However, when he put it into words, she felt instinctively he was right. It was just the stamp of approval that she required. The approval in bed was entirely mutual.

Joshua Logan, however, was concerned only with her professional abilities. He was planning his film version of *Fanny* and wondered whether Jane wouldn't make ideal casting for the title role. He had no plans to repeat the stage musical version of the classic story (based on a French film trilogy) of two aged men from Marseilles and the girl in the striped jersey which had for a time given a certain amount of pleasure to audiences at London's Drury Lane Theatre. This was going back to the original story, although there were those who wondered whether even with Charles Boyer and Maurice Chevalier – Hollywood's definition of Frenchmen – this should be made in America at all.

Jane, at a stage in her life when, rightly, anything went, was game enough to accept Logan's offer. Her problem was possibly because, with her Method experience, she 'thought' French and to her, French was Paris. The test microphones picked up a French accent which was possibly a little too much Berlitz and not enough Marseilles, but would have passed most other people's tests. In fact, Logan was sorely tempted to sign her for the role, until he wondered whether an American girl fitted in with the Chevalier-Boyer combination.

He told writer James Brough that he was frightened he would be 'stabbed in the back' for hiring Jane. But as he said, he was stabbed in the back anyway – he used Leslie Caron when the movie was finally made in 1961 – and wished he had had Jane after all.

Logan was determined there would be no second thoughts about the casting for a new Broadway play he was planning as the cameras were readying to roll for *Fanny*. He had bought a play by one of Hollywood's leading scriptwriters, Daniel Taradash, who had written the film versions of both *From Here to Eternity* and *Picnic* and was now anxious to achieve as much renown with a live production on the Broadway stage.

Both he and Logan thought he had his opportunity with *There Was a Little Girl* – which told a story that might be considered to be more relevant to the climate of public opinion in the 1980s than it was twenty years earlier. In recent years, rape victims have been subjected to a degree of suggestion that they themselves usually bring on the crime. Women's organisations and many other civil-rights groups have been fighting the notion but increasingly – and to public horror – a number of judges have made the allegation. This was basically what *There Was a Little Girl* was about – with Jane playing the 'little girl' rape victim in question.

Henry didn't approve of his daughter going into the part at all. He was to say later on that he was concerned that it was a badly written part in a bad play. Jane, however, took it that he was trying to run her professional life and that, above all, he disliked the idea of his daughter having anything to do with a rapist, even on the stage.

'He questioned the taste of the play,' was how she put it, somewhat delicately.

Once offered the role, however, she was not about to turn it down. She saw things, she maintained, from the viewpoint of the actress who needed a break. Henry himself hadn't been in that position for years. He was used to having producers begging him to perform in their plays, putting off openings to fit in with his Hollywood and Broadway schedules. That wasn't his daughter's situation at all. 'What my father didn't realize,' she told the *New York Mirror* at the time, 'was that if I refused the role, I'd have a hard time getting other jobs. I'm not a star. But once I took it, he said nothing. He always plays it right.'

The excitement leading up to the play's opening was as acute as it had been for *Tall Story*. Once again – and still inevitably – the Henry-Jane connection was the one that was emphasized. 'Here Comes Another Fonda,' shouted the normally sedate *New York Herald-Tribune* on the front page of its entertainment section. To the left of and beneath the headline were pictures of Jane in rehearsal – including one in which Logan demonstrated the kind of hold he believed the rapist (to be played by actor Rian Garrick) should have on Jane's arm and throat.

There were other opportunities for plugging the play. As her name was flashing in neon, the words 'Jane Fonda' were spelled out above nearby movie theatres playing *Tall Story*. In fact, the names of two Fondas were blazing in lights. While Jane starred in *There Was a Little Girl* at the Cort Theatre, Henry was down the road in the lead in Robert Anderson's new play, *Silent Night, Lonely Night*, at the Morosco Theatre.

Henry had invested in his play and it seemed sure of running for as long as he could stay in it, but he warned Jane that hers was a turkey. When he heard that the traditional opening night party was planned at Sardi's – the theatrical restaurant opposite the famed Shubert Alley, a place where the walls are decorated with caricatures of the great Broadway figures of the past and which is as much an institution thereabouts as the theatres themselves – he begged her not to go. But she insisted on all the trimmings of being a rising young star opening on Broadway, including the masochistic act of being there when the newspapers' first editions came in. Now he was playing it right simply by not keeping his own counsel and telling Jane what he thought of the play – not what he thought of his daughter's acting – and imagining the reactions of the critics,

Henry knew what they would say – and he was right. At least, he was partly right. The New York *Daily News* said she herself was a new Sarah Bernhardt – or at least would be in 1990 – but, like all the others, hated the play.

As Henry noted: 'Sardi's is a great place not to be when your show has just been panned.' It was an experience Jane had to learn for herself. 'Jane's eyes crossed a little when she read [the reviews]. Then she smiled at me. I knew then she was a real professional.'

Henry smiled himself when he read that bit about Sarah Bernhardt of 1990 and some of the other nice things the critics were reserving for his daughter. As Jane remembered, his face was shining: 'More than it did at Dennis. And it was more beautiful.' That was pretty nice for a young professional to realize as well.

More important, she was a real professional who was being recognized as such. For this first Broadway role in a play that was indifferent, to say the least, she won a New York Drama Critics Award – even though the Butchers of Broadway had their say and the show came off after just two weeks. But she herself was more than vindicated by what the critics handed her that year.

There was not much encouragement anyone could give to Miss Fonda after that.

She knew that she was already, at the age of twenty-two, on the way to the top. And she was looking forward to getting *Invitation to a March* under way. 'I'll murder anyone who gets in my way for the part,' she said. Hollywood was close to murdering anyone who got in the way of the Fonda film career. She was being boosted as the most exciting new find in years. It was something said of a dozen other actresses every summer, but somehow the people who knew about such things seemed to believe it.

Jack Warner gave a cocktail party for his new find. Ms Parsons gushed about that, too. If they didn't have cocktail parties to report and to gossip about, they were in a bad, bad way, these amazons of the Press whose columns were distributed to practically a thousand different newspapers and magazines.

Films and Filming wrote a piece about her and headed it 'Person of Promise'. They used a still from *Tall Story* in which Jane looked more like Brigitte Bardot than herself – which was seemingly quite symbolic.

Ms Parsons hadn't the slightest reason to think about that sort of thing.

'A week later,' she reported, 'Jane paid me a visit. I shall never forget the way she looked when she breezed into my house from the beach where she had spent the day trying to get a suntan. She was wearing a white blouse and yellow skirt, with her hair wrapped in a tight turban, which she called her "babushka". In her hand, she carried a bright blue balloon which she found on the kerb outside my house – the colour effect was most becoming.'

She remembered that Jane looked about fourteen. But what she said was quite mature. There were the usual stories about her drama school, about Vassar, about boyfriends – yes, she said, she was in love with one at that moment – but her reply to the requisite query about marriage was revealing. Beneath the cliché was a yearning: 'When I marry, I want it to be for all time.' Every starlet who ever was has been quoted as saying that. But she added: 'I have grown up with divorce and I want to feel sure before I marry.'

'Quite a girl, my old friend Henry Fonda's daughter,' concluded the columnist who had also elicited that Jane loved tennis, swimming and painting and had a fondness for classical music as well as progressive jazz and rock'n'roll. 'Beautiful, talented and charming. I invited her to come and see me again soon and she promised she would.'

Failure to obey a command like that was close to professional suicide. Jane wasn't contemplating that kind of suicide any more than she was any other. Her psychiatrist would have been interested if she were. But into her fifth year on the couch, she was not letting anyone talk her out of regular visits to her shrink.

'My father says I need it like a hole in the head, but I believe in it very strongly. Why waste a lot of time feeling guilty as so many of us do? It's helped me a lot and I know it can help others. That's why I'd like my father to go. Any man who's had four wives must be unhappy.'

Henry regarded that sort of statement in the same way he reacted to his daughter's emotionalism. He tried to ignore it.

Of course, he knew that the Louella Parsons interview was just a beginning to the sort of things that were about to happen to her; part of the requirements of the trade like his own posing for pictures with Frances, Jane and Peter in the old days.

Jane didn't like either some of the publicity pictures she was required to do – like posing in clinches with Tony Perkins. But that, too, was acting.

Henry didn't even raise an eyebrow – which, admittedly, for him could be a costly undertaking in terms of emotional expenditure – when she was quoted saying things like: 'I'd like to have a child now, but I don't want a husband yet, so that's out. I think it's good to be a young mother. I was brought up by a very young stepmother and it was wonderful.'

Afdera couldn't have been too pleased about that. Nevertheless, Jane was gradually formulating her – for 1960 – exceedingly revolutionary thoughts on human behaviour. She told Hedda Hopper that she considered marriage to be totally obsolete, anyway. She accepted that it was probably all right for some people. But she said: 'If you're going to get married, it should be done properly. You must be able to make compromises and sacrifices, and I'm not ready to do that. I couldn't maintain such a relationship.' Then she added: 'I don't think I'll ever be able to do it and it doesn't bother me too much.'

The man constantly asked to give an opinion on Jane was Joshua Logan, who said that he was very proud of what he had achieved through her.

'I was suspicious of her career at first,' he said in 1960. 'As one always suspects newcomers who have successful parents. But she matured, she became so beautiful I didn't care. I asked her why she didn't seriously try the theatre. She said, "Not interested." I had to wait for her to make up her mind.'

Well, now her mind was made up and she wasn't allowing her Hollywood debut to interfere with her plans for a career in the live theatre. To Jane's credit, she was happy enough to continue to learn her craft off Broadway.

When the call went out in 1960 for an Actors Studio production of what was described as 'an unusual summer package show' at the Lyceum Theatre on West 45th Street, Jane could hardly be held back.

Her relationship with Timothy Everett came to an end – prompted, it was said, by her distaste for the shabby way he dressed; whatever the reason, Jane was tired of him and his feelings for her were so possessive that she felt stifled. The Lyceum production was a perfect way of demonstrating her desire for change.

It was an opportunity to join the Actors Studio, after all those years merely sampling what it had to offer through her classes with Strasberg.

These summer stock companies usually concentrated on well-known works by leading authors which had starred big personalities. Instead, this Lyceum show was *No Concern of Mine* by a virtually unknown English writer, Jeremy Kingston. It had been rejected by a number of top Broadway managements, so Kingston was pleased to accept the offer of director Andreas Voutsinas to produce it at the Lyceum.

It wasn't commercial and, in fact, Jane said that she couldn't understand it at all simply by reading it. She played a young drama student constantly in conflict with her brother.

'It took a lot of guts to do this play,' she said – and she wasn't referring to herself. Her praise was all for Voutsinas. What few people realised at the time was that Jane and Voutsinas were, as the phrase of the time put it, 'an item'. More significant than that, though, was the power he had over her. He was another Svengali in her continuing role as the Trilby of contemporary theatre.

Jane knew that was unhealthy. 'I guess I'm a kind of slave type,' she was to say of the relationship she had with this man of Greek ancestry she had met at Strasberg's classes, where he worked as a sort of unofficial assistant.

No one could have seemed a less suitable companion for the personable, attractive and still so young star. He looked like one of the figures film musicals such as Fred Astaire's *The Band Wagon* and *Funny Face* used to enjoy making such fun of – dressed from head to foot in black, wearing a black beret and smoking from a long cigarette holder. He was also considerably shorter than Jane herself.

None of this mattered to her. She needed influences like the director the same way she needed her psychiatrist, and for virtually the same reasons. She was unsure of herself. She needed people to point her in the right direction, the same way older, more sophisticated women needed interior decorators to plan their room designs. She wouldn't do anything unless Voutsinas thought it a good idea. Her confidence in him was enhanced by the fact that he and she shared the same analyst.

When it finally came time to play in *Invitation to a March*, she believed their relationship was at its zenith. In fact, it wasn't. He was intended to be Arthur Laurents's assistant director, but the two men didn't get on. So Jane had to face up to life without him.

The play was trumpeted along the length and breadth of the country – mainly because of its impressive cast. Newspapermen were encouraged to think of the amazing phenomenon of a young, pretty, highly talented girl who just happened to be the daughter of Henry Fonda. At the same time, they could speculate how she would get on with the rest of the cast – Shelley Winters and another offspring of a potential theatrical dynasty, James MacArthur, son of playwright and screenwriter Charles MacArthur and the legendary lady of the American stage, Helen Hayes.

The play was put on by the Theatre Guild. Arthur Laurents spent most of his time, apparently, telling people that he had written the part of Norma just for Jane.

It opened for a pre-Broadway run at the Colonial Theatre in Boston and followed it with another two weeks at the Cass in Detroit. But it was a distinct box-office flop wherever it played, though it managed to run for a few months in New York. None of this, however, affected her relationship with the Greek 'Svengali'. Neither did she make any attempt, or see any reason, to hide her feelings for the director, who has later become known for his part as the homosexual in Mel Brooks's sardonic comedy *The Producers*.

'I've been in love with Andreas for over a year,' she said when they both arrived in London in July 1962.

6

Together Jane and Andreas had gone to Athens. He stopped by there to see his parents.

The sophisticated Miss Fonda, at twenty-three, had seen more of life than most people do at three times that age. It was as if with Andreas, seven years her senior, she had changed entirely her old thought processes. With John F. Kennedy in his second year in the White House, it was a time when people thought about things being well ordered. The First Family were attractive. The emphasis was on family.

She was taken with the simple life, she said. Once more, it gave her an opportunity to reflect on her own hopes for the future, perhaps for the far, far future.

Seeing Andreas's family was an eyeopener. That was when she referred to looking forward to raising grandchildren and of being a character. A number of people had begun to think of her as a character already, but not yet as a grey-haired grandmother.

'You know,' she added in an interview with Susan Barnes in the London *Sunday Express*, 'I was brought up to be afraid of growing old. I used to be petrified of it. Now I have got over this fear. Now I'm actually looking forward to being old.'

Was Jane saying too much about marriage and the way her future was going to be? She undoubtedly was, but then it was one of the things expected of a young woman and she was content to play the part of the star and do everything that was required of her. Her days of refusing to do the predictable thing and of telling the Press what it could do with its interest in her were for the future.

In one interview she said that she was totally off male company. An astute journalist noticed her walking into Schwab's drugstore, the place where Lana Turner was supposed by legend to have been discovered, with the paper containing the interview under her arm – and three handsome and apparently eligible young men dancing attention to her like worker bees around the queen.

But the only one she was interested in now was Andreas. 'It's marvellous to be able to admire and work for somebody you are personally attached to,' she said.

Perhaps that was particularly the case after some of the things that had recently happened to her – like being featured on posters all over the United States, declaring her to be 'Miss Army Recruiting 1962'. Later, when help to the armed services didn't really fit in with what she was saying and thinking about the war in Vietnam, she would have reason to regret that. She did so by alleging that the pictures were phony – that her face had been substituted on another girl's body.

Plenty of her appearances had, however, been strictly on her own. She was featured as the star of a TV colour special, a version of Somerset Maugham's *A String of Beads*. But that was a mere fill-in, like an appearance she made at the Palisades Amusement Arcade.

No, she was now a serious actress and Andreas Voutsinas was the man who was guiding her. A slave or not, being with him was what interested her most.

In later years, she would doubtless conclude that she was also a slave to the film industry, although at the time she was glad enough to move from one movie to the other at the speed of contract players working in the studio system of old. *That* was virtually at an end now, but Jane flitted from each soundstage to the next as if she were a secretary employed by an agency and changing offices every other month. She not only appeared to do what the producers told her but made no complaints about it either, despite all she might later say. She still posed for all the pictures she was required to have taken, including a ration of what looked like cheesecake – except that an essential part of her equipment was a set of falsies.

There were still those who were whispering – not many were strong enough to come out in the open – that Jane's success and the career it spawned was something of a falsie itself. Others made the not unreasonable comment that Jane in fact was a lot better than the movies she had been given.

If Voutsinas had been doing what he took as almost his divine responsibilities sufficiently to heart, she would not have made them. For much of the time she would refuse to go on a set unless Andreas was with her, smiling at her, willing her on like a boxing trainer punching with his 'boy' from the ringside or a football coach seeing that the instructions he had so painfully mapped out before the start of a match were carried out.

It has been said that Voutsinas's principal contribution to the way Jane was developing was to turn her aside from the mores of Hollywood and make her enthusiastic to appear unlike the cheerleader she had been in *Tall Story*. That pays insufficient credit to Jane's own acting abilities and what she wanted for her career. She was just right as the cheerleader. When she played a rape victim on the Broadway stage, that was not because of Voutsinas. Joshua Logan knew she could do it and Jane knew she could do it. The critics plainly knew she could do it, too – and winning that award with a bad play was even harder than winning it with a good one. Nevertheless, when the 'slave' Fonda was told that Voutsinas was responsible for a change in her professional personality, she accepted it. There was undoubtedly a spell he wove around her and she was caught in its web. Andreas told her she needed him and she believed it.

After Athens, they went to London together – officially to talk about a new play and for more work on the film she had started making in Greece with Peter Finch, *In the Cool of the Day*. She found it a levening experience, in all sorts of ways. It was her first working trip abroad and since most of the technicians and others involved with the movie were British, she learned some of the ways of the British film industry, its own ideas on perfectionism, its restrictive practices, its tea breaks – and above all its language.

Bernard Shaw said that Britain and America were two countries divided by a common language. She saw just how divided, and suffered the complications of attempting to learn Greek (not easy by anyone's definition) at the same time as cockney rhyming slang. She discovered the intricacies of enclosing her plates of meat (feet) inside her Tilbury docks (socks) and with them climbing the apples and pears (stairs). They didn't teach such things at the Actors Studio. Certainly no one at Vassar would have lifted a titfer (titfer-tat – hat) to the idea.

This was a time when her feminist instincts came to the fore for the first time. The unit manager was a woman – a woman who was punched in the stomach by their driver. Both were Greeks, but Jane was incensed that a woman could be treated in that way. She thought she had learned an appropriate swearword to help her convey what she felt, but she obviously came out with the wrong one. Nobody turned a hair – and that in a country where men are supposed to be very careful about the way they talk to ladies, let alone punching them in the stomach. She felt less frustrated about the language in Britain.

She also had a certain respect for English actors (and the Australian Peter Finch was considered an honorary Englishman by her). Audiences were about to see her film *Walk on the Wild Side* at about the time she was making this new one. Joshua Logan had lent her to producer Charles Feldman for this picture and a lot of Jane's admirers – including Henry and Andreas, for totally different reasons – dearly wished that he had not.

Henry hated the idea of his daughter playing a prostitute as much as he had disliked her being a stage rape victim; Voutsinas wished her to play the part as though she really was snarling at all men while taking her clothes off for them and letting them do with her as they would. In a later generation, that would be called 'over the top'; fortunately for most people concerned, including Jane, the director Edward Dmytryk made sure that her acting was below the top.

Bosley Crowther said in his *New York Times* review that the film gave Jane a chance to be 'elaborately saucy and shrill'. But it was 'a poor exposure for a highly touted talent'.

He said of Dmytryk's direction that it 'makes you wonder whether he read the script before he started shooting. If he did, he should have yelled.'

Jane did her share of yelling. In this picture, she starred with Laurence Harvey and snarled her way through a number of powerful scenes that were reminiscent of the young Elizabeth Taylor at her steamy best.

Another featured player in *Walk on the Wild Side* was Capucine, a sexy French actress who was most men's cup of coffee at the time, though now remembered mainly for *The Pink Panther* (1964). Barbara Stanwyck starred, too.

None of the women on the set seemed to care for Mr Harvey. 'It's like acting by yourself – worse than acting by yourself,' Jane said. They got on together by all accounts like a fish meeting a worm – with a hook and line attached.

She accused him of underplaying scenes; of making faces and with each grimace unnerving everyone else. It was an indication of how far she had come in her own career that she was able to talk like that.

When I interviewed Harvey not long after the experience of making that film, he had much the same to say about Jane. 'What a strange girl!' he said. 'She seems to be suffering from the Hollywood disease – get yourself a big name and there's no need to live up to it.'

He was dismissive of her success. 'She has a few things written about her and she comes to the conclusion she's the biggest star in the movie business. You can't tell her anything. Two hours on the set and she's playing director and running the outfit.'

Harvey died in 1973. He was only thirty-four when he made *Walk on the Wild Side*. Already he then had eleven films under his belt, including *Expresso Bongo*, *Room at the Top* and *Butterfield 8*. It is true he was being put in some highly unsuitable productions, including *The Alamo*. But he had already proved himself to be a film star. Jane took the view that being a star did not make everyone a good actor and that was what she respected. Even so, Andreas was around all the time and if he took a dislike to Harvey, then Jane as a matter of course would, too.

Peter Finch in *In the Cool of the Day* was different. It was good politics to talk nicely about one's co-star in a current production, but by all accounts they seemed to get on well enough.

She admired his professionalism, his lack of 'monkey business'. And there was no romance between them. 'If an actor and actress want to have a great wild thing, that's their affair,' she affirmed. 'But it is not necessary in order for them to act love scenes well.

'It helps if you have some rapport with the person you are meant to act with romantically. But this doesn't mean if you are acting a murder, you have to actually murder someone. You just have to realize that sometimes you want to murder someone. There's always a little bit of transference, if you like an actor and you're working well together. But what the hell do you do if you are an actress and you fall in love with your leading man? You get a little sloppy.'

Perhaps she was getting a little sloppy over Andreas. Henry certainly thought so, although his own romantic attachments gave him little right to comment, let alone to pass serious judgments on her. But he hated the Greek director and all that he stood for; mainly he hated what he thought Andreas was doing for his daughter's career. After complaining about her being a rape victim and a prostitute, he sighed audibly at her playing a woman with problems that she reveals for the pages of a sex survey in *The Chapman Report*; which was heralded as the sexiest movie ever to be made in America. It was nothing of the kind, but people still remembered the Kinsey Report and the publicity for the picture made some sex-starved individuals salivate at the possibility of seeing all that come to life on the screen. The picture was tame and so was Jane's portrayal of one of the young women taking part in the survey. It got close to boring, even with George Cukor directing the picture. However, he admired the young Miss Fonda.

'I was extraordinarily impressed with this young lady,' he told me shortly before he died. 'I always had a terrible prejudice against children of famous stars. It is not difficult to believe that they get where they do simply because of parental influence. This was definitely not so with Jane Fonda. All the women starring in the picture, Jane, Shelley Winters, Claire Bloom and Glynis Johns, were real actresses.' And that from a director who had a reputation for creating real actresses and developing those who had been created already – like Katharine Hepburn.

From this film, she went into yet another, *Period of Adjustment*, written by Tennessee Williams. She should have adjusted herself out of it. She spent a great deal of time crying in this picture, a fact she tried to forget when working with Peter Finch. Being with Andreas didn't help her. It was evident that the relationship was not likely to last. Possibly Jane knew that. For the moment, however, she walked with him with stars in her eyes. Maybe she did need to be a 'slave', but there were still the stories being told by her past loves of being consumed by her. 'She swallows you whole,' said one in an age when such a statement about a woman's relationship with a man was taken strictly metaphorically.

When she returned to New York from London, Andreas seemed to vanish from the scene. She was booked for her third Broadway play, *The Fun Couple*, a dramatization of a new novel about an attractive young pair and the world in which they live, fairly oblivious of everyone else.

For a time, with Voutsinas off the scene, she was a freelance in the love stakes – a catch for anyone who had the chance of getting close enough to find her phone number.

In early 1963 Roddy McDowall and Jane were seen with each other everywhere that counted. The bearded McDowall – the hirsute look was for his role in the Biblical epic *The Greatest Story Ever Told* – took her to the best Hollywood parties and they danced and necked at the Coconut Grove. One night there, Henry – who had broken off with the fourth Mrs Fonda by now – was sitting at another table with a young girl who Jane was certain had finally justified her bet with Peter – by being younger than Jane herself.

But if she did feel a little peeved about it, she kept that to herself, too. She was no longer going to give any personal interviews and particularly she was not going to claim, as she had, that marriage was obsolete. As she said: 'I found it hurt people near to me, especially my father.' The impression that she cared so much about her father – a man whom she still didn't really understand and who reciprocated entirely – showed a sense of caring that was not always visible. But in public she was now saying what was right and flattering, particularly about Henry. 'How would you like,' she joked in 1963, 'to have a father who grows younger every year? Do you realize what that can do to a woman?'

She was not sure that she really did enjoy the sort of people with whom her business put her into contact. 'Actors are so boring,' she said.

So she moved away from them. In fact, she moved away from America. In 1963, she was in Paris – working in French films and being seen a great deal with the man she had met at Maxim's, Roger Vadim.

7

I f Jane had previously needed a Svengali, in Roger Vadim she had a Pygmalion – a sculptor who breathed life into his works of art and then fell in love with them.

When I met him, he encouraged the view that Vadim Created Bardot (after having married her and starred her in his film *And God Created Woman*). In fact, he liked to think that he equally created his common-law-wife, Catherine Deneuve, who in 1963 gave him a daughter. After 1963, he was saying he created Fonda.

There are grounds for taking him at his word. Jane changed after coming under the Vadim spell. Certainly, Bardot and Deneuve did, too – out of all recognition. So did his second wife, and Jane's immediate predecessor, Annette Stroyberg.

He created them in his own image of what a woman should be like – the innocent little girl look; the blonde gamine; the hair either upswept or hanging loose over the shoulders; the mascaraed eyes. Sometimes they looked so alike it was difficult to tell them apart.

They called Vadim a womanizer. 'I love women,' he told me, 'but I am also a feminist. I am far from a male chauvinist pig.'

The feminist called Vadim was born of mixed French-Russian aristo-cratic parentage in 1927. His full name, Roger Vladimir [Vadim] Plemiannikov.

He started out as a journalist, became a screenwriter and then a director. His first film, Bardot's *And God Created Woman*, made his name as well as that of his star and wife.

By the time Jane came on the scene, he was established both as director and as womaniz ... er ... feminist.

It later turned out that their first meeting at Maxim's had been far from auspicious. Jane, the teenager feeling her way in the capital of a strange country, was faced with the self-assured husband of Stroyberg, who believed that women were creatures on whom he could weave a magic spell.

He and his heavily pregnant wife were at Maxim's, the centre – as seemingly always – of everyone's attention. That did not mean, however, that he couldn't look at anyone else – and when there was a pretty girl around, his eyes stared transfixed. As much, it would appear, at her feet as well as at her face or the rest of her body. Surprisingly, the conclusion to which he came was that she had thick ankles. He didn't just think so, he wrote the 'fact' down – on a slip of paper and passed it to her companion, the film actor Christian Marquand, who was also his best friend. 'She has swollen ankles,' he scribbled in French.

Marquand took up the paper, looked at it, screwed it up and threw it to the floor. Jane noticed this and when Marquand was looking in the other direction, picked it up and read it. She smiled – according to Vadim.

They met again in the United States, when Roger was looking for a star for one of his new films and Jane was already established as that – a star.

At the Beverly Hills Hotel – not in the swank Polo Lounge, a room so dark that one can have a detailed conversation with a complete stranger without realizing it, but in the coffee shop: Vadim needed to see his women.

Jane was in one of her hard-to-get moods; kittenish, teasing as young women like to do when they know they are being stalked. Vadim's reputation was more well known to her. She had studied the director as though he were part of a university course. He knew it – because he had studied her. Consequently, their meeting was like a tennis championship. Every exchange of conversation was a game. The end of each sentence was a set. Every full discussion was a volley between them.

Vadim was the sophisticated Frenchman in the world's movie capital, trying to set up a film. Jane was playing the casual student from UCLA or USC, wearing old clothes and no make-up on her face. Both enjoyed the meeting for their own reasons – Jane for making herself so difficult to waylay that she knew she would be able to bring him to her lair whenever she wanted; Vadim for being able to plan the next stage of his campaign.

The tall Vadim, with horn-rimmed spectacles, was perhaps not handsome in any traditional way, but he was intensely masculine and his very determination to show he was in charge, combined with a Gallic charm a woman underestimated at her peril, made him very attractive.

They got on well enough, smiling, giggling in what to any observer in that coffee shop looked extraordinarily like the first stages of the act of courtship. Jane couldn't be persuaded and since he had other things to do, bringing her – professionally speaking – into one of his studios was not at the top of his priorities.

Making love to Jane, however, was – even if it were not an occupation that would come just yet.

For a time they contented themselves with contemplating the almost-was and the still-might-be. Jane was partly still under the authority if not quite the spell of her Greek mentor. If she wanted to rid herself of his influence, this was plainly her opportunity.

In meeting Vadim, Jane proved to herself that she could do without Voutsinas. In fact, she no longer wanted him. She daydreamed about Vadim as he did about her and she got on with her career.

One thing is certain: it was from the beginning a mutual feeling, even if neither was making any official statements in the matter.

Years later, Vadim said what it was about Jane that so appealed to him. 'The vulnerability hiding behind the appearance of strength and self-confidence, her honest search for her true identify and, of course, her face, her body and the fact that we were perfectly compatible physically.'

Just how compatible would take a little time to develop. There were those, however, who helped them along without realizing it. The *Harvard Lampoon*, a prestigious college magazine, decided to present Jane with their award for Worst Actress of the Year for her role in *The Chapman Report*. They were not terribly wrong. *The Chapman Report*, despite and probably because of the hype it had received for a salaciousness which was never there, was a pretty dreadful film and Jane's own performance not a great deal better.

Besides, the *Lampoon's* strictures were not much to worry about. In Hollywood lore, it was almost as valuable an award as the Oscar – dozens of highly successful and artistically capable performers had received similar 'accolades' and survived to make another million or two at the box office. Vadim noticed her inclusion and decided it added a new dimension of charm to her personality. He liked it.

It certainly did not prevent the work coming in, MGM reputedly offered her $100,000 to play in *Sunday in New York*. Her decision to take the offer was sensible. It proved to be a highly rewarding exercise, both financially and in showing the public a new Jane Fonda, the one they would want to see again and again.

In this, she was the very bright, slightly abrasive young thing who always seemed as much good fun as she was sexy. That was a commodity that didn't come in too many packages in the early 1960s, particularly since the death of Marilyn Monroe. Fonda was never a Monroe – for one thing those breasts of hers still owed a great deal more to the padding provided by the wardrobe department than they did to nature. Her sexiness was a lot less sultry. Girl-next-door was the hackneyed phrase to describe the kind of femininity she offered.

Actually, hidden in the very adult sex comedy was the kind of story most people would like to find out about their neighbours. A brother (Cliff Robertson) and sister are each involved in the sort of affairs they don't fancy the other knowing about.

Robertson gives every impression that he is perfectly chaste, the kind of brother every girl next door could look up to. He is an airline pilot and Jane, of course, has no idea that he finds ways of taking off with every girl he meets. She tells him she is 'the only twenty-two-year-old virgin alive,' and asks: 'Is a girl that's been going around with a fellow a reasonable amount of time supposed to go to bed with him or not?'

Robertson (who feels differently about the girls he meets, although he wouldn't tell his sister) replies with a firm 'Not.'

Jane herself had no reason to worry. She gave the kind of performance most actresses would be very happy to advertise.

Unusually for this time when the young Fonda was finding her feet, when she still lacked the security of meeting her father on his own terms – he continued to say some pretty unprintable stuff (although much of it *was* printed) about Andreas – she was as much liked by her fellow performers as she was by her audiences.

Rod Taylor, who co-starred with her and Robertson, was extremely taken with the girl who played his love.

'It was just a fun thing,' he told me. 'It seemed to me that whatever was going on up there on the screen was what happened in real life. We got on like a couple of lovely kids.'

It was the turning of a corner. Before long, most people with whom she acted would say much the same thing about her.

'I honestly believe she falls in love with the parts she plays,' said Taylor in our interview. 'Therefore, a lot of that love reaches out to the people around her. As far as I know, it seemed as though it were a labour of love to her. *Sunday In New York* was just a frothy, wonderful time.'

There was another reason why Taylor enjoyed working with her so much, he told me. 'She wasn't into her political bullshit.' In those days, that kind of 'bullshit' was not even contemplated as being a compromising factor.

What did seem much more of a problem was the continuing story of the relationship between the Fondas. She and Peter still seemed to have a lot in common, although his drug-taking did appear a little excessive even by her standards, but Henry was no more supportive of her lifestyle than he had been before. What was different was that for the first time she was willing to talk about it to comparative strangers.

Taylor was among those who were well aware of it.

'I know from our talks that she was very concerned about Henry. I told her, "Come on, don't be so fucking silly. You know you're madly in love with him, go and cuddle him."'

She kept saying that they disagreed about their lifestyles, although Taylor had the feeling, he said, that Henry was quite 'Godlike' to her.

As for the relationship between Taylor and Jane during the filming of *Sunday in New York*, it was like 'a silly giggling adolescent romance – although it wasn't that, because we were totally platonic.'

But there was chitchat – 'high-school romance stuff'. There were more professional incidents, too.

One was a scene shot on the Rockefeller Center skating rink in New York. 'I had to tell her a funny story, which was kind of offbeat and dirty. The story in the script really wasn't very funny at all. We were chatting about it in rehearsal and I said, "Just let's roll the cameras." They did and the cameras caught us in the kind of bubbly moments we had experienced at lunch or dinner with each other. We both ad-libbed the whole thing and it worked perfectly.'

The critics certainly seemed to think so. *Time* magazine, glorying in the words that at the time seemed more important than informed judgement, said it was 'another brightly salacious Hollywood comedy about the way of a man with a maid who just may.'

It went on, 'As usual, winking wickedness turns out to be mostly eyewash [this *was* 1964], but the plot – more to be pitied than censored – gets a buoyant lift from stars Jane Fonda, Cliff Robertson and Rod Taylor. All three abandon themselves to the film version of Norman Krasna's trite Broadway farce with disarming faith, as though one more glossy glittering package of pseudo-sex might save the world.'

The film, said the anonymous critic, 'scores on style'. It was frequently funny – even 'the obligatory we-were-just-drying-off-in-the-bathrobe scene'. This, said *Time*, was because Jane 'in a plain blue wrapper, looks so honey-hued and healthy that her most smouldering invitation somehow suggests that all she really has in her mind is tennis.'

What she really had in mind for much of the time was Roger Vadim, who found ways of writing and telephoning her and of getting over messages that he was quite taken with her.

The reviews of *Sunday in New York* – which were much more comforting than those of *In the Cool of the Day*, released at much the same time – helped her think more casually about extracurricular prospects, and Vadim was at the top of the list of these.

They next came into contact when he was asked by the French producer Francis Cosne to offer the intriguing young Fonda girl a new part.

He reacted even though he knew that Voutsinas was still in tow – Jane had not yet decided to make a final move in that direction, although it was uppermost in her mind – and that he was with her when she flew to Paris to make a new picture. By now, Vadim knew that the Greek offered little competition, but the fact that he was still ostensibly on hand made the chase he now savoured like a hound in a fox-hunt all the more exciting.

They came to the French capital because Jane was to co-star with Alain Delon in a new film, *Joy House*.

In this, she played a rich American (what else?) who was trying to kill her boyfriend. *The Love Cage* was another title for the picture – in France itself, it was called *Ni saints, ni soufs* – and if Jane had not succeeded so splendidly in *Sunday in New York*, it might have seemed by far the most appropriate title for a picture that seemingly trapped her in a cage of confusion. Was it a Hollywood film, or was it a French picture made by an American company? And what sort of an actress was she? That was an even more pressing question.

She was determined to prove she was her own girl, who could cope with new surroundings. She took with her a travelling companion, a woman who would speak only French to her for two months. It was a very different situation from the one surrounding the young girl who Henry had hoped would be having a finishing-school education. In every way this was a different experience.

On the surface, it was not one of her happiest professional experiences to date, But there were compensating factors that made it one of the most significant in her life. She was not, however, telling herself that as she battled with her first few days under the hot lights of a French studio.

She was five feet seven inches tall and for once that seemed very short indeed. For reasons difficult to understand, she felt a pygmy surrounded by giants – actors experienced in French, the eminent director René Clément, the equipment that for once seemed to tower over her.

But it was Clément's methods that concerned her most.

Because she hadn't spoken English at all for two months, the prospect of facing the French publicity machine and, on Clément's instructions, talking to reporters was perhaps the most daunting factor.

As she said a few years later: 'I didn't speak very good French then and I never really understood much of what was going on.'

To make things worse, 'there was no script and it's just never the same. Too much playing it by ear for my taste. But Clément is still wonderful.' That did not, however, make the film any easier to comprehend. And those who did understand it when the picture was finally released were not her kind of people at all, she confided.

'The only people who really dug that movie, for some odd reason, were junkies. They used to come up to me and give me a great big wink. But I'm awfully glad I did it.'

At first the reason she was glad was simply because it got her to France. Later, she could add that the principal reason was that it also got her to Vadim. For the moment, however, her main cause to be glad – or certainly the *official* reason – was that it gave her an opportunity to see Paris in a new light and to broaden her professional experience by studying how the French film industry operated.

Hollywood made her a star in her own right, but also as Henry Fonda's daughter. Going to France, taking advantage of the offers to film there, provided a unique opportunity to set the record straight, to establish that she was her own girl, a star who would succeed because she was a good actress and had the charisma to justify the term.

Vadim knew this and was determined to snare her. It was all the more his intention when rumours started to circulate about Jane. She had sent Andreas packing – perfect for Vadim, although he never really doubted that Voutsinas offered no real competition. Now, though, the stories were that Jane and Delon were romantically attached. More of a difficulty – except that Jane, while immensely enjoying the image ascribed to her, denied it and so did Delon; however, since the French actor was in the midst of the break up of his marriage any woman seen frequently in his company was an obvious threat. With every rumour, Jane seemed to enjoy it more – especially since she knew Vadim was after her.

They came together at this time ostensibly for purely professional reasons. He wanted Jane to take the title part in *Angélique, Marquise des Anges*. The producer had failed to sign her because Jane's agent had sent him a telegram saying that she wouldn't do costume roles. This was another challenge for Roger. He took the idea of trapping her into a new film role as seriously and as avidly as that of bringing her to bed.

Professionally he failed to persuade her. But that was just another phase in the courtship process. They talked at a party given by a mutual friend for Jane's birthday. They did more than talk. Jane's former stepmother Afdera has said that when she saw them together, they talked, touched and did everything but perform the act of love in public, not caring.

On this occasion, they were hinting that that was what they wanted to do then, too. It would become an easily recognizable pattern. Nobody was left in any doubt that the pair were ideally suited to each other and were enticed by what each represented.

It seemed to bode well for a future professional relationship, too. They went out together; they went to bed together, not always, according to Vadim's own book, entirely satisfactorily; and everyone who knew them could see that before long they would be working together.

They did, when Jane finally agreed to make a Vadim film. This was, in fact, a remake of *La Ronde*. Arthur Schnitzler's play of love and sex had been going round the French and German theatre circuits since the days when men wore frock coats and top hats and women laced themselves in so much corsetry that only the most avid seducers were able to achieve their aims without losing the inclination.

To people who were themselves enticed by movie sex, Max Ophüls's 1950 version of *La Ronde* held a near-sacred role. It was the first imported French film of postwar years to whet the appetites of American and British audiences. Women were not seen to bare any breasts and there were no scenes of simulated intercourse in the versions that reached either Britain or the United States. But it was a superb production; cheeky, sophisticated and great fun. Simone Simon and

Simone Signoret epitomized a kind of sex not seen on Anglo-Saxon screens and the film was a huge hit in areas where the very idea of a French film was in itself a huge turn-off.

This was the film Vadim now wanted to remake, again in French. Jane took up the idea like a duckling introduced to its first park lake. She did it because she trusted Vadim as well as loved him. The movie also represented the kind of independence she had so long craved – far, far away from Henry's influence and the guilt it still brought, and away from any stereotyping she believed Hollywood wanted to create for her. Vadim told her she could do better than she had even in *Sunday in New York*. As for *In the Cool of the Day* . . .

Alas for them both, *La Ronde* didn't exactly prove it.

Catherine Spaak and Claude Giraud were among the other stars of the movie, but none of them was able to make the picture a success. The original French film – with the added advantage of Anton Walbrook's narrator spinning the roundabout of love as he spoke/sang his witty commentary – was as light as a soufflé. This one was heavy as an omelette that had stuck to the frying pan.

It didn't alter the relationship between Vadim and his American star, however. They were constantly seen in each other's company and most of their time away from the public eye was spent with each other, too. The film had introduced her to the idea of appearing in bed – and without too much in the way of clothing – in public. It was not a strange Jane to Vadim.

'She was not yet a star,' Vadim said to me. 'But she became a really big one after three or four years.'

Vadim is happy to talk about his love affair with Jane, as it was at this stage. 'People who have read what I have written say, "My God, they ought to erect a statue to you. You have been so kind."' He has always thought of his women as 'great, great women' – and certainly Jane is in this category.

As Vadim said in his review of his three celebrity loves, *Bardot, Deneuve and Fonda* (Weidenfeld, 1986), the problems of consummating their love had now gone.

Jane was, he maintains, 'searching for new roads leading to the discovery of her identity'.

He saw that straight away. For the moment, there could be no certainty that they would get together on anything like a permanent basis.

She was convinced her love for him would survive a long enough time without the formalities of getting married. 'I wouldn't marry him,' she told a whole succession of reporters. To one, she added: 'And I wouldn't lie to you.'

But his reputation *was* a lie, she added. 'When you get to know him, he is charming. He often lands in trouble because he is kind-hearted and this translates into weakness.'

Her own feelings for him were certainly not seen that way.

He plainly released her from a great many of her earlier inhibitions – and has never been reluctant to talk about that either. As he once said, 'she had so many bachelor habits ... she cannot relax. Always there is something to do – the work, the appointment, the telephone call. She cannot say, "Oh well, I'll do it tomorrow."' But he added: 'Jane has a fantastic capacity for surviving. She learned long ago how to be lonely ... For me, what was attractive was her attention to other people.'

Vadim now took it upon himself to educate the latest woman he was moulding. Neither Vassar nor her 'finishing' in Paris had been enough, he maintained. She needed to know more about culture. Since he said it, she was more than happy to go along with his notions. Read more books, he said. So read them she did. Books like Gorky's *Mother*, *L'Espoir* by André Malraux, and *The Prince* by Machiavelli. He later found out that she couldn't finish Machiavelli. She wasn't interested in politics, she declared. They were more words she would be having to eat before very long.

There were those who believed that Educating Fonda was proving as stimulating to Roger Vadim as their sexual relationship. It was, however, merely part of his creating process. Shaping her mind was every bit as vital a part of the sculpture as organizing her wardrobe or deciding how her hair should look.

They went around Europe. In Amsterdam, they saw the red-light district. Jane became the feminist. The whores were degrading womanhood. He had to push her away to prevent Jane becoming involved in a one-woman protest demo.

Vadim went back to America with Jane – mainly for the release of *La Ronde*, which was now being called *Circle of Love*. The change of name was fairly indicative of the kind of movie it was.

Their own circle of love, however, got wider. It spread from the United States, through France, to the Soviet Union.

They flew into Moscow, arm in arm, barely able to take their eyes off each other – even to take in the scenery, the Kremlin, the uniforms, the people old and young.

Going there was Vadim's idea. It was his ancestral territory and he wanted to see the place from which his father had hailed. Jane, for her part, wanted to see everything that could be regarded as forming a piece in her lover's story. They saw *War and Peace* being made on a set that looked like part of Hollywood and heard the assembled film crew tell her how much they enjoyed her father.

Vadim was to say that he found the people warm and friendly. But the country was exactly how he had imagined it. There may not have been much in the way of opulence but he couldn't see any evidence of extreme poverty either. Jane, on the other hand, expected to see open signs of oppression. When she heard they would be watching the May Day parade, she was convinced of it. Russia was a militant nation that suppressed any ideas of opposition. Not that any of that really concerned her. She was far more concerned with being with Vadim. If he wanted to see his father's birthplace, she was going to enjoy seeing it with him.

There was no other motive involved. By the time she returned to America, however, Jane had changed. Suddenly, she saw in a new light a country she had grown up to despise. Now she heard stories about the Soviets only wanting peace and being misunderstood by the West, who really didn't want to think anything else. She accepted a great deal of it.

'I couldn't believe it,' she said before the snow had been wiped from her boots. 'All my life I've been brought up to believe the Russians were some alien, hostile people sitting over there just waiting to swallow up America. Nothing could be further from the truth. I was amazed how friendly and kind and helpful they were.'

And once the amazement had gone, she contemplated what could be done for international peace. There was no better way, she thought, than for other people to follow her example and see the place for themselves.

A change was needed in international relations.

For the moment, though, neither she nor Vadim was thinking of changing their own relationship. They were clearly in love – even if this seemed a fairly prosaic, everyday term for the kind of people they were and the sort of life they lived. But neither were they any more inclined than they had been before to make their relationship more permanent by going to the altar or to a justice of the peace.

Back in America, Jane was once more subject to the inquisition. And strangely, the newsmen still wanted to know more about her relationship with her father than with Vadim – which is a further indication of how journalism has changed in the last two decades.

'I really admire my father's acting,' she told one interviewer. 'He's never bad, no matter what he's playing in.' For the moment, that was not the kind of record she could yet claim for herself.

Vadim set about trying to change all that. His trouble – and Jane's – was that he was much more enthusiastic about keeping his own image intact.

Their base now was a home they had taken in Malibu. If Jane was beginning to talk of wanting to be away from the usual idea of Hollywood stardom, Vadim was enjoying every moment of it. The French film industry was different. Hollywood, as far as he was concerned, set the example by which any self-respecting film man should expect to live.

As for Jane, she was still endeavouring to prove that this was the life she had chosen for herself – and if she was doing it back in America again, that was to relieve herself of the title she had unfortunately been given as a result of making *La Ronde* and living with its director – 'the American Bardot'.

M. Vadim may have been tickled by that. After all, it confirmed his Pygmalion role very nicely. But Jane was not. If she hadn't cared for him so much, she would have run away simply to escape that sort of appellation.

'I've a lot of respect for Brigitte Bardot,' she said – which was the kind of thing she would be expected to say. She was also expected to qualify the statement. And she did. 'But I don't think I'm like her at all. And in any case, I prefer being myself. That's what really got me in Hollywood. I ended up no longer knowing who I really was. I was like a prefabricated product and a prisoner of the system. So I decided to escape all that and get out from under my father's shadow.'

To a great extent she was doing that, although she still worried about what Henry would say about her latest love and she *knew* what he would say; even though his own life was far from the general idea of what a father's style should be.

And she was constantly, even now, dogged by those comparisons with Henry. She didn't treat them kindly, as statements like this revealed: 'If you're Henry Fonda's daughter, you're immediately vulnerable. You're watched and expected to be a hit or a flop right away. If you're Miss Nobody from Ohio, you can get away with a flop. That's what held me back so long.'

She was in love with the film business almost as much as she now was with Vadim. She saw sometimes two pictures a day, including her own when possible. She was also getting to see her father's films, some for the first time. It was at this time that she first saw him in *The Grapes of Wrath*. It was not only a great film, but also politically sound.

'I knew my father made serious movies and that in his heart he is a very progressive person,' she said at the time.

'I think it's the most brilliant acting I ever saw. It's a perfect movie, the kind of thing I would like to see. All my life has been a privilege,' she said a number of years later, when she herself was in a more 'serious' phase. 'You can be a privileged movie star, or you can commit yourself to the idea that people can change their lives and can change history. I want to make films that will make people feel stronger, understand more clearly, and make them move forward – women and men. That's what I'm interested in.'

For the moment, in 1965, she was more concerned with the Jane Fonda who was making films with Roger Vadim either behind the camera or providing his influence from further afar.

'The disadvantage with films is that one day's rehearsal on a studio set is the equivalent of a New York play opening with all that long, careful preparation. But the marvellous thing about pictures is that you can prepare a specific moment. The camera can do subtle detail work and maybe grab a good accident just that once. It's a director's medium unquestionably. He has to control everything at once.'

And Vadim was doing his share controlling Jane.

Vadim had taken over from Voutsinas. What he recommended for her, she was willing and able to do. A whole string of ideas poured into their mail boxes every day. Producers were constantly on the phone. Every time they dined at a Beverly Hills restaurant, they were surrounded by agents and other producers. They knew that the two were in demand as much for the novelty they represented – and the publicity that went with it – as for their art, but it did not matter.

They were part of the culture of their times and both enjoyed it. If writers would forget about her being the American Bardot – and as long as she stayed in California, they would – she would help them not to remember her relationship with Henry Fonda.

Vadim was delighted with his new creation. And he still is. For him, she represented not just a new woman made in the image he thought perfect, but the perfect lover.

He had also begun forming her in the image he thought was right for her. Bardot he had created from a girl who dreamed of being a ballet dancer. Catherine Deneuve he turned into the star of Jacques Demy's *The Umbrellas of Cherbourg* at the age of twenty. He told me: 'Producers would not have given the money to go with this actress if she had been totally unknown. Because of the years we were together, she had an exposure to the press which she cultivated so well that she was going to be the next big star.'

The situation with Jane was not that different. 'When she left Hollywood, it was because she wanted to make a name on her own. She was a little starlet, the daughter of Henry Fonda. Some journalists compared her with Brigitte Bardot and she hated that. She was right to hate it. She came to France to try to make a name of her own. That was very courageous and typical of Jane – usually people go the other way, to Hollywood, to try to make a name.'

Sometimes, the name wasn't all she might have hoped.

When the American distributors of *La Ronde* decided to advertise the movie with a huge poster over the Broadway theatre playing the film, purporting to show a totally naked Jane, she sued.

She said through her spokesman – using legal, press-agent's talk – that she suffered considerable 'anguish' seeing her person so exposed. She also felt 'shame'. Enough anguish and shame to be worth $3 million, it was decided by the law firm of Paul, Weiss, Rifkind, Wharton and Garrison.

The offending parts on the giant eight-storey billboard at the DeMille Theatre on 47th Street were covered up. with what Jane called a 'Band Aid' – in fact a large strip of canvas. The poster was finally removed.

Mr Walter Reade, head of the company owning the theatre, Walter Reade-Sterling Inc., said he couldn't understand what all the fuss was about – while thoroughly enjoying the publicity which was at least doubling his daily take. Vadim couldn't in his heart of hearts have disliked it all that much either.

Said Mr Reade: 'We are not in the pornography, cheap and salacious business.' The artist had worked from stills and his picture was 'in very good taste'.

It may not have been intended as such, but it served to confirm the change Vadim had made in his new mistress. Even if she didn't like the title herself, it rubbed in the message that she was the new Hollywood Bardot.

Vadim knew its value – as that of everything else he did when advising and recommending the next work she should do.

'I did help her. She was charming in *La Ronde*, *Circle of Love*. The movie did very well in Europe,' he told me.

The American critics were not so sure at all. Writing of Vadim's new version of the classic film. Eugene Archer said in the *New York Times*: 'His dubbed *Circle of Love*, which rode a crest of exploitation yesterday into the DeMille, Coronet and theatres all over town, is a dull, pointless, ineptly acted vulgarization of a distinguished play with nothing to recommend it beyond some attractive colour photography by Henri Decae ...' He hated the dubbed voices.

'The only tolerable voice in the collection belongs to Jane Fonda who uses her own – though it has no relationship to her lip movements, since she played the part in French. Wildly miscast as the discreet and timid matron, the part Miss Darrieux made hers for life, the improving Miss Fonda plays against type. With some comic skill, she creates a perverse imp who speaks modestly while her gestures and expression pointedly belie her words. In the film's most diverting episode, Miss Fonda cavorts in bed with the student, Jean-Claude Brialy – where despite those billboards, she remains strategically covered by a sheet at most times ... The rest are a sad lot and after Miss Fonda's early exit the film careers violently downhill.'

That was not, however, what could be said about her relationship with Vadim, who continued to frame the kind of woman he thought she should be. He may have protested that this was not his intention, but it only confirmed the notion that he was making an American Bardot out of her.

Vadim would always deny that that was his conscious aim. But as her lover he took on the familiar role of manager of her career as well as of her private life. Andreas had done this before, but with Vadim there was a new depth to this relationship, a more obvious sense of caring and a new equality of status.

They took a home together near Paris in a village called St Ouen-Marchefroy, the kind of place made famous in Jacques Tati comedies, the sort where you expected to see the mayor opening a 'Clochemerle' public convenience.

Actually it was, she said, 'about forty-five minutes from Paris, the way I drive.'

Their home was an eighteenth-century farmhouse, with three acres of grounds and two buildings making up the home. 'I fell in love with the colour of the stone walls – a kind of beige honey colour like an Andrew Wyeth drawing.' But everything wasn't quite as simple as just moving in. 'Just try telling ten workers in your French how to modernize a place and yet keep its original beauty.' She tried and on the whole succeeded. Friends who went to see them there came back to Hollywood in near-ecstasy.

For a time, even Henry seemed pleased. Jane was at Orly airport when she spotted a tall familiar figure wearing dark glasses. 'It was my father,' she reported, 'on his way to West Berlin for *Battle of the Bulge.*'

Henry was to say that he wasn't so keen on those stumbles into airports. Even when Jane was not around someone was going to ask him about her. As he said: 'I'm between planes somewhere and a reporter has a clipping that says Jane Fonda thinks her parents led a phoney life. Or that she thinks her father should have been psycho-analysed thirty-five years ago. Now it's all right for her to think it, but I don't think it's right for her to say so in interviews. After all, I am her *father.*' It was a continuing story.

He had got so unnerved by Jane's behaviour at times – or at least, the kind that was reported – that he snapped to a reporter: 'Daughter? I have no daughter!' It sounded like a line from one of those films from the days before even he started making them, when the girl with a babe in her arms would be sent out into the snow while the pianist in the pit played 'Hearts and Flowers'.

Subsequently, he modified his remarks even though Jane signally failed to change her ideas or her lifestyle.

Jane's brother compared Vadim with their father. 'Vadim is kinder and more open,' said Peter at this time. 'But I think my sister married my father.'

It was not a statement that endeared the two 'brothers-in-law' to each other. 'I think your brother hates me,' Vadim told Jane when he heard that.

But compared with Henry, to Peter, Vadim was honest, above board and totally reasonable. Peter related his father's objections to Jane's living with Vadim to the senior Fonda's own behaviour.

'The only difference was that he'd send his chick home at night. His duplicity blew our minds.'

Vadim couldn't quite be sure about his relationship with the head of the family. He said he liked the older man and although he himself might not be considered to be an ideal suitor, Henry was the first to recognize that he was a considerable improvement on the other men in his daughter's life.

Nevertheless, Vadim was certain that Jane's father would hate him. He certainly was anything but pleased that the Frenchman was living with his daughter. 'He wanted to dislike him,' Jane later reported. On the whole, he did – although he didn't discover her and her lover in any compromising situations. And, by most accounts, he before long softened, too.

When, out of the blue, Henry phoned them in Malibu to ask if he could come over, Roger was scared out of his wits. But Henry came, the two men shook hands and when he saw that Vadim was fishing, everything was all right. A man who liked fishing had to have something right about him.

There was no doubt that Jane thought so, too. So did their ever-widening social circle. To them, Roger and Jane were the ideal, extremely enviable couple.

They believed so, too, with apparently ample reason.

Their life seemed idyllic, but she still denied she had any intention of marrying. It would have shocked the Louella Parsons and Hedda Hoppers who just a few short years back screeched about her sentiments on marriage, but now it really did not matter either to her or to Vadim or, strangely, to her public.

She didn't see marriage as a source for stability. How could she?

'In any case, it's not really necessary for a family unit to be tight and close. It can be split up and so long as we all love each other, it's all right. I mean we're all very close and we never see each other. Just bump into each other at airports.' Which gave some indication of how important that meeting at Orly had been for Jane. But Vadim was her uncompromised love.

When she went searching for a white cashmere sweater for Roger in London – 'It's got to be cashmere because the poor lamb gets kinda itchy with ordinary wool' – it was like listening to any young bride talk about her husband. There just was *no* real difference, the way she saw things.

She had given up her sessions on the psychiatrist's couch at last. 'I was travelling so much that I didn't have time. And when I did have time, I found I didn't need it any more.' And the reason? She was 'terribly happy.' With Roger Vadim.

'I'm happy because I'm in love. And whether a woman is happy because she's in love or just happy, she's a better actress, whoever she's working with. It influences everything.'

They were planning a new film to be called simply *Love*. It didn't happen, but that was no cause for worry.

As much as anything she loved him because of what he had done for her career. In a strange way, he had made her see that it was not the most important thing in her life.

'I'm much more relaxed now. I used to work all the time, making three or four films a year. I used to think then that my career was the really important thing in my life. But now, I've questioned myself and I know it's secondary. I could never sacrifice anything for it. And oddly enough, because I'm more relaxed, I'm a better actress. I used to be so nervous before a film, I used to come out in boils – pretty, huh? Now, I'm just nervous.'

Part of being accepted as Jane Fonda, Film Actress and not simply Henry Fonda's daughter was doing her own thing. But she did it with Vadim's help.

And the American Press were pleased to add whatever little assistance that they could.

'Ever since de Gaulle threw out NATO and the Johnsons (President and Mrs Lyndon B. Johnson) fired their *chef de cuisine*', wrote Gerald Jonas in the *New York Times*, 'one of the last remaining ornaments of the Franco-American alliance has been a blonde, blue-eyed bilingual actress named Jane Fonda.'

She may never have figured herself as part of an Alliance, or at least a political one, but she was certainly happy with the alliance with Vadim.

When she was offered the title part in a spoof Western, Vadim grabbed the opportunity on her behalf. Nobody said it, but in *Cat Ballou* she was Brigitte Bardot in Tombstone City.

The film was described as a *Tom Jones*-type piece.

It was another big Fonda success. In later years, it would prove such a hit on American television that Columbia's TV offshoot couldn't run off sufficient copies to cope with the demand. She was not thinking of its TV potential when she made the picture, however.

'It is not only my first Western,' she told the *New York Times*, 'but I think it's also the first of its kind ever made.'

It was the story of a girl who vows vengeance when her father is killed – the kind of thing Jane probably would have done herself if anyone tried to murder Henry, for all the things she had said and thought about him.

Lee Marvin, in a dual role, had reason to regard it as a big hit for himself, too; and if the ideal partnership in a movie is when both co-stars feel as though they have hit the jackpot, then ideal this tale was – the story of a has-been gunfighter, his evil brother and the woman who likes to think she could have beaten Annie Oakley in any shootout the folks thereabouts would care to organize.

She also would have beaten, with her bare knuckles if necessary, anyone who made a pitch for Vadim. Now there was a new security when she showed him her Hollywood and she loved bringing him to the parties and the other top attractions of the film capital in much the same way as he had been in showing France to her.

The critics plainly thought that the effort was worthwhile. Now she was receiving the kind of plaudits she had hoped to expect as her due after *Sunday in New York* but which were so prominent by their absence for *La Ronde*.

In the *New York Herald Tribune*, Judith Crist said:

'Well, let's get those old superlatives out. Jane Fonda is just marvellous as the wide-eyed Cat, exuding sweet feminine sex appeal every sway of the way.'

Jane swayed that little sexy behind of hers in all the best places – and in some of the least fortunate ones too. The row over the poster continued and there were sneaky attempts to put it up elsewhere. They didn't succeed.

Briefly, the couple went back to Europe. But the call of a new Hollywood offer was enough to ensure more tickets were bought for America. This time, Vadim approved the script for a film in which Jane would star opposite one of her idols, Marlon Brando.

Any actress influenced by Strasberg and his Actors Studio school of performance had to admire Brando. His early performances – the famous Brando 'mumbling' in *A Streetcar Named Desire* and *On the Waterfront* – were the first introduction the general public had to the world of the Method. Jane knew what this represented to herself and to her profession, and working with Brando was an opportunity she was not going to spurn.

The Chase was a Lillian Hellman screenplay, from Horton Foote's novel. The authorship of the script was another attraction to Jane; a third was that Sam Spiegel, one of the names most respected in Hollywood was producing – with Arthur Penn as director. Brando played a Texas sheriff, fighting the Deep South mentality of a lynch mob.

Jane played the unfaithful wife of the escaped convict who was about to be the victim of that mob, Robert Redford. Redford hadn't yet earned his image of the suave debonair heir to Robert Taylor and Clark Gable. It was Brando whom Jane described as being 'sexy'. Not as sexy, though, as Vadim who was always around in the studio, if not on set – Brando let it be known he didn't want Roger present while he was working. He intuitively feared the impact Vadim's influence would have on his co-star.

Jane had an equally intuitive notion of the part she was playing. 'This woman, Anna, is all I think a woman should be. She has reasons to be frustrated, loving two men two different ways at the same time. But she can't stand pointlessness and dishonesty. She's one of those rare women who has put her life in perspective.'

It wasn't a great success, but it *was* a new extension to her career. Now there was to be another. Together, she and Vadim took off for Las Vegas – to get married.

8

I n a way, it was part of Vadim's feminist philosophy. Jane
deserved what she wanted; and if she now sought the security
of married life, then so be it.

It was totally contrary to all the things she had been saying,
and not just to the Hollywood amazons. She later admitted that she
had made her original statement to Hedda Hopper about marriage
being obsolete because she knew it was good copy. But she did believe
in the general sentiment.

'I was speaking theoretically and on that level I still believe it. It
seems amazing to me that two people can coexist at all. Why does it
have to be put down on paper, as if people were possessions.'

She still believed that marriage didn't make much sense. It was
'something superfluous – like the human appendix. I'm sure that in
the future, like that organ, it will be eliminated because it certainly
doesn't protect anything as far as the couple is concerned. We're all
fickle. Why have the added burden of marriage? Maybe women do
need the security.' Well, not this woman. Or did she? 'I don't know,'
she said.

She was to say that she did it more for Henry than anyone else.
There is reason enough to believe it, and to believe her when she said
that two days before the appointed date with marriage she panicked.
'I wanted to call the whole thing off.'

Vadim denies that it was his idea that they got married. As he wrote
in *Bardot, Deneuve and Fonda*: 'It shows a lack of understanding of Jane

86

to imagine that she would be capable of taking such an important decision through weakness, weariness or simply kindness. She has never let anyone make the important decisions in her life for her.'

He denies most vociferously that it was part of a gigantic publicity stunt. He also maintains it was too important a part of his life to treat so casually. That was why when she said she planned to call it off, their more intimate acquaintances gave it serious thought.

But she didn't. And Henry was one of the reasons why. No matter how infrequently they saw each other – and how many of the times when they did get together that they spent those meetings arguing – she still desperately sought his approval for most of the things she did and wanted it for those where she did not go out of her way to seek his acquiescence.

'I knew I was hurting him,' she said.

Henry meanwhile showed his opposition to Jane's lifestyle by refusing to see any of her movies at this time. (She took that as a slight, which it might have been, but he claimed to never see any of his own either. He always said he hated the sound of his voice.)

Now there would be less reason for Henry to complain. It would also make life easier for the children they planned to have. When they took Vadim's daughter (by Annette Stroyberg) on a trip, she revealed somewhat tactlessly that other children would delight in telling her that her parents were no longer married. This way, there would be none of that sort of worry – and, besides, they themselves would find it easier to get into hotels.

If, however, people believed that this was a concession to total conformity, to old world values, to the mores of the society Jane hailed from and which Henry claimed to espouse whenever he married a girl just about old enough to be his daughter's elder sister, there was reason enough to sit up and think again.

The marriage ceremony was in Las Vegas, an outpost of taste and serenity, usually devoted to a totally different kind of gambling. However, since marriage itself is something of a toss-up, it is perhaps not unreasonable that Las Vegas also specializes in providing instant weddings – and, in turn, practically instant divorces.

Vadim and Fonda went there because, once having made up their minds to marry, they saw no reason to go through the formalities required elsewhere. However, it did not mean that they treated the whole thing as an occasion for excessive solemnity.

Jane was to say that she was sleeping through the day. She could not understand why she had gone to Vegas to go through, of all things, a form of marriage. She kept repeating to herself: 'I honestly don't know why I'm doing it.'

The ceremony was performed at that temple of the extravagant, the Dunes Hotel, a place that boasts it serves breakfast at any time of the day and refuses to display a clock in case any one should be worried about ordering it in the middle of the afternoon.

On this occasion, Justice of the Peace James S. Brennan performed the ceremony.

Henry, to nobody's surprise, was not there, but Peter did turn up with his own new wife, Susan. Roger's mother, then Mme Antoinette Ardiouze, flew over from Paris for her son's third marriage. She acted as matron-of-honour, which was only one of the unconventional aspects of the occasion.

Christian Marquand and his wife, Tina, were honoured guests, as befitted Vadim's closest friends. He had a particular reason for honouring Mme Marquand. She was the daughter of the eminent French actor Jean-Pierre Aumont.

It was fortunate that they were there. Both Jane and Roger had been so carried away with the occasion that they forgot one of the most important parts of the arrangements – their joint wedding rings. The Marquands lent the couple theirs for the occasion.

The ceremony itself was in a six-room suite on the hotel's twentieth floor. Peter played the guitar, while a five-piece orchestra of girl violinists – all wearing skin-tight blue dresses positively floodlit with sequins – provided live muzak.

The marriage register she signed as 'Lady Jane Seymour Brokaw (her mother's maiden name) Fonda Plemiannikov.' The name 'Vadim' did not appear with reference to her.

The honeymoon was spent in reasonable Las Vegas style watching the Dunes stage show, which appropriately enough for Vadim took the theme of the French Revolution; a revolution in which the major characters looked more likely to lose their naked breasts at the guillotine than their heads. The couple then stayed up all night – and if you were to believe the publicity which they nevertheless managed to provide for the anxious press, that night was spent gambling.

But they were soon back to another kind of making money – in the movie studio. If their marriage was going to mean anything at all, they were going to have to show they were as compatible in the workplace as in the bedroom.

Together they went back to their eighteenth century farmhouse and planned the next picture they would make in the Paris studios, a movie

Jane – the first movie. On the set of *Tall Story* with co-star Anthony Perkins.

Jane in France.

The provocative Jane Fonda – mid-Sixties.

Vadim and Jane in Malibu.

Jane on the scaffold in *Cat Ballou*.

The kind of pose she would later hate herself for. Behind Perspex in *Barbarella*.

Jane in the mini-skirted world of fashion. Before she lived in jeans and sweaters, Chanel had a very good customer in her.

Her one film with Peter Finch – on location in Greece for *In the Cool of the Day*.

Husband and wife; star and director. Jane and Vadim working on the set of *Barbarella*.

The trap. Jane suffering in *Barbarella*.

The Vadims – Jane, Roger and their new baby Vanessa.

Henry in reflective mood while Jane plays entertainer with a 'mobile' for Vanessa (who is out of the picture).

Under arrest. Signals of defiance from an upstairs window with Elisabeth Valliard and Mark Lane at Fort Meade in 1970.

No good cause would escape her attention.

The Army didn't like her demos one bit. Time and again she was escorted off the bases.

Not all her audiences approved of Fonda demos. Here she leaves one spattered in paint.

which Vadim was sure would exploit both his wife's talents and her body. He had no inhibitions about the necessity for her to reveal her physical attributes and she was willing to take his advice, despite all the fuss over the Broadway billboard. It was, after all, his trademark and was a way of ensuring that the American Bardot was going to justify her image.

For all her growing sense of independence, her developing devotion to feminism, she was totally in his hands – metaphorically as well as physically.

She was aware as much as anyone that people were going to look for a new Bardot, whether or not that was Vadim's intention. As she said: 'Odd, you know. As soon as it's known one's making a film with Vadim everyone says, "Oh, another Vadim". Well, it's true I look different from myself in *La Ronde*. But that's because Vadim likes his women to look a certain way. When I asked him how he liked a girl to look on the screen, he just said, "Luminous!" The truth is that Vadim pays more attention to how an actress looks than any director I've ever known. Now I see how very different the Hollywood look is from the European.'

It was one of the reasons she had first decided to leave America. 'If I'd stayed in Hollywood, I'd have just been my father's daughter. Here I'm a separate person. And I've learned so much while I've been here; about life and about the business.'

The Vadim look was different, because he knew that the censor, as a matter of principle, always cut things out of a Vadim picture. So there was a game afoot. He planned scenes for every one of his films knowing that the censor was going to get to work. In fact, he did very little in the next Fonda-Vadim movie.

The new film was based on the Emile Zola story, *La Curée*. But a Jane Fonda film now automatically meant an American – and therefore a British and other European – distribution. For these, he already had an English-language title, *The Game Is Over*.

One should not come to the conclusion that he thought his own game with Jane was over. But perhaps there *was* something worth thinking about in that title. Was he trying to say that his Pygmalion game was now at an end?

Despite what may be evidence to the contrary, Vadim is determined no one has the impression it was all merely a retread of an old tyre.

'It had nothing to do with the Bardot image this time,' Vadim assured me – a view that was not shared by most people who saw this story of a young married bourgeois couple caught between their relationship with each other and the husband's son, Jane's stepson.

Jane told everyone how keen she was on this new project – her first full-length role in a Vadim movie. 'This movie's very important to me.' And no, she said, she wasn't going to appear nude in it all the time.

Having decided that there was no more mileage in Jane the girl everyone now expected to get undressed, reporters started asking her about the reverse topic, the clothes that she did wear.

She never aimed to get on to any best-dressed-women's lists. 'They're boring,' she declared as though making any other anti-Establishment statement. 'I get the impression that in a lot of cases, they're rich people who play it safe. I know some women who work to get on that list.... I can think of so much more interesting things to do.'

She had bought a number of suits from Chanel while in Paris but she cut all the skirts into minis. 'Chanel would die!' It was still the age when women wore stockings. Tights were a rarity. Jane told everyone she had a leotard beneath her mini skirts, and the information was flashed around the world.

Woman gasped. Men mumbled words of disappointment.

But she was right. There were more interesting things to think about – even though, with the best will in the world, *The Game Is Over* could hardly be one of them.

Jane did her own dubbing – into French as well as into English. She loved this extension to her career, apparently an example of her growing self-confidence. It was confirmation that she had mastered the French language; and, professionally speaking, it enabled her to 'say things you wouldn't dare say in English'. That was one way of looking at the foreign-language film business.

More people were to see the film than could at first have been imagined. And a lot more were to see part of the movie than ever actually paid for a ticket at a theatre box office.

It proved that the familiar publicity game, if nothing else, was certainly not over.

In one ten-second scene in a Turkish bath, Jane is seen naked – revealing (then, the most daring thing imaginable for a film actress) her breasts.

She had ensured that the set would be closed for this scene. What she did was for her husband's eyes and those of the most essential technicians. Nobody else was going to see more than would actually appear on the screen. It wasn't quite to happen that way.

Scenes from those ten seconds were printed outside the studio laboratories. A photographer, it seemed, had hidden in the soundstage rafters.

The shots then found their way to what readers of *Playboy* magazine knew as The Desk of Hugh M. Hefner. For him, they were like the gift of the Crown Jewels to a pretender to the throne of France. He published – and once again Jane sued.

Again, Jane said that she had thought she was only going to show her back on screen and nothing at all for the readers of *Playboy*. Again, she complained of 'mental anguish' and said that she suffered 'intense humiliation'.

The price of that 'intense humiliation' was $9.5 million.

The lawyers said more in court. 'She has witheld from the public glare her nude persona likeness and refused to permit any photography which used the exposed portion of her body.'

The action was ultimately lost.

She, naturally enough, had to answer charges that to take her clothes off at all meant a licence for pornography. Not at all, she said. She made the film, feeling 'relaxed and free'. Pornography was different. 'Pornography begins when things become self-conscious.'

Later, she told the *New York Times* – in an article headed 'Here's What Happened to Baby Jane', a gift at a time so soon after the Bette Davis-Joan Crawford movie *Whatever Happened to Baby Jane?* – that she was not at all naive about the way films were made. Publicity was essential and she thought that there was something perhaps pleasant about all this publicity. 'I think it's nice if people think I'm some kind of sex symbol. But I'm not responsible.'

She didn't blame her husband for the pirated pictures. 'I knew Vadim would protect me in the cutting room,' she declared. Finding out that a photographer had hidden to take the pictures 'rocked' her: 'It's a simple matter of breaking and entering and invasion of privacy.'

She knew what Vadim was making of her, but what he wanted to do most was to say something about society, she believed, and she was willing to let him say all he wanted to. Her sexy appearance was essential to Vadim's message – and Roger underlined what she told the *Times*'s Gerald Jonas: a conscious repudiation of 'the Christian sense of sin' and a celebration of the human body.

Two more Hollywood movies followed close on *The Game Is Over*, neither of them exciting enough to cause the slightest degree of controversy as far as Jane's body was concerned. Politics and prejudice were another matter.

Hurry Sundown, based on an intelligent novel by K.B. Gilden, did, however, deal with a controversial matter, black-white relations in Georgia. It was even more controversial because it saw things from the point of view of the downtrodden blacks who were being oppressed by the whites.

Perhaps, though, the most controversial thing of all was the fact that the movie was made at all. Otto Preminger produced and directed the film, which gave every sign of showing that his once-deft touch had practically disappeared. (His total destruction of *Porgy and Bess* had turned out to be Sam Goldwyn's last film.)

Jane played the lead in the picture – with Diahann Carroll in almost as big a part; the first time when black and white actresses had competed for top billing.

John Phillip Law, one of her co-performers, remembers one outstanding thing about Jane in this film – her energy. 'I was amazed at just how she could run around from place to place,' Law told me.

The picture was about good and bad, about integrating the races, and the cast was intended to mirror the story – with Jane playing the wife of a plantation owner portrayed by Michael Caine. Jane was supposed to ooze sex with every pout, and she did. But sometimes you believed that it owed more to sweat than libido. That, though, was not what worried the populace of Baton Rouge, Louisiana, where much of the movie was shot.

When she was seen kissing a little black boy in the street, she was told by the local sheriff to get out of town as quickly as possible. Most people felt the same way about the picture.

The acid reviewer Rex Reed commented: 'Critic Wilfrid Sheed wrote recently that no film is ever so bad that you can't find some virtue in it. He must not have seen *Hurry Sundown*.'

And *Cue* magazine wrote: 'Preminger's taste is atrocious. His idea of erotic symbolism is Jane Fonda caressing Michael Caine's saxophone.'

Indeed, Caine held the saxophone between his legs, and Jane was sitting on the floor in front of him. Vadim, as before, advised Jane on taking the role. He said she should go ahead.

He was exercising his rights as a husband; to be her confidant and adviser. In truth, of course, he had demonstrated those rights together with all the others for quite some time. He was happy enough being married, but he maintains to this day, as he told me, that he has no great admiration for marriage as a way of life, let alone an institution. Plainly, there is little that is institutional about Roger Vadim.

She wasn't too worried about the doubts. She had faith in Preminger. 'I did *Hurry Sundown* because I liked the character and Otto Preminger was directing. I like to be told what to do and Otto knows exactly what he wants.' The pity was that Jane wasn't so well assured herself.

Her next film had a great many more redeeming characteristics. *Any Wednesday* (in Britain it was called *Bachelor Girl Apartment*) now ought to be remembered as Jane's only real brush with the Hollywood system of old. It was made for Warner Bros. at the time of the studio's twilight as an independent studio and with Jack L. Warner exercising one of his final spasms of authority as the Last Tycoon – in 1966, he was the only remaining mogul from the big studio era.

Adapted from Muriel Resnik's Broadway play, it was the story of a millionaire's dalliance with his mistress – every Wednesday. He sets her up in her own smart Manhattan residence, which is written off – much to the evident distress of his wife – to his business. It is the only known time in history when Jane Fonda might have been described as a tax loss.

It could have been a heavy-handed affair, except that the screenplay was written by the producer Julius J. Epstein, who had shared an Oscar for the script of *Casablanca*, gone on to write some of the deftest comedies in film history, and treated Hollywood movies as his own kind of dish. He remembers Jane Fonda, he told me, with great affection. 'A delightful young lady,' he said.

Epstein had written the script of her first movie *Tall Story*. His memory of her on both pictures was of a 'strict, strict professional' even at this early age. 'She knew her lines. She didn't demand changes. She was not in the least bit temperamental. I guess she got that from her father. I did a picture with her father once and it couldn't have been a better experience. He was also the true professional. I would think that was a family trait.'

One thing Jane was very concerned with was the clothes she was going to wear: 'She wanted to wear clothes by her own French designer. She was right. The clothes were wonderful.'

The head of the studio was not quite so sure. Indeed, Jane's big memory of the picture is more, it would seem, of Jack L. Warner than anything else, and what he said about her body and the clothes with which she draped it. He told her that he did not like the size of her bust.

Mr Warner measured breasts by the amount of space they would occupy on a CinemaScope screen. The message was transmitted to her on Warner's behalf by the wardrobe department. 'When I told them I didn't wear a brassiere,' Jane later reported, 'I was told "Mr Warner...."'

Mr Warner said she had to wear a bra. In truth, similar demands had been made by movie moguls since the days when Hollywood films were shot in open-roofed barns; a few years earlier Harry Cohn, head of Columbia Pictures, had insisted on Kim Novak's supporting her bosom with an undergarment she hated wearing. Jane could only assent.

Also Jane wanted to wear polka dots. Out. Mr Warner, she was advised, did not like polka dots.

Vadim was in Paris while the movie was being shot. But every day – and frequently more than just once a day – he would phone the studio from France and she would take the call on the set. 'Usually, he would call at about two in the afternoon, just as we were getting back to work after lunch,' Julius Epstein remembered for me. 'They would be on the phone for between forty-five minutes and an hour, while I would be pacing up and down on the set. That was the only chink in her professional armour. She was crazy about him.

'But she was so good and professional in every other way, we let her do it while we went on with doing something else. We accommodated ourselves to it and gave ourselves time to set up the next scene.'

The film was eventually completed and previewed in the time-honoured Hollywood way, unannounced in a neighbourhood theatre, with the audience invited to complete cards on which they scribbled their not altogether articulate or knowledgeable comments. The least printable were those that were not written down – by M. Vadim.

'He wasn't very pleased,' Julius Epstein told me. 'There was no sign language. He came right out and said so. He told us he didn't like the picture. She was all right. We were the ones who came in for all the criticism. She just stood in the background like a very, very loving, devoted wife' – which, of course, was precisely the sort of woman being deceived in the picture. Rosemary Murphy played the wife in the film and Jason Robards Jnr, her husband, the one who set Jane up in her apartment for use on Wednesdays. Dean Jones provided the younger male interest.

Julius Epstein remembers the picture as being 'not very good'. On the whole, that was not the view of the critics. *Time* magazine described it as 'a kind of sexual string quartet, arranged for four players'.

Of Jane's role in the movie, the magazine's critic – unnamed in those days, which heightened the mystery but didn't usually say a lot for the publication's honesty – wrote: '*Wednesday*'s girl of the hour is Jane Fonda. Looking tempting and wholesome, she cries a lot, but wears her tears like costume jewellery. Produced on cue, the drops are merely decorative, unrelated to any real passions or real truths about the plight of a 30-year-old spinster who has a sneaking fondness for bright balloons, babies and a big business tycoon.'

How about that! At twenty-nine, Jane Fonda was already playing a thirty-year-old. It was only one way in which she was defying Hollywood convention, the principal rule of which is that you are always at least five years younger than the age on your birth certificate. But that was not a problem. In fact, Wardrobe and M. Vadim apart, the picture seemed to have sailed through without too much trouble.

There were even fewer difficulties with her next movie – another picture about the Big Apple, but very reminiscent of *Sunday in New York*, if only because *Barefoot in the Park* showed the same bright, funny, pretty New Yorker of the earlier picture.

It had the added advantage of a Neil Simon script about a couple of newly-weds (Jane and Robert Redford) battling with poverty for the sake of love. They were so good, seemed so much in love, that all over the world young couples started queuing for marriage licences. Being poor and married and young had never looked a more attractive proposition.

Charles Boyer made a cameo appearance which turned out to be one of the most charming of his long career – it was also one of his last – and Mildred Natwick as Jane's understanding, indulgent mother did more for the mother-in-law business than anything since the days of Naomi and Ruth.

It was another event in Jane's miniskirt period – black tights with black leather boots; a blouse invitingly unbuttoned. She looked prettier than she ever had before. That itself was different. She had been attractive, devilishly attractive, some might say; but now she was pretty. There was a difference and people who saw *Barefoot in the Park* could detect the variations.

Above all, Jane had never been better. She was proving something that wasn't easy to show – that a girl could in the span of the same career be funny, be beautiful, be sexy and be intelligent. She had the art of taking a script and putting on the right face and using the right voice to fit the written words in front of her.

There were not many actresses who could do that. Jane Fonda was not going to be typecast. She was available for any good part that might come her way. Many players like to think of themselves as actresses as much as stars. Other people were now to think so of Jane, too. It had been a fight, but the battle seemed won.

There was, however, a more significant tussle on the way. Jane was going to show she could bring a cartoon to life – a cartoon that showed quite as much as even Jack Warner liked of the female anatomy, and actually discussed sex.

9

The amazing thing about Jane Fonda early in 1967 was precisely how many Janes there had already been.

Fifteen films in seven years had revealed several before the pretty 'Barefoot' Jane, the sensual, exciting, sophisticated, puzzled girl-turned-woman: Jane the cheerleader; Jane the Western outlaw; Jane the *femme* who was not quite *fatale*. Many of them showed the influence of whichever guru happened to be on hand at the time. Now, though, Jane was proving she could be influenced by a strip cartoon.

'Barbarella' was not most people's idea of a comic strip – at least not to those living in America, where for many people a session with 'Blondie' went along with the cornflakes and orange juice. In Britain, comic strips were their most daring in 'Jane', she regularly took off her clothes in the *Daily Mirror* and had been doing so since before the Second World War, but she was never more than a little bit 'naughty'.

Cartoons in France, however, were a different matter entirely. The French were used to sexy strip heroines who were different in the same way that French movies were still different from those made in Hollywood or Elstree.

Barbarella was like many of those French heroines, although she *did* appear in America, in the magazine *Evergreen Review*. Not only did she regularly display her naked breasts, but sometimes even a touch of her pubic area. She was always being shown in bed – and not simply for the purpose of sleeping. And she went far and wide for her troubles.

In an age when people had just begun to talk of the 'jet set' crossing the Atlantic, Barbarella went from planet to planet looking for sexual stimulation. More than that, she went from galaxy to galaxy.

Roger Vadim thought that converting this kind of strip into a new sort of strip of film would not only be highly commercial, but would prove a perfect vehicle for his new wife. Jane, as always, agreed that what Vadim thought was right was good enough for her. When he said that she should be seen totally naked in the opening minutes of the film with some of the more enticing parts of her anatomy concealed by the letters of the credits, she found no reason to argue.

He didn't originally plan it that way, but the costume Jane was supposed to wear failed to turn up, so Vadim said that it would represent a perfectly satisfactory introduction to a movie in which everyone *expected* Barbarella to be naked all the way through.

Jane later had a lot of explaining to do with that picture. It plainly did not fit into her ideas of not just feminism, but women's protest. Her explanation, with the gift of that hindsight which is not only her prerogative but which figures in the stories of practically everyone everywhere who has ever made a mistake, was that she didn't think she could protest about anything.

'When I first became an actress, I was told that I didn't look right. That I wasn't right. I had to dye my hair blonde, I had to wear falsies, my lips were repainted. That all helps to make your mind alienate you from what you are, not only inside, but outside.

'You can't protest. It is not patriotic and all the people that you see who are protesting are either kicked out of school, fired from their jobs, called up in front of the House Internal Security Committee as my father was. Frightened. People were frightened during the '50s. It was like a country that was frozen. You were put in a category. You became a blonde movie star. And I was a drop-out. I left. I went away. I lived in Europe because I didn't see any way out.

'Nobody ever sat down and said to me, "You know, there *is* a way out. These are society problems. If you sit down and figure why they exist then perhaps you can find a way along with your fellow country people to change things. I didn't think so. And besides, I was a woman. I felt that a woman can't change things. I became *Barbarella*.'

Vadim told me that he fully recognized that Jane wasn't happy with the *Barbarella* role – but only after digesting it: 'After that, when she got involved in other movies, of a different character, with a social meaning, she for a while was upset with *Barbarella*. She was saying that women shouldn't let their bodies to be used. Later on, she told me that she regretted saying those things. She said she had been a little excessive in her comments. "I looked good in it," she told me. I said, "Yes, you look good".'

The truth of the matter is that it wasn't until the film was fully into production that anyone remembers hearing Jane talking about changing society; certainly not about changing the movie itself. Vadim didn't want to do so; as far as he was concerned, there was no need to do so. She went along with him.

Vadim had to admit that *Barbarella* was a Bardot type role for Jane.

'It looks more like a Brigitte Bardot type of movie, it is true. Sex is there,' he told me. 'But not graphic sex. It is fun. There was a lot of camp humour and fantasy. People have completely forgotten that Jane became Jane Fonda through some other movies that helped her before *Barbarella*.

'But all people remember is *Barbarella* – because *Barbarella* looks more like a Bardot movie in a certain way. But it was just one of the movies that Jane could do.'

He was glad that she did – and not simply because it became such a hit for both of them. The reason is not nearly so obvious.

'One of the reasons I was pleased that she did it was because she was not very secure as far as her looks were concerned. She didn't feel that she was in any way sexy.

'She was insecure about her body and her face. People may not believe that, but it's true. *Barbarella* gave her a certain sense of confidence. She didn't have to prove anything.'

No one could doubt, however, that everything about the movie had what would today be described as 'sexist' stamped all over it. Sets and costumes were made to resemble human organs. Chairs looked like sculptured nudes. Glasses were shaped like female heads, with wine pouring from the lips. Girls – nude, of course – were seen smoking a huge bubbling water pipe, labelled 'Essence of Man'.

Vadim himself told the *New York Times*: 'What interests me is the chance to escape totally from the morals of the 20th century, and depict a new futuristic morality. It's a very romantic story, really.'

It was a new kind of romance, this. No one who was close to the set or who was even to see the finished movie would really think of it in those terms. Being brought up on a more conventional Hollywood diet would make most people think twice about giving this science fiction anything like a 'romantic' label. There wasn't a lot in common between Barbarella and, say, Garbo, Bergman, Elizabeth Taylor or all the other ladies who looked beautiful and feminine, fulfilling the requirements of the fan magazines.

It wasn't easy for the men, either, to contemplate or identify with those who were able to make love to a woman who resembled nothing more than an explosive secret weapon. She was so tough, a whole football team would have dissolved in her presence – not out of love but from sheer terror.

'Barbarella has no sense of guilt about her body. I want to make something beautiful out of eroticism,' Jane declared, boldly. But it wasn't easy for her to achieve that ambition.

She hated getting undressed for her role, mainly because, as Vadim told me, she didn't think she looked her best in that situation. The technicians who vied to get into the normally closed set might have convinced her otherwise.

In fact, the technicians were the cause of a certain amount of trouble – particularly the assistant make-up man who told too many people how many times he had caressed the Fonda form. He went into graphic detail about the breasts, bottom and inside thighs he had magically touched with the paint and powder he was paid to apply. Too much detail for his wife, who bought a gun and threatened to kill him. The man didn't remain in his job but did stay alive.

But getting dressed wasn't any easier for Jane. The perspex bra she wore was so uncomfortable that it resembled medieval torture. If Jane's political awakening was close by, this costume alone made her sorry for the future of mankind – or at least womankind.

She was, however, assured that what she did only glorified her and her sex. Jane felt she couldn't argue about that. 'Vadim,' she said, 'loves science fiction and he's gotten me interested.' The diction was American, but the sentiment showed the French influence brought up to date.

'In a way,' she said, 'the cinema is the natural medium for it, but up to now the technical gimmicks have been treated as the *raison d'être* of the science fiction film.'

The film was shot in Rome, with the leading players in the movie all sharing the same house, rented by Vadim, with Jane, quite unusually, acting as a mother hen.

'Everyone gathered there,' said John Phillip Law, who again was co-starring with Jane. He played her blind, platonically affectionate personal welfare officer – a social worker dressed as an angel. And, by all accounts, thoroughly enjoyed the experience of working closely with the Vadims.

To him, Jane was the perfect co-star and hostess. She wasn't yet involved with politics, although Peter's activities even before his motor-cycle role in *Easy Rider* had established him as a spokesman for the new politically-aware generation (who later would see the powered two-wheelers as their escape from contemporary society and all that it entailed).

But Jane was ready to be influenced. She had established friendships with Joan Baez and Vanessa Redgrave. They were spending more time condemning war than practising their respective arts and, in odd moments, were telling Jane their ideas. She nodded approvingly, but said little more. For the moment, she was concerned with making *Barbarella* and with living with its director – a man she described as 'terribly vulnerable – and like a puppy dog who wants to be loved and patted'.

So she did her best to love and to pat him: 'I think one of his great qualities is his ability to accept love, which is as important as the ability to give love. To accept love well is not an easy thing to do.'

In those heady, hot months in Rome, that was quite enough to occupy Jane Fonda, free at last, so it seemed, from the guilt and the inhibitions about being the daughter of her father.

It was plainly a happy time for her – perhaps the happiest of all times she had known so far. She was accepted for herself while still enjoying being part of Vadim's life. Nothing she did, however, was without his blessing. Still, she wasn't so secure as to believe she could do anything serious without his advice. On the set of *Barbarella*, he was husband as well as director. At home, in the big house shared by the leading members of the film's cast, he was director as well as husband.

He said he appreciated Jane as much as she loved him. 'For the first time,' he declared, 'I'm married to an adult.' But although she frequently beat him at chess, he wouldn't go so far as to say that she was intellectually brilliant – even though, with Jane's bank account clocking up $400,000 every time she signed a new contract, she was able to understand how to make money and support herself in the manner to which she was determined to stay accustomed. 'Too cerebral a woman is unsupportable,' he said. And he wanted to support her.

Once more, it was Jane's energy that struck John Phillip Law: 'Jane was sort of running a big house and in those days she would simply run around all the time.'

And not just run around the house. Every morning before the Roman dawn cracked, Jane would drive into the centre of the city and take a ballet lesson. 'Just to get herself in shape and unwind,' said the actor. He recognized that for what it was – 'the seeds of her aerobics'. Jane had made a discovery which, in financial terms, would before very long be as important as the knowledge that putting her before a camera and shouting 'Action' could make her an astonishingly good actress (after she had like all graduates of the Strasberg Method, 'felt' her part and studied her script).

There was nothing forced or false about her. It was as though she realized nobody was about to take *Barbarella* terribly seriously and she was going to enjoy having a good time and the money in the bank it would bring her.

There was, in addition, a special bond between actress and actor. When Jane starred in *The Fun Couple* on Broadway, Law played with Van Johnson and Caroll Baker in the Garson Kanin play, *Come on Strong.* Both opened on the same night. It gave him a sense of cameraderie with her from then on.

As so many others around her felt at this time stress, there may not have been any indication of her political awareness yet, but John Phillip Law now realizes these were 'the formative years'. 'I am sure all that activism was incubating at that time,' he told me. 'But the only awareness I had about her aspirations in those directions was the fact that she was always socially conscious.' Yet, when he thinks about it, this was quite clearly the start of it all. She was anxious about the world.

Just how 'socially conscious' was revealed – casually, it seemed and without anyone noticing the significance of the events – the evening when he brought Joan Baez to dinner at the Rome house. The conversation turned to the then ever-escalating Vietnam war. Joan told everyone at the dinner table just how strongly she felt about the conflict and how vital it was for America to get the hell out of the place.

Joan did the talking and Jane the listening. 'Jane was like a little child,' John Phillip Law told me. 'She looked the way I did when I met the astronauts – in awe; starstruck, I suppose, is how you'd call it.'

Strangely, it was Peter Fonda who was more responsible than anyone for making Jane start – very tentatively at first – thinking about the wider political world of the late 1960s.

As Law added: 'The awakening was going on all around her at that time.' And the real interest among her set seemed to be centred around Peter's progress. John remembered: 'Everybody seemed to spend most of their time with Jane asking her about her brother. Ironically, Peter had made more money from one film than his father had in his entire career at that point. I think Jane realized the impact *Easy Rider* was going to have on the kids and she was having a dawning sense of her own social responsibility.'

So that was it. It was all beginning. A dawning sense of social responsibility because she was getting to find out something about people younger than she was and less privileged, too.

But her feelings for Vadim were certainly much more critical in her make-up now, although this was not always noticed. 'She was so much in love with him,' John Phillip Law recalls. In love or under his thumb?

'I don't think you could say she was in any way under his thumb. She just seemed a loving wife.'

So loving that when Vadim had his birthday, she showed her love so bright and clear that everyone involved in the movie could see it: she bought him a Ferrari. That was love indeed.

The police were not so pleased with the purchase. One night, Vadim arrived home very late – with an uninvited police escort. He had driven all the way to their villa going in the wrong direction up a one-way street. Jane didn't let a thing like that spoil her love for both the man and his car.

'But the main way she showed that love,' said Law, 'was in the way she took her responsibilities running the home in that house in Rome and taking care of all his friends while she was filming *Barbarella*.' That was fairly remarkable, since she was in practically every scene, which necessitated her being on the set all day.'

Yet as we have seen, she came to regret a great deal about *Barbarella* – exposing her anything-goes philosophy as well as her breasts. It didn't fit with what she would later say about women's lib. If she said at the time she didn't wear a bra, it was to demonstrate she was proud of the fact that she didn't have to augment what nature had given her – notwithstanding Jack L. Warner or the falsies she had been made to wear for her first film role. Burning bras was a different game altogether, although before very long she would be supporting the women who allegedly did that, too.

It was an opportunity for people to make much of the fact that Jane was showing a great deal more than was usual for American actresses – and more than in the other French movies that she had made.

Quite surprisingly for the kind of publication it was, *Newsweek* magazine published in November 1967 a semi-nude picture of Jane on its cover.

Jane wasn't happy about it. Acting in the nude was a different thing. What she did in a studio was only for the benefit of the picture itself.

If the director – who just happened to be her husband – decided it was necessary for the movie, then she would go along with it. However, allowing her half-clad body to appear on a magazine cover was a totally different ball game.

Some of the watchdogs of the nation's morals plainly believed something similar. At Meridian, Idaho, the District School Board voted unanimously after that publication to remove *Newsweek* from the list of 'recommended supplementary news publications for use in social study courses'.

That put Jane in an unusual situation. For the first time, she was in agreement with a do-good morals group with whom she normally had absolutely nothing in common. But, as she is not on record as saying, that's show business.

She might have thought that the ladies and gentlemen of Idaho had the right idea. Indeed, what is surprising is that, actually, she didn't dislike the exploitation more. When she came to producing her first *Workout* book a generation later, she proudly displayed a still from *Barbarella* showing her dressed in the full glory of her fortieth century get-up with John Phillip Law looking on approvingly. Mr Law now enjoys that – but sees the irony of the situation.

But then this was a film never to be taken remotely seriously. Vadim himself was to describe it as an Alice-in-Wonderland kind of tale. Although the Queen of Hearts by AD 3967 might have found a more effective way of execution than merely saying 'Off with her head.' 'Direct the ray gun' might have been more in her mind.

What was similar to *Alice* was in the way Barbarella took charge. The sense of superiority and ridicule was there in every frame.

Indeed, Jane once said that she felt more 'pulled together' – about two hundred times more – since Vadim came on the scene and convinced her that *Barbarella* was right for her. He himself thought that most Americans were too 'puritan' about their attitudes to sex, certainly about the way it was portrayed on screen.

When the film came out, Jane said: 'I'm certain that, deep down, I still have no confidence. Really that's no bull. If a situation begins badly, if I feel I'm being boring or that I don't look good, well, I crumble. You want to hide, but the old ego won't let you. So you go on to a stage or a screen and hide behind the mask of a character. You're safe, but people are still looking at you.'

Vadim told me he recognized all that. She once asked him: 'How can you love me and respect me? I'm nothing.' Clearly her Roger did not think that of her.

There was someone else around at the time who plainly didn't either. Proving that love knew few boundaries and even fewer conventions, Andreas Voutsinas was on hand, too – acting as dialogue coach. The amazing thing is that he was able to be as close to Jane – and she to him – and consider his relationship purely professional. How Vadim thought so, too, showed the degree of his belief in sexual liberation.

Others in the picture who enjoyed loving and respecting Jane as she flew around in her pink spaceship were equally unruffled.

The cast was impressive – Marcel Marceau as a wizard and Claude Dauphin as the President of Earth. Jane wanted her father for that role. Henry was quite interested – he was anxious for anything that would bring his now fractured family together again – but then he hesitated; 'Will I have to take all my clothes off?' he asked. He wouldn't, but he decided that discretion was the better part of valedictory and chose not to want to be remembered for taking part in what was bound to go down in history as a sex epic. M. Dauphin, suitably reassured that he could remain fully clothed, took the part and seemed grateful for it.

Nobody, however, looked happier than David Hemmings. The script decreed that he was the one most anxious to remove her from the spaceship and place her firmly in his bed; to which she did not object at all.

Barbarella has been held up as the perfect example of Vadim's role in shaping the women who were to be his. As he told me: 'I really did help their careers. I didn't create them because you cannot create people. They are there. But with Jane as with the others I helped the process along, to go faster.

'Jane knows that I did help her in her career. She needed to be Jane Fonda when she came to Europe. Afterwards, as we say in French, there is no return. When you help people, do you think they ever give anything back? Never. It's like when you lend money to a friend, do not expect to get it back – what I did, I did for Jane and for those other people.

'It would have been the easiest thing to have contracts with those women for four or five pictures after I left them. But I did none of that. People attach their success to me. It is a glorious shadow on me. It's a little bit disturbing and frustrating. To be remembered more as a promoter of great talent is not like being remembered as a director.'

That was his view in 1986. At the time of *Barbarella* in 1967, he was saying something rather different – either because that was what he truly believed or because it made more commercial and political sense to say what he did then.

In January 1967, he told the *New York Times*: 'What interests me is the chance to escape totally from the morals of the twentieth century, and depict a new futuristic morality. It's a very romantic story, really.

'Barbarella has no sense of guilt about her body. I want to make something beautiful out of eroticism.'

Jane's fight with *Playboy* continued, the lawyers being busy while she worked on the soundstage. She wasn't denying, though, that she did appear nude in the film, but perhaps a little more nude than she really was. 'Vadim has a way of making a girl seem more undressed than she is. People accuse me of being nude in my pictures. But of the sixteen I've made, maybe three show some of my figure. It irritates me. People get an idea and then it starts snowballing. I don't think that actors playing a nude scene are objectionable if it is part of the story. Vadim always has taste in his nude scenes.'

She was not anticipating any problems from the censors – indeed not even *The Game Is Over* had had any censorship difficulties (except in Italy) and there was no reason to think there would be any now. 'When a picture is a commercial picture and seen by the masses, we have to approach it in a different way than an art picture. *Barbarella* is a picture that can be seen by everyone. People are saying the story is sadistic, but Vadim is primarily lyric.... There's a lake that swallows you up. Dolls bite you. But Vadim has given a fairy tale quality.'

This, though, was going to be a different experience as well as a different kind of science-fiction movie. She was glad to be part of it. In fact, she gave the impression now of being glad of practically everything that was happening to her and had happened in the last year or so.

She was totally convinced that the best thing she had ever done was marrying Vadim – well, almost as good as having him direct her.

'It's extremely relaxing to work with Vadim,' she told Sheilah Graham, one of the last of the big Hollywood columnists who hadn't yet heard that her day was supposed to be over.

'How he manages his calm in a movie like this (full of space-age special effects) baffles me. If it were me, I'd be in constant tears. Actually, it's not easier to work with Vadim, but I'm much more relaxed because I know that I'm completely protected. It isn't only that he's protecting me, his wife, but all the others.'

Even though Jane was meant to be a character living in the fortieth century, there was little in the way of technical gimmicks. A beauty test between Jane, wearing fibreglass armour that seemed to resemble most of all a long-line solid transparent bra, and a robot with a television antenna on its head, was plainly no contest.

She said that she was going to leave the details of her appearance to Vadim. She did and was clever to do so.

It would turn out to be one of Jane's most famous films, one that from that moment on would always be associated with her. Mention her name in print in the late sixties or early seventies and the name Barbarella would always be coupled with it.

The importance of the movie in the Jane Fonda story was recognized even at the date of the movie's release.

Part of its significance, however, was that it was the first American picture to abandon *all* the inhibitions drawn up by the Hays Office, the self-censorship body invented by the studios under the headship of Will Hays, a former Postmaster General. It had imposed the codes of conduct – the length of a kiss; the depth of a neckline, the fact that a husband and wife could never be seen in the same bed – that stayed in force for more than thirty years.

Vanessa Redgrave had bared her breasts in the British picture *Blow-Up*. After *Barbarella*, it would be the thing to do in Hollywood, too.

Time magazine headed its review 'Sex Odyssey, 40,001'. Variations on that theme were to be found in almost every other review; and for much of the film it looked more like a prehistoric epic than something so far into the future.

Reported the magazine: 'Comic-strip buffs, science-fiction fans and admirers of the human mammae will get a run for their money in *Barbarella*, and will probably provide *Barbarella* with enough money for a run. Other moviegoers need take no notice. The only break-throughs in this husband-and-wife collaboration of Actress Jane Fonda and Director Roger Vadim are made by Miss Fonda's shapely torso through an assortment of body stockings.'

The stockings were not intended as a form of protection – either physical or mental.

'These,' wrote *Time*, 'are ripped and ravaged by – among other things – a team of sharp-toothed mechanical dolls, a flight of angry budgerigars and a machine designed to kill its victims with sexual pleasure.'

There were those who felt that Jane's role was going to compromise her feelings for feminism, particularly since now she had the reputation of being something of a High Priestess for that 'movement'.

It was the age of pot-smoking – 'grass' and LSD – and of flower-wearing hippies. Jane was dressed in Paris, made up like the film star she was and she gloried in her husband's Ferrari and the success it represented. But none of that was any reason to give up what was becoming her natural constituency.

It all sounded – and sometimes looked – outrageous. But the sixties were still swinging and Jane was certain she was not going to be left out of anything.

As we have seen, she was interested in politics. Making *Barbarella* had not altered that one little bit. On the contrary, she shared Vadim's view that by demonstrating woman's unique beauty, she was enhancing her status. Not many men who had Jane Fonda on a particularly high and shining pedestal at this time would find reason to quarrel over that.

So what *was* the link between Jane, Brigitte, Annette and Catherine – apart from Vadim himself, that is? Said Roger: 'All the women I've married or lived with had three things in common: they were actresses, they were beautiful and they dyed their hair blonde.'

That last statement said it all: he liked his women to be blonde and they were all willing to please him in this regard.

More significantly, Jane was getting concerned about civil rights, about what was happening to the American black community and to the Indians. She and Vadim read the American newspapers as well as those in France – and were getting different messages about the war going on in the part of the world which had once been part of the French Empire, Indo-China, now Vietnam.

Vadim has described the political 'metamorphosis' that Jane experienced at this time. The political ferment in France which was to lead to the resignation of General de Gaulle – who seemed up to then virtually immortal and likely to remain in charge of France for the next century – led to her comparing the stories she had heard about the French in Indo-China with what was going on in Vietnam.

She met some Army deserters and realized she felt not shocked but at one with them.

The Vadims were in the American Embassy in Paris the night the Democrats nominated Hubert Humphrey to oppose Richard Nixon for the US presidency. Quite possibly, this was the night she thought she saw a particularly black cloud descending on Washington and spreading outwards in most directions.

It was also the night the television cameras saw a young politican being arrested. His name was Tom Hayden. Jane noticed him, but no more.

Others thought this was the dawning of a new glorious golden age. That 'social conscience' of Jane's was affected by what she thought would be a walk-over for Nixon. Even if Humphrey were elected, he would only escalate the Vietnam struggle (and the fights at the Democrats' Chicago convention served to confirm this). Nixon, she believed, would be much, much worse. Jane Fonda suddenly realized that the war and its effect on her country were more important to her than her next film. But for the time being she was keeping quiet about them.

The causes of the Indians, the blacks and women still seemed to worry her more, although as yet she was doing nothing about it. She was concerned with ecology as well, although that was a term not yet in general use at the time. While they were in Rome, the landscape around their French house was being put under the bulldozer, to provide, so it was said, views similar to those to which she had grown used in America. Fifty fully-grown trees were planted round about the house. 'They don't cost as much as an evening dress,' she explained, as though apologizing for the money all this entailed. There was not enough concern, she believed, for the land, in France or anywhere else. She was just doing her duty.

Vadim has said that he was brought to invoke the quip from the American radio and film wit Oscar Levant that if God had had a bank account, he would have made that garden.

Jane had her own account, needless to say – and equally needless to say, it was in sufficient credit to delight the hearts of bank managers the world over.

Barbarella successfully behind her, Jane announced she was going to take some time off. One of the main reasons was that she hated Rome. 'A girl can't walk down the streets alone. The men never stop insulting you.'

There was here a perhaps unconscious declaration on behalf of the future women's movement. Jane wasn't used to insults, but what she really meant was that she had come across the issue later to be defined as sexual harassment.

Before, however, she had a chance to think about those problems of the world and what Jane Fonda could do about them, she had a more personal concern, one that was for her and for Vadim alone and one that would prevent her making a new film of any kind for the time being.

Jane Fonda was pregnant.

10

She wasn't sure how she was going to take being pregnant. Somehow or other, the most natural of functions seemed to have connotations of the bourgeoisie that she feigned to despise.

It was her age, she said, that persuaded her that it was a step that ought to be taken. As she said: 'I was thirty and I thought, "Well, if I'm ever going to do it, it better be now."'

However, when 'now' arrived, she wasn't certain whether she should be as glad as she was or whether she wasn't quite as happy as she believed herself to be. Such were the complications in the condition of mother-to-be. Other women in that state experience hormone changes that make them crave sardines and marmalade. Jane craved an inner contentment that ran counter to the lifestyle she had made for herself and tried to believe was precisely right.

'Before I know it,' she told herself, 'I'll be forty. And it'll be harder.'

But did she really want a child at all? She wondered about that. 'I didn't want to know it,' she later recalled, remembering the trip home from the doctor's office after the rabbits had done their job and confirmed what she knew already.

As she explained: 'I felt so vulnerable. I realized how I had always, strangely enough, rejected femininity because it represented to me vulnerability and a lot of things that scared me.'

Saying that, Jane was revealing much more about herself than she might have understood. What she had rejected was not femininity, but the kind of femininity she now, quite suddenly, believed was the right one.

There was very little that was not feminine about the characters she portrayed on screen – and not just the curvy creature in *Barbarella*. The weeping costume jewellery of *Any Wednesday* had been worn by the most feminine performer seen in years – at least since *Barefoot in the Park* and *Sunday in New York*. But, as people who had worked with her could testify, including those who positively loved her for it, she was strong. Her very professionalism in knowing her lines and turning up on time was somehow not considered a feminine trait. As she now recognized, her strength was merely a sign of her weakness.

And now it was all working. The hormones were proving a good excuse for the changes she was willing to admit in her life.

She explained: 'During the process of becoming a mother, I completely overcame this. I became so proud and so aware that I would give and die, and it didn't matter, that I was an animal.'

What started out like a passage from *Parents* magazine now seemed more like a learned contribution to *American Anthropologist*. But that earnestness in stating how she felt was further proof of her *desire* to change, which in itself was a symptom of the vulnerability she had tried to pretend she despised so very much.

The Pregnancy of Jane Fonda was so important that she could have written a book about it. In truth, it was not uneventful. She caught mumps, but she never even thought of abortion. The baby was considered to be formed by then and her gynaecologists saw no reason to believe there was any risk of deformity.

In her French farmhouse, she considered her role in life and decided she fitted in perfectly with the pastoral scenes around her. All about, she later recalled, 'all of the animals were whelping and foaling. The dogs were giving birth and the cats were giving birth and the rabbits and the chickens. We were all kind of all together. It was really kind of marvellous and it was a very peaceful, beautiful period for me. I just realized that I am a female animal. I just came to terms with myself and my body and my fellow women. Truly, my relationships with women have changed since then and consequently with everyone.'

It did not mean, however, that her nightmares were over. The farmhouse was not relaxing enough for the size and location not to have its impact in her sleeping hours. The worst dream now was of being left alone there, its vastness being made worse by an inexplicable feeling that it was freezing cold – in the midst of summer.

A constantly recurring dream was of seeing dogs being run over.

She still walked in her sleep, too. One morning she awoke to find that she had moved all the furniture during the night.

Her relations with men changed even more than those with women in her earliest months of pregnancy. That, she said – but it could have been bravado on her part – was the hardest part of all.

Her father was part of the change as well. He was as confused about it all as was his daughter. When Henry Fonda heard that his daughter was pregnant, he could only think that grandfatherhood would bring a new dimension that other men in his situation might not think about: his daughter would now of necessity have to be more stable. For that he, quite reluctantly, had to be grateful to his French son-in-law; a man he was not sure he liked now any more than he had previously.

Pregnancy, however, was not providing Jane with totally new outlooks on life. She was unconvinced that being married to a man she loved passionately meant she had to be monogamous. For instance, she liked several of Vadim's own friends – and was not totally turned off by the notion of going to bed with any of them.

There were, however, governors to her behaviour; the way of life she followed made people think that she was somehow immoral. That was not the way she saw herself at all, although she knew that there were limitations to her character, especially when she was compared to her husband: 'I'm just not as nice a person as he,' she admitted.

One of the reasons was those feelings she had for the other men in the Vadim set, like his close friend Christian Marquand. She was not beyond musing on the possibility of more than just bedding Marquand but actually having a child with him. 'I think that it would be nice if you could have babies by all the men that you love and respect. There are a few of Vadim's friends that I would love to have babies with, but the trouble is that it takes too long.'

She was just into the stride with her own pregnancy, care of Vadim, and did not yet know what it felt like to go the full nine-month stretch.

'It would be wonderful,' she said, 'to have a son of Christian's, but I mean, nine months ... If a pregnancy lasted two ...'

So if it were not just for that, she would have been happy to consider it. Vadim was not asked for a comment at the time but the betting is he would have found it somewhat difficult not to feel a little disturbed – in private. In public, he would have said that she was quite right, he fully understood what she meant and good luck to her.

In fact, he himself had suggested to her that they should practise a form of sexual freedom. He saw no reason for monogamy and was having other dalliances – all of which he duly reported to his wife. She, however, even before pregnancy, couldn't cope with that kind of lifestyle.

'She has told me she felt humiliated and guilty,' he said. The guilt was about being a woman – because she couldn't really accept his ideas of freedom.

That was when Vadim believed that their marriage was threatened. The baby, however, was going to change that – for the moment at least.

But as the months went by, spent mostly in St Tropez, Jane's emotions were becoming more maternal and less ambiguous. She had made up her mind she was going to breast-feed her child when it arrived. St Tropez was the place where no well-undressed women would dream of being seen anything but topless on the beaches. As she contemplated the scene, she said that she couldn't stand women – particularly film actresses – who refused to provide the best food possible for their children simply because they feared the effect it would have on their breasts.

They went back to Paris, Jane getting bigger by the day.

For months, Vadim had predicted that his child would be born on 28 September, Brigitte Bardot's birthday. That was all Jane seemed to need. She was worried to the point of almost being frightened of all that that would involve. The haunting by Bardot – poor innocent Bardot who knew nothing about it; nice kind Bardot who frequently visited the Vadims at their summer home in St Tropez just before they moved back to Paris to await the birth – continued.

If all this was imagination bordering on extreme fantasy, so were some of the stories told about the process of Jane Fonda giving birth. One story has it that when the evening of 28 September arrived with no sign of birth approaching, Vadim pretended to call on the invocations of magic. He said be could bring on the event by leaning gently on Jane's abdomen and saying a few magic words. It had the desired effect: labour pains began.

Vadim gently – more gently, it seemed, than the way he had pressed down on Jane's extended stomach region – helped his wife to his car and drove towards the Paris hospital. Another story has it that they were in sight of the building when the car stopped. The man who could prepare movies from the initial idea to the final product, who had guided his wife's pregnancy as though it were as much a detailed operation as any film, had forgotten to put enough gas in his petrol tank. This seems as much fantasy as the story of the 'magical' powers.

He drove right up to the hospital in his Citroen – the Ferrari did not seem suitable for such an occasion – and called the former Mrs Susan Fonda, who was in Paris, to be with them on this important night in their lives.

It says a great deal for the fondness Jane still felt for her stepmother – Henry, meanwhile, had been divorced from Afdera and was now married for a fifth time, to Shirlee Adams, a former air hostess.

The baby was born later that night, a girl they called Vanessa. The story is that the child was named after Vanessa Redgrave, whom Jane admired so much.

Vadim has said that it was a good name to choose because – once they no longer had to think about a name for a boy – it was about the only one they could think of that sounded exactly the same in English, French or Russian.

More likely, they simply just liked the name. 'VV,' said the baby's father, contemplating her initials.

'VV Born on BB's Birthday,' reported one newspaper headline.

11

Vadim was to say that motherhood suited Jane. She revelled in the baby clothes, in preparing the nursery at the farm-house, in the idea of bringing Vanessa home to show Henry and Peter, and above all, apparently, in breast-feeding the new arrival in the Vadim family.

Friends poured into the flower-filled hospital room, where Jane looked pink and ecstatic, and the father as proud as a director just told he has won an Oscar, scored a record at the box office and had a producer's offer of a seven-picture contract that is about to make him the richest man in movie history.

Somehow, this was the finest production of his career. More excited, friends reported, than he had been when Catherine had given him his first child and undoubtedly more so than when Annette had produced hers (which was after they had parted).

He become more demonstrative. There was the morning, for instance, when Jane was still in the hospital and he showed a love that is the private domain only of new parents.

He slipped into Jane's bed, lifted up the baby and put her on his chest – almost, one might think, an attempt to provide an immediate mother substitute for the baby, or at least to demonstrate his role as strictly one of equality. It was none of these things. Simply a gesture of unadulterated love.

He allowed the baby's fingers to wind themselves around his. As he did so, the tears flowed from his cheeks on to Vanessa's soft, silky hair.

It was a quiet interlude and one that Jane and all the people who soon would be reading so much about Ms Fonda would hope to recapture. For the moment, however, she was thinking of herself simply as a mother who also happened to be a film star. Somehow or other, she had convinced herself that there was no reason why one should compromise the other. There was absolutely no reason why she could not be both.

There was a slight, nagging thought that she was not totally content with life as it was, even though she had absolutely everything. It could have been put down to postnatal depression, which was not restricted to Jane Fonda in this state of her life.

Ask her whether she was happy and she was ready to respond: 'For me to say I'm not would be ungrateful. I've got everything anyone could ask for, everything I've ever wanted ...' At that there was a wistful look in her eyes, a sentence that was not difficult to complete – but how? Even Jane didn't know.

It was one of the things that would later, and not very much later either, concern Vadim more than any problems he had ever had professionally until then. He tried not to think too closely about it; and by all accounts, he did not put his doubts or concerns to Jane any more than she was willing to spell matters out for him.

This was going to be one of those difficult times that are familiar to many married couples. Is it wiser to leave things and pretend that nothing is wrong, or should they talk about it? Neither seemed to know. Certainly Vadim would say that he didn't.

He began to notice 'warning signs' that things were not going quite as right as they should have been. In an earlier book, *Memoirs of the Devil*, Vadim put it like this: 'A tenuous shadow, an indefinable sense of drifting apart, as though some cold barrier was growing between us, made me feel that I was living a walking nightmare.' However, he added that the sensation was only 'fleeting' and by the time it had passed, he had convinced himself it was all an 'illusion'.

Jane, for her part, gave no formal indication that she felt anything of the kind. On the contrary, she had made up her mind that everything that happened to her was going to be entirely normal and uninterrupted.

But then quite suddenly she met a German woman journalist – it was one of those moments that seemed to creep up on the seemingly mature and adjusted Miss Fonda when she was close to another woman, someone who had the look of 'Please confide in me' on her sympathetic face.

To this sympathetic face, she said: 'I've been thinking about getting a divorce.'

Now, Vadim may have noticed the warning signs, but Jane had never said anything of the kind to him. Yet she had found a theme that was worth warming to – and once warmed, would be heated still further and then damped in a totally illogical way. No one ever claimed that Jane had to be in the least bit logical: 'Maybe a divorce would be good for our relationship ... Of course, we'd go on living together.'

Vadim might have been reconciled to that, but then his wife never gave him an opportunity to contemplate such a move. She had exercised her motherhood rights to the full. But she was not totally certain that she was glad that the birth-giving process was over.

She missed being pregnant – to the point of feeling jealous of those women who still were. This was also part of a continuing process. The seemingly strong, tough Jane Fonda had enjoyed being able to prove that she was 'just' a woman with the needs other women felt. Pregnancy had given her that. Now she didn't want anyone to think she was any less of a woman for being the person she was now.

'As my belly grew bigger, I became more feminine and less agitated,' she said reflecting on why she now felt jealous. 'I've never been so elated.'

It wasn't difficult to see the evidence, although there were those who put down her more strange thoughts to the changes brought on by the birth. But she didn't hold back at all in explaining why. She spoke of the pain of childbirth and seemed to relish it: 'The pleasure and pain were so extraordinary that I try to hang on to every memory of them.'

Vadim may have concluded that his principal rival was his daughter; and indeed it appeared that Jane had thoughts only for Vanessa, to the point where it wouldn't have mattered terribly if he had taken her at her word, applied for a divorce and then enjoyed one of his admitted affairs with less concern and perhaps conscience than he undoubtedly felt.

Everything was based on Vanessa – a state of affairs that many another new mother would recognize but which, as usual, Jane seemed to carry to excess. 'When I read the papers, it's with an eye to how the news will affect Vanassa,' she said. 'I am two hours late to appointments,' she admitted, reflecting on a situation that was beginning to worry business associates, the people who watched her pregnancy and subsequent delivery with a view to the effect it would have on their own professional plans.

Usually, she had a practice of being strictly punctual – precisely fifteen minutes late for *every* meeting. Now, though, people had to accept her as she was – two hours late. It was all because of Vanessa, looking after her, feeding her, watching and instructing the nannies. There were more important considerations than mere work. 'Nothing can make me care,' she said, with the kind of honesty that people in the film business had previously respected, but which now began to worry them. Was the *most* professional of actresses now going to change her principles?

Jane was ready to think about going back to work and Sydney Pollack and a production consortium he was co-heading, Palomar Pictures, wanted her desperately. The only problem was that their schedule required a virtually instant return to the studio floor for Jane.

They had a picture all ready for her that was going to do more for her than anything she had attempted before. She saw that, but she resented the requirements of the filming process and the effects they were having on her personal life, which she protested was so much more important than anything she did in front of a camera. Nevertheless, she agreed to make the film. It was a wise choice – if one was only thinking about her career.

The picture was *They Shoot Horses, Don't They?* and in making it she recognized that there would be no more *Barbarellas*, no more sex romps like *La Ronde* and, also for many of her friends, no more *Sunday[s] in New York* either. The gamine who loved being a newly-wed had had to hang up her going-away dress for ever and settle for the approach of middle age.

Well, perhaps not exactly middle age yet. But the part she played in *They Shoot Horses, Don't They?* was of an embittered woman, not a girl – a woman who had been through torments which showed on her face and, most of all, on her swollen feet.

Perhaps Sydney Pollack was wise in choosing a woman in midst of obvious stress for this part. The emotions she felt naturally were ideal for this role. It didn't make her any happier to have to do it so early after Vanessa's birth, however.

One instant requirement was that she had to stop breast-feeding the baby. She hated Pollack and the business brains behind *They Shoot Horses, Don't They?* for that.

'They took away what belonged naturally to [Vanessa],' she complained. So she had to devise new foods specially for the child. After five weeks of life, Vanessa was eating wheat germ, blackstrap molasses, animal brains and fish. Nutritionally that was good enough. But Jane resented it. 'To think,' she said in the midst of her pique – was *this* also the effect of her hormones? – 'that I would have been-breast feeding her all this time!'

It was not the only change made in her body system. No woman's body is the same immediately after giving birth, whether she has been breast-feeding her child or not. Jane set about toning up her body as though she were an athlete – and that was precisely, of course, what she was. She started an intense series of massages, working at it and suffering with it in the way she had her pregnancy.

It was a hard, hard slog. But now, according to Winnie Long, the masseuse, she suddenly became as professional a massage client as she was an actress. She went to Louise Long's salon at Panorama City in the San Fernando Valley, where Louise and her daughter-in-law Winnie danced attention on her alternately.

Winnie told me: 'She was very much a professional, very con-scientious about what she did. She needed to slim down and to do it as quickly as possible. She was very serious, as serious about that as she was about her work.'

One tends to think that this was the germ for her concern for 'Workouts' that would come later on. But Winnie Long takes no credit for that: 'My mother-in-law was very serious about the need for dieting and that was what she talked about. My mother-in-law put everyone on diets, eggs and grapefruit for breakfast and eggs and tomatoes for lunch. That was highly cholesterol. I'm not sure if Jane did that. She was always very careful about what she ate.'

Jane appreciated the 'heavy massages' she got there – and the facials. Those heavy massages required something of a tough constitution: 'But Jane was always in good shape.'

Sometimes she used to go over her lines while she was on the slab. But there was usually time to talk. 'We talked babies,' said Winnie Long. 'I'd just had my fourth and she'd had her first.'

What she was about to have was a baby of a different kind – a more mature movie than anything she had done before, an amazingly effective cine-dramatization of the horror days of the Depression, when people would do anything to make a buck, and 'anything' seemed to multiply into 'everything' with a craze of that mad age, marathon dancing.

It was to prove one of the most important movies in her career – her role as Gloria won her the New York Film Critics' Award and an Oscar nomination; that alone was the sign of having finally arrived.

As Gig Young, who *did* win an Oscar for his role as the seemingly heartless MC – so very different from the fluffy light-comedy parts he had previously regarded as his natural domain – said in the film: 'There can only be one winner, folks. But isn't that the American way?'

Jane may not have won the coveted piece of bronze, but the fact that she was being named for one was proof at last that she was appreciated by her colleagues – at least, for the time being. This was, in fact, the last movie she made before other matters would take on a higher priority with her.

The professionalism that Winnie Long had noticed in her massage salon was spotted a thousandfold on the set – and from all angles. It was undoubtedly the hardest part she had yet undertaken. Her clothes stayed on, but her emotions were bared for all to see; Gloria was caught up in the horror of deathly endless clinging while a band played and the public watched – to see who would be carried out next.

The fact that eventually some couple would be declared the winners and would walk away with a few dollars was hardly relevant; the public came to see sweat and blood and tears – they didn't really want anyone to win.

Johnny Green, who also gained an Oscar as musical director of the picture – he was associate producer, too – remembered the marathons well.

'I went to one in the worst possible way,' he told me. 'At their height, it was fashionable for so-called upper-class people to go to see these terrible, terrible displays of human bestiality – as they would go to the Colosseum in Rome. It was the same debased, human venality. It was terrible. You went to see people tortured. But you went in black tie. You went to a black-tie party and then you went on to one of these things. I remember the host and hostess of the party I went to had a bus to take people to see this Nero circus. I stayed for half an hour. It never occurred to me I would be involved in a film in this way.'

He didn't want to do the picture, but then couldn't resist it – among others, he couldn't resist working with Jane Fonda.

Because she had just given birth to Vanessa, because it was such a different role from *Barbarella* and all the rest, and because the film only helped add fuel to the social awakening others had noticed, it was both difficult and important for her that she did well in it.

Others connected with the picture noticed that. Johnny Green got to see a great deal of that professionalism. It was a film with, as he puts it, 'wall-to-wall music', so for the months in which it was shot, he practically lived with Jane Fonda.

To a man who had known Jane since she was a little girl – Green's association with Hollywood, particularly during his years as head of music at MGM, goes back almost as far as her father's – *They Shoot Horses, Don't They?* (the title would be spelled out at the picture's end, but it was easy to work out) was an eye-opener in so very many ways.

Jane's Gloria is, in a strange perverse way, a Fonda type; a girl so determined to go on that she allows nothing to stand in her way. Gloria even carries on to the extent of dancing with a corpse. She won't stop even when her sailor partner dies on her.

At the end of the film she herself dies. She tries to shoot herself, but can't. Another dancer, a hillbilly who has come to the big city for the first time and, with good reason, hates it, takes the pistol and does the shooting for her. He explains he has good reason. 'They shoot horses, don't they?' he says.

Sometimes the actors and the director felt they wanted to shoot the musicians. As Johnny Green told me: 'We had to deal with problems that had never been faced by music people before. Three-fourths of the action takes place in the dance hall, while these people are going through the torture of one of these marathon dances.'

He explained how it worked: 'In the background there's music playing and there's a bass player in camera and he's plucking the bass. You know the psychology of subliminalism ... on the screen, the bass player is plucking the strings in the silent places between the action while the dramatic scene is playing in the foreground.'

That was the kind of mood in which Jane had to work – with the 'joy', as Green put it, of having Sydney Pollack directing.

The Santa Monica pier, the setting for the picture, was rebuilt on a sound stage at Warner Bros.

'Jane is a very private person,' said Green. 'But what I can tell you about is her approach to her work, the study that she puts into a part, the kindness, the understanding, the intelligence and the consideration with which she co-operated with me and my staff – and the patience that she showed.'

She would do a 'dramatically wonderful take' only to hear Green, the music expert, whisper to the director, 'Sorry, Sydney, it ain't going to work.' Those musical beats had to be more than the usual kind of background sound. For once in a film, it was not enough to be able to dub the music after the dialogue. This time, there had to be a marriage between the two.

'Something had gone wrong music-wise that would have crippled Sydney if he had tried to use that take and there would have been no way in which I could have rescued it. A temperamental actress could have made life impossible. Instead, Jane made *everything* possible. She was interested. She was understanding. She was fascinated by it all. I'm not saying it didn't try her patience – it tried mine.'

There was another factor – perhaps the most vital of all: 'Jane was very keen on getting the picture made. Not only in those terms, but in all kinds of ways. The picture represented the torture of the human soul. But to Jane it showed her professionalism and she was wonderful in it. It was well before she became politically active and started saying things to which I am radically opposed. But I knew then that she was absolutely honest and for that I put her on a pedestal.'

Everything about the picture had to indicate the period in which it was set. If one couldn't smell the blood and the sweat, sitting in the audience at the movie had to be as close as possible to being part of the crowd watching the dance marathon, and crying for that blood, yearning to see the stretchers brought in.

Make-up, hairstyles, to say nothing of the costumes, had to be exactly as they would have been in those hideous times of 1932.

It was not the only thing that was strictly as-it-was. Totally unusually for a multimillion-dollar budget picture, it was shot strictly in sequence, with the first day's shooting being restricted to the estab- lishment of the characters and of the first tenuous but confident steps they took. They looked fresh on the screen, and they felt fresh, if a little apprehensive. They were meant to be apprehensive in the picture, wondering how long it would take, how they would do – no matter how certain they were that they could hang on. But these actors were doing no more than show precisely how they felt at the beginning of what they knew would be a tough shooting schedule. When they shot the first actual dance steps to be shown on screen, they *were* the first steps the cast took, too.

One of the actors with whom Jane worked on the film, one of the dancers experiencing the torture chamber of Santa Monica pier, was Robert Dunlap. 'I can't tell you about the boredom of the first day,' he told me. He was then 25, and played a college kid, one of the principal dancers involved in practically the whole picture.

What sorted out the professional dancers from the actors and actresses who merely took a few steps on the floor as a purely acting job were the preparations they took: 'You could see them stretching as they limbered up for their work. Jane was among them. It was then I first realized the ballet and modern dance experience she had had – as she taught us how to stretch. I could see how knowledgeable she was about dance and about the human body and its parts. She would say, "Keep this body portion straight … don't do this …" These were the seeds of the Workout, obvious right from the start.'

She talked acting as well as dancing. She also talked about her relations with her father. 'She said that they had very different acting methods, but their aim was to get the same result. I remember her saying that they had different maps to get to the same place. They may have both intended going east but they took different routes to their destinations. "My map would take me sometimes through Phoenix and Washington to New York. His map would take him through St Louis. But we both got to New York." I thought that was a very interesting analogy.'

But she wasn't keen on 'chit-chat'. She had to go 'into preparation' before a scene was shot. That to her was as important as the scene itself.

But Jane, the Method actress, sometimes did things that were not the result of any preparation. In one scene, Michael Conrad – playing the mobile umpire, taking frequent looks at each of the competitors – roller-skated up to Jane and her partner.

'I've got my eye on you,' said Conrad, playing a fellow who suffered from a stigmatism. 'Which one?' asked Jane. The whole company broke up – and because it did, the filming had to come to a stop. The extemporary question was lost.

It was a strange picture. 'I really felt,' said Dunlap, 'that after the first week or so, we were taking part in a competition. It seemed that all the couples were vying to get into camera.' That also helped in getting the right atmosphere for a picture that needed authenticity almost as much as good acting.

'Everyone knew,' Dunlap told me, 'that this picture was special. There wasn't time to talk about anything but the film, the acting, the make-up. It was the kind of film you couldn't wait to get away on vacation once it was all over.'

A *Playboy* Playmate who worked on the film as an extra, lost something like forty pounds in weight by the time it was finished. 'We were supposed to burn out – which we did.'

Another one of the 'dancers' was the eminent character actress Jacquelyn Hyde, who remembers the picture with affection and Jane with a degree of admiration that does not automatically come with working with a star of international reputation.

'I expected her to be snobby,' she told me. 'She wasn't at all.' There was clearly a sense of co-operation between star and supporting actress that others in similar situations would envy.

It was Jackie's second film – after working with Woody Allen on *Take the Money and Run*. There was nothing about taking the money and running on this picture. They walked round a track and they danced but no one had any energy to run. The money was strictly earned. It was a gruelling slog for everyone concerned, not least of all for Jane.

'She was in many ways quite different from the woman we know now,' recalled Jackie, 'Although there were a few sides of her that were quite familiar.'

Jane would come in for make-up in the mornings wearing slacks – slacks that cost $200. 'You could tell that they cost $200, even in 1969. I would watch her because she was always impeccable and very involved in fashion – yet there was that other side that we got to know soon.'

So what was there about her that attracted so much admiration? 'When I think of her,' replied Jackie, 'the words that come to mind are "determined", "disciplined" and "very fair".'

There was another factor, too, that attracted Jane to less successful performers. 'She loves talent,' replied Jackie. 'It sounds like ego, but I remember turning on the *Tonight* show while we were making the movie and heard Jane say that there was "wonderful talent" in the cast, and she mentioned my name. I thought that was so kind. Nobody knew who the hell I was at the time.'

She would invite Jackie and other performers to screenings at the studio after filming. 'Although God knows how she had the energy after that gruelling work.'

Of course, each day Jane was still going to her sessions with Louise Long. Every morning at five-thirty she was on the slab having her massages. 'She was slowly dragging other people around to do that, too,' Jackie told me. 'It was indicative of her discipline, to be of fighting weight, perfection.'

Jacquelyn Hyde told me she recalled only one blow-up on set; a quarrel between Jane and the director over the interpretation of a scene she shared with Gig Young, who called 'Yowsah, yowsah, yowsah ...' into his megaphone.

'Jane blew at Sydney Pollack – and she blew! She became a Star, demanding to do things the way she thought they had to be done.' Gig Young had told her he thought she was taking too long over a scene. That didn't fit in with her Method ideas and the way she now intended interpreting them on the set of *They Shoot Horses, Don't They?*

It was a very intimate scene. In the end, it was shot in two different ways. Jane's way won, of course.

'But that was unique,' Jackie Hyde now recalls. 'She was the Star then, but she never acted as the star of the picture.' There *was* a difference. Requiring the right to be respected for her knowledge and experience and status is different from claiming or pretending that she was superior to others below her in the cast, which she appears not to have done. 'I found her a worker – eminently fair,' said Jackie.

There was another factor that came out in the course of the work on the picture. 'I sensed,' Ms Hyde told me, 'an element of personal unhappiness.' Though Jane never talked about Vadim, she gathered there was something happening there: 'Her face would drop. Somehow the woman who had been there was off in her own world. Her vulnerability was allowed to show until she caught herself and realized what was happening.'

When Vadim came on the set – as he did frequently, sometimes spending whole afternoons there – Jacquelyn Hyde says she 'sensed a kind of distance between them'. As she explained to me: 'There wasn't a lot of touching.'

Vadim's visits increased as work on the film progressed – to give encouragement, to study Jane at work on another man's picture, perhaps to reassure himself that everything was still right between them. Sometimes he came for a whole afternoon. Occasionally he brought the baby with him. Vanessa's first visits to a film set were not necessarily intended to give her the feel of the movie business.

'A lot of the seeds of what became Jane Fonda were obviously there.' And part of that was the determination of Jane Fonda. 'She followed a straight line going after what she wanted. We grew older as the film went on. We started young and ended up old. She completely immersed herself in the part. She was not a major talker on the set, but she was concentrating on her work all the time.'

It was not a funny film, and there were few funny, light moments off the set. In some pictures, stars and lesser performers let their hair down between takes as a kind of mental refreshment. This was not one of those pictures. 'The few social things that went on, like the screenings, were rare moments.'

Her kindness to other players extended to extras, too. Other performers complained that extras drank from the same coffee pots that were reserved for the stars. Jane never did.

Jacquelyn Hyde remembers this as the time Jane was 'just tipping into politics'. 'The dichotomy between this left-winger and the girl who wore $200 pants struck me as quite amusing.'

'I felt that Jane was a woman who was living two lives,' said Jackie. 'In one she was Madame Vadim who lived in Malibu. Then there was the other, the actress. She was obviously being driven by something. She would take off those $200-dollar pants and put on the *schmatters* [old clothes] we all wore. And her energy!'

Once she had to pick up actor Red Buttons who, as the script dictated, collapsed. 'I remember thinking she wouldn't make it. Her face was ashen. But she did it.'

But which was the more likable Jane Fonda – the actress or the lady in the $200 pants? 'I think I preferred the actress,' said Ms Hyde. 'I expected to be intimidated by her. I wasn't at all. I found that she and Gig Young were two of the nicest people I knew. There was the friction between them, but separately they were wonderful people.'

Since the film was shot in sequence, the actors and actresses really did feel as though they were dancing a marathon. They would stop for lunch -- with Jane having little more than the carrot on which she would munch, seemingly, contentedly.

At the end of the day, the company broke up, went home – and almost felt as though they were cheating. Marathon dancers did not go home, sleep in beds. Once in a while, the make-up man came and painted circles on the faces of performers who had slept too well.

It was a stunning picture with stunning performances from everyone concerned, notably Jane, Gig Young and Susannah York, who was the third lead and as one of the marathon dancers has never been better.

Susannah, who played a contestant not out for the prize money but for the chance of being spotted by a movie talent scout, used to curl up between scenes on the top of an electrician's ladder, eating an apple and reading a book.

Sometimes she and Jane would snatch a moment's relaxation with the other players, lying on a makeshift camp bed in one of the rest rooms used by the dancers on the screen in the brief breaks they were allowed during the marathon.

As for Jane, she *became* Gloria, the girl in the marathon, the dancer and the one who had to don running shorts for the even more gruelling part of the torture, the marathon walks round and round and round a wooden track – another feature of the life 'lived' by the exhibits in the gladiatorial colosseum.

'I don't know how we survived those fourteen weeks on the set,' Jacquelyn Hyde now remembers.

Time magazine noted: 'As Fonda plays the part, Gloria is a born survivor, a cork of a woman who would bob to the surface of a sewer or an ocean ... As a footnote to American history, *They Shoot Horses, Don't They?* is invaluable. The entire cast – particularly Young and Fonda – understands the era when existence seemed one long bread-line. The pencilled eyebrows, marcelled coiffures and bright, hopeful faces change by degrees into ghastly masks ...'

But the critic wasn't entirely satisfied. 'The film makers should have known better than to cling to unidimensional symbolism and stylistic conceits. They shoot movies, don't they?'

/**12**/

J ane may have been shot dead at the end of *They Shoot Horses, Don't They?*; but in real life, she survived to tell a very fascinating tale indeed – how the difficult, anti-Establishment child of the great star had reached maturity and was able to take on the world on her own terms and be loved by all as a result.

That, certainly, was how it seemed at the dawn of the new decade. Her so-called 'liberal' views were being spread around the dinner tables of the wealthy and on the beaches of Malibu – but nobody seemed to take it at all seriously. Her opinions on baby-rearing and on the latest couture collection from Chanel were much more serious topics for conversation.

The most serious of all, of course, was Jane's career – and there was reason a-plenty to talk about that. An actress who had just won the New York Film Critics' Award was now one to be given every consideration. Like the best roles.

Her biggest problem was simply the most difficult – not making too many mistakes. *They Shoot Horses, Don't They?* was undoubtedly a wise choice. But there had been other, negative decisions, which not many people knew about, that perhaps were not quite so sensible. She didn't believe that – at the time. But there were moments of what-might-have-been that make one think. She seemed so right for a couple of movies which were put before her.

Nobody blinked in Hollywood when Jane was called to her agent's office and presented with the opportunity of playing a character who dressed not an awful lot differently from the one in *They Shoot Horses, Don't They?*; a girl who also got shot, after spilling quite a bit of blood herself; a girl out of America's Depression history. Jane read the script, took a while to consider whether she wanted to be a gangster's fighting moll and turned down the chance to play the female lead in *Bonnie and Clyde*. Faye Dunaway would have reason to be grateful to Jane Fonda for that, but Jane herself made a meal out of eating herself up for months afterwards.

There was another film that the people who run the business side of things in the movie business thought was up her section of Malibu's main street – a story of a crazed girl who had just been impregnated by the devil. Jane didn't think *Rosemary's Baby* was much of a film. Mia Farrow thought otherwise and most people now agree that she was probably right.

With time to reflect, Jane conceded she had made two great big mistakes – the kind of error that needed a *They Shoot Horses, Don't They?* to put right. Her decision to take on that role had been wise; she might not have made it had she not seen the folly of her previous ways.

Now she was determined not to make that sort of error again. 'I'll take anything,' she declared in February 1970. 'Even a musical.'

Jane doing a musical was a tempting proposition. With her ballet experience, it may have seemed only a natural development in her career, the kind that Shirley MacLaine was now making all her own. But it wasn't going to be Jane's route.

Nor was the one of happy, contented marital bliss. More people were now detecting a change in the set-up with Vadim and his wife. Others were noticing what those on the set of *They Shoot Horses, Don't They?* had discovered: they were not quite so loving – or perhaps doting is a more appropriate word – as they had been. Jane liked to kid people, herself included, by saying that their baby had brought a new dimension to their lives. She maintained that they were closer. But that was only so when they struggled to stand side-by-side in a crowded elevator. Mentally they were growing further apart, with Jane leading the drift.

Unusually for Vadim, he more and more looked the innocent party, just waiting to be dropped and left at the wayside. None of the other women in his life had ever put him in that position. It wasn't comfortable for him, but he didn't know what he could do about it.

Was she perhaps blaming Vadim for not taking those two films – the ones that could have made her career even more successful? No one would ever know the answer. But in those days, it had been a different Roger Vadim. At that time, he was the boss, and Jane was not just content to run to his command, but she positively enjoyed it. It gave her security. That was when it was his word that went. He told her what films were good for her, which ones enhanced her acting talent, and took advantage of that prodigious beauty, the one that she was never really sure she possessed.

The signs were fairly clear now for most people who knew the way the Vadims lived and worked. The couple who so embarrassed Jane's stepmother by almost performing the sex act in public now barely held hands in other people's company. More than that, they were just not very often seen together.

Vadim, a friend told me, felt as though he was just hanging on, staying in Jane's life for the ride. That was the most unusual situation of all for him and one he hated. He was still the same man. But Jane was not the same woman.

Yet she constantly tried to say that she was — and if things weren't as they had been, that was as much cause for concern for her as it was for her husband. And she said at the time: 'I worry a lot about Vadim and me.'

Vadim seemed, on the whole, to regret it more than did his wife. 'I do much more giving than Jane,' he said in 1970. 'In a way, in our relationship, she is the man and I am the woman.'

When asked about that relationship by *Time* magazine in February 1970, Jane countered: 'Forever is a very difficult word.' It was another public admission that things were not at all right.

That was not, however, the only thing that worried her. She was also concerned about her career — 'or if I'll ever be hired again.' That may have been more of a worry in the days when she had turned down the two films. Now there didn't seem to be much risk of finding herself in the dole queues.

She was more frank on some occasions than on others. Jane liked to tell people — close friends, acquaintances or the newspaper folks who didn't allow her to talk to the milkman without deciding it was an 'item' for their columns — that Vanessa had done nothing to change their lives. No one will know whether that was true — or if, with her increased sense of confidence, Jane was now standing on her own two feet and didn't need anyone else's.

What is certain is that Jane enjoyed the role of the protective young mother. Vanessa was her cub and she was going to shelter her from the law of the jungle. She not only read newspapers with an eye to the effect of the day's happenings on her baby, but everything she heard about, she put into the context of the year-and-a-bit child. 'Will they,' she asked, 'find a way to clear away diseases of old age by the time she's thirty?'

She was aware of the pitfalls of motherhood. 'I'm hoping when she grows up, I won't be doting or overly possessive,' she declared at a time when that was hardly the concern on most people's minds.

Nor was it the subject that concerned *Time* or why she was communicating with the magazine. For the first time that any of them could remember within the past decade, the three Fondas were getting together, courtesy of the magazine, and talking show business. On the whole, they talked of little else for a cover story that endeavoured to show that all was now lovely in a garden that had been covered with weeds for much too long.

The cover itself was one of those pseudo-chic collages that looked as though it were done in junior school on a bad day. Jane was seen smiling wearing a flowing scarf (Jack Warner would have hated it; it was in polka dots) dominating the page in a distressing psychedelic wash of reds, green, blues and yellow. Henry had to be content with an inch-and-a-half square in the bottom left-hand corner and Peter was riding his motor cycle, covered in purple, at the other side.

The article itself was not very much more revealing – except for the fact that it took place at all. The main piece dwelt on the remarkable family – not like the Barrymores, it declared; the Fondas had their own ideas on dynasties. As Peter said, 'We're not a theatrical family. Someone else may think of us like that, but my father is Henry Fonda, a peculiar, incredible person on his own.' (Things were getting better; Peter hadn't said anything nearly as nice about Henry in his whole life.) 'My sister is Jane Fonda, but she could be Jane Seymour, see, and she on her own is incredible. And I'm Peter Fonda. I could be Peter Henry and still be doing my number.'

The article tried to work out how they all did their various numbers. Alongside it was a detailed questionnaire going into their thoughts on the theatre – and themselves.

It was the week nothing more important had happened than a visit by President and Mrs Nixon to Chicago and the death in Wales of the philosopher Bertrand Russell. So the very fact that the Fondas were together made news – sufficiently so for there to be an editorial about it, too. Peter told writer Mary Cronin that he was agreeing to the interview because he had 'diarrhea of the brain when there's somebody there with a pencil or tape recorder'.

Jane was so wrapped up in just being there together, she said, that it made her reflect on how lucky she was. 'I felt like I was three years old, all over again.'

With bottles of beer in front of them at Henry's Bel Air home, they contemplated the Art of Being Actors. Jane talked about her commitment to that Art. 'I think there are very rare, genius actors that believe totally what they're playing ...' She spoke of the actresses who didn't merely play Juliet, they *were* Juliet. 'I know it has happened to me – there will be just one scene where you don't have to work on it. You just *believe*.'

While Jane said that there was nothing more exciting than experiencing the immediate response of a live audience, Peter, without needing to resort to his verbal 'diarrhea', defined it in one word – as 'orgasm'.

To Henry, a live performance was easier to 'grow into' than one before a camera. Jane admired her father's stamina – both she and Peter were only saying the most adoring, respectful things about their parent – but knew she couldn't emulate it (apparently, the agonies and torture of *They Shoot Horses, Don't They?* wasn't as demanding). 'But I haven't got the discipline or the technique. Having to do it every night for me was death. What Dad does, I'm totally in awe of.'

Jane, though, was somewhat more anxious to follow through her film work by actually seeing the results. Henry, as we have seen, didn't see his films; Peter threw up when he saw one of his. But Jane conceded, 'It is so different with me. I see every movie I do. I don't see them twice if I can help it, but I always see them once.' It was, she said, an education. She learnt by sitting in a cinema and watching her movies as the audiences who buy tickets would see them.

'I don't like the way I look either, except that I don't look at it as me. I look at it as a character that I'm playing.'

That might have seemed false modesty if Vadim hadn't told me precisely the same thing. (He was notable for his absence from this conversation. No conclusions need have been drawn from this; Peter and his wife were, it seemed, ideally suited, but Sue wasn't there, either.)

One thing that came out of the discussion was that it wasn't all sweet and light between the sibling Fondas. Jane and Peter disagreed heartily over many aspects of their talk.

Jane was convinced that the mass murderer Charles Manson was influenced, in his group family and the orgies he held, by what he had read. The 'incredible orgies,' Jane said. 'They weren't incredible,' said Peter.

Jane had seen *The Wild Bunch* and decided that the director Sam Peckinpah wanted to show what it felt like to die. 'That's absolutely not true,' responded Peter. 'I think he knew, going in, that it wasn't true. I think he knew he was making violence in such an acceptable form that we would all groove into it as voyeurs ...'

Interviewer Jay Cocks wanted to know about their public images. Henry said he only knew about *his* because people told him about it – the 'middle-class American morality that is Henry Fonda' was how writer-director Joseph L. Mankiewicz had put it to him.

Peter wasn't sure about his image either. 'All I do is want to create questions in the minds of the audience. I just want them to say Why? or What?'

And Jane? 'I don't think I have an image and when people try to give me one I think they're making a mistake.' (She would be thinking that much more only months ahead.)

They were asked if they saw themselves as the First Family of American cinema.

'We're not,' said Peter.

'I think it's very nice,' corrected his sister. 'Terrific.' Then she went on: 'It's unusual that three people in the same family have made it.'

'No, it's not nice at all,' said Peter, sounding like a little boy arguing with his elder sister over the price of a lollipop. 'If that makes us special, let's find another family, quick.'

Jane had by now decided she knew some of the recipes for success in the cinema. 'You have to keep some of the mystery,' she said – sounding like a clothes designer who favoured a one-piece bathing suit in preference to a bikini.

She herself had stopped wearing miniskirts, much to the delight of the House of Chanel. Was this part of the mystery, too? Or was it just a sign that she still followed the diktats of the world of fashion? No, she looked upon it thoroughly intellectually.

'I think it's sexier when people are saying it with their eyes, fully clothed,' she explained.

Mystery affected every aspect of life, especially the important ones, like love and sex. As she explained at this time:

'If you bring a plastic penis into the classroom, as they do in Sweden, that removes all the mystery. If you go to bed with *Human Sexual Response* under your arm, things can get very boring.'

The *Time* writer took that all unquestioning, unemotionally. He was impressed with the new Jane Fonda now being presented to the public. There was admiration for the girl who – thanks to her sessions with

Louise and Winnie Long – had thinned down so much that she could explain: 'I like to feel close to the bone.'

Much more to the point, the writer noted in this second month of the first year of the new decade: 'In the '70s, the daughter will dominate the screen far more successfully than the father did in the '30s, '40s, '50s or '60s. Her bony body and lean, clean features can attack grin or grim pictures with equal ease.'

No one could have known the extent to which Jane Fonda would dominate the screens in the months and years to come – and not just in feature films. News programmes, too, would be featuring that 'close-to-the-bone' girl before the month was out.

/13/

One thing was now very clear – as the *Time* interview indicated – the three members of the family were more united than they had ever been before, with Henry providing the most unexpected offers of support hitherto unimaginable. For the moment – it would change again – he was saying things like 'We're very close now, closer than we have ever been.'

He implied that it was a two-way street and Jane was as much responsible for the situation as he was himself. 'She doesn't talk about me the way she used to do any more,' he said. 'She's got this marriage to Vadim and the baby, and my God, that girl has maternal instincts she never knew she had. She's grown into an extremely intelligent, attractive woman.'

That in itself was tremendous praise. Henry Fonda knew an attractive woman when he saw one. He even approved of her lifestyle. 'Look at the kind of home she's created, look at the life they lead out there in Malibu. People coming, people going all day long, open house all the time and Jane handling it all so beautifully, making people feel comfortable ...'

In fact, Henry didn't know that the marriage with Vadim was not so marvellous. Vadim appeared to be the also-ran in their household for some time. He had even stayed at the studio at nights when Jane was too tired to go home after filming *They Shoot Horses, Don't They?*, and hoped that by the time it was all over, they would return to that marvellous home in Malibu and everything would be as before.

In fact, it was not. Jane didn't want to stay in Malibu for long, either with Vadim or even with Vanessa.

When a friend announced she was going to make a tour of India and Nepal, Jane said that she would go with her. Vadim stayed with the baby while Jane decided to go 'in search of herself'.

Above all, she seemed to go in search of the poverty of India. It looked as though she was in some way trying to appease her conscience, that gnawing feeling that a privileged, young, successful, white woman ought not to have so much while others had so little. In fact, she was genuinely appalled by all that she experienced – even though, in Sikkim, she stayed with the king and queen in their palace. But seeing the vast differences between rich and poor – greater than anything in America, and there had been nothing approaching it in the Soviet Union – awakened her feelings of disquiet about the state of humanity.

Vadim himself was much more concerned about the state of his own humanity and the effect her absence might have on their marriage.

On the surface, things couldn't have been better, given that they were separated by a few thousand miles of ocean. It was a situation which only looked confirmed by the correspondence between them. Jane sent Vadim a long love letter from Nepal in which she declared, according to his own writings, 'that she loved me, that she would never allow life to separate us again. She needed me and wanted to be worthy of our happiness.'

But he says he knew that all was not right. In fact, the very length and the very loving nature of that letter convinced him that all was over. He could read between the lines. If she had really loved him, he said, she would have written begging him to come and join her.

When she got back to Los Angeles, they decided to take a 'honeymoon' suite at the Beverly Wilshire Hotel, one of the smartest of the West Coast hostelries. There they experienced a deep, profound love, 'a strange and intense physical rapport' was how he described it in his book *Memoirs of the Devil*. But immediately afterwards, they decided to separate – and no one knew.

People didn't know because they told no one; and even to Vadim himself Jane behaved, he reported, 'very kindly'. Vadim has hinted that if he had been suicidal, that would have been the time to do it. Jane, he said, was a very good nurse, 'but cholera cannot be cured with cold compresses'. Vadim got on with his cholera alone, and Jane with her own kind of unhappiness, which to the outside world didn't necessarily appear to owe much to her marriage.

At the time she put it all down to the pressures of being Gloria and playing in *They Shoot Horses, Don't They?* But ever since her days on the set of that film, the Malibu house and all it entailed was less a paradise than her father and practically everyone else who came into contact with them believed. As she said: 'I'd walk to the door and ... auugh! So I stayed away. Of course, Vanessa would stay with me every now and then. Still, it took me months to get over it.'

In fact, now that the 1970s had got into their stride and her relationship with Vadim had ended, those who knew her were not sure she had got over anything at all.

But at this stage of her life, you had to know her fairly well to come to that conclusion. Nobody had yet called her a superstar, but that was the way she was being treated. Everything she did seemed to interest the newspapers. And there was nothing that interested journalists more about stars than their views on clothes – or, as in Jane's case, on going around without any clothes at all.

Writing in the *New York Times*, Jane Cook noted how Jane was down to her last mink coat, which was all of two years old. Most of the time, she loved maxicoats – and the day they met, she was wearing a black and beige print blouse, black pants, matching ankle boots and a silver and turquoise Indian belt. 'Gold hoop earrings dangled from underneath her short bob,' reported Miss Cook.

Reading that, there wasn't much else to worry about in the world – certainly not the part of it inhabited by Jane Fonda. She was giving every impression of having her own ideas on clothes, and that it was a vitally important issue for her.

'For so long, it was rigid, the little-black-nothing dress and everybody looking the same,' she said, the way any film star would say it. But she admitted that her ideas were not exactly conventional. As she said: 'I never really fitted into any proper fashion category – so for me this individual way ... is fine.' As to the current craze for nudity: 'Once the human body is accepted, dressed or not, all the permissiveness in movies and plays will be *déjà vu* for a while.'

That feeling of *déjà vu* was fairly obvious in most of the things Jane said at this time. One could only guess at the changes that were likely to be afoot before long. Not even the hoary old tale about the relationship between father and daughter was ready to die yet awhile. 'I felt that being Jane Fonda people would be judging me from a certain angle,' she told one journalist. 'I'd have to be great or not at all.'

As she collected her New York Film Critics' Award and the Oscar nomination for *They Shoot Horses, Don't They?*, most people seemed to agree that Jane really was great – and on her own merits.

When she was told about the award, she was actually staying in New York, borrowing her father's Manhattan apartment after a gruelling few days plugging the film in London.

Reporters had called with the information, but the maid wouldn't wake her up. 'I will make sure she sees it the minute she wakes,' the woman told them. 'But it would be more than my job is worth to wake her now even with such exciting news.' Presumably she was enjoying sweet dreams that were pleasantly interrupted a few hours later.

She discovered the news on a piece of paper placed on her pillow by the maid. It said simply: 'You have been voted actress of the year by the New York critics. Congratulations.'

Of course, it gave her extra confidence. But the mere notion that she could be riding horseback on the reputation of others – or with too much help from others – continued to be galling.

To some, it seemed that she would do anything to try to be understood for what *she* felt about the things that mattered. People, as we have seen, were keen enough to find out what she felt about the cinema and the fashions that went with it.

Not, though, Jane Fonda's view on the international scene. While she accepted the norms of the showbiz publicity game, she had other things on her mind – among them now was letting people know precisely how she felt.

Her visit to India seemed to govern practically everything she did. She was full of the need to fight poverty. At the same time, the anti-war fever that was beginning to grip America had caught her in a tight vice. And she was still perturbed about the status of America's Indians. When a group of what are now known as Native Americans staked their claim for full federal recognition of their rights, she told them they had her support. Why a young (some would say politically immature) white actress's concern would ever matter is one of the mysteries of our century, but matter it did – if only because of the publicity value it entailed.

The Indians decided to invade Alcatraz. Jane told them she was with them all the way – to the extent of, amazingly bravely, going to the former prison island in the midst of San Francisco Bay to see the occupation at first hand. She joined a procession of vehicles that travelled to the bay with signs attached to their sides reading: 'Custer had it coming' and 'Red Power'. She said she thought they were wonderful. Later, she led a delegation on their behalf to the California state legislature.

She had got to hear about it all in an article in *Ramparts*, a magazine which she had taken since the late sixties and which influenced the way she thought politically in much the same way that other women of her age were influenced by fashion publications.

The magazine had a reputation for left-wing thinking and she read and believed most of what it said. The pro-Indian cause was not merely close to her heart. Apparently it occupied *all* her heart. And most at the time welcomed her gestures of support as not-to-be-sneezed-at sustenance for their public-relations campaign.

Her views on President Nixon and his escalation of the Vietnam war were kept mostly to her own circle; but, as in the ripples of a pond, the circle got wider and the words managed to find ways of leaking out.

So did her relationship with her father – which was suddenly back to square minus one. Henry had done what was to Jane the unthinkable. He had gone to South Vietnam to entertain the troops. That had been a showbiz tradition ever since there were troops to fight wars.

Since the end of World War Two, Bob Hope and his entourage had gone every Christmas to perform for servicemen, an act that branded him as a prize hawk. Henry went to Vietnam not to express sympathy with Nixon's policies but simply because he thought there was an audience who needed entertaining. Jane didn't see it that way.

Once more, the Fondas were in conflict – a battle that brought back all the old insecurities that Jane had once possessed by the bucketful. She no longer wanted her father's approval; but she did desperately want to approve what he did – and now she plainly did not. The elder Fonda was unapologetic.

'Before I went, I wasn't anti-Vietnam,' Henry said. But he admitted he was 'anti-card-burning and flag-burning'. And significantly, he added: 'I think a lot of the unwashed who go into these demonstrations are protesting for the sake of protest.' He may also have added that he himself was fairly 'apathetic', but that bit about the 'unwashed' (even if meant as a dig at hippies) was revealing. So were his conclusions about it all.

In effect, what his trip to Indo-China proved, as far as he was concerned, was that he was not apathetic any more. 'My eyes were opened,' he declared on his return. Both Jane and her friends who were making themselves more and more active in the peace movement couldn't quite understand that. In fact, they came to the conclusion that Henry Fonda's eyes had never seemed so closed. And that they would before long find ways of demonstrating the fact. That was not what Henry believed. 'I discovered it was my morale and America's morale that needed strengthening, not the troops'. This has been said before – and I couldn't agree more – that every time there's a parade or peace rally in this country it will make the war that much longer, because it doesn't escape the attention of Ho Chi Minh.' So what now of the man who had pricked America's Depression-laden conscience with *The Grapes of Wrath?* Henry could see no conflict. 'But I'm still a liberal,' he said, and could see no reason why that should be doubted.

Jane could have had doubts about it, but Henry was adamant. 'I don't feel I'm a hawk because I'm for our involvement in Vietnam – and I don't agree that we should bomb the hell out of them. But you can't be there and come away and not at least feel, well, obviously we should be there and the job is being done and it's a good job.'

His daughter had come to the conclusion that it was a pretty lousy job and before long she would be stating loud and clear just how lousy she thought it.

Sometimes she was a great deal more open with what she did and said than most people had yet come to think. When she gave an interview with Rex Reed in the *New York Times* she had no inhibitions whatsoever.

The interview was supposed to be the standard talk-with-the-stars type of piece – more of the fashion chatter, words about the film she was making next and about family life – and gave no indication that it was going to read like anything but a normal conversation with a celebrity.

In the article, she talked about the future, about her child: 'I've learned so much from watching my daughter Vanessa. I never knew how to use time before. Now I do. I don't want to work for a while. I've learned photography and now I'm learning speedreading and autohypnosis. There's so much to do in life.'

Vanessa herself was a 'constant source of discovery'. And part of the discovery was no doubt her family: 'Listen, whatever Peter has told you is his story, not mine. Whatever the Fonda myth is supposed to be, I do not hate my family.' And as for Peter, 'I'd like him even if he wasn't my brother.'

That statement came as a sort of bottom piece of the sandwich. The top part was her view on the world.

'This is the end of a decade,' she told Reed, 'and I find it reassuring that in my adult life I've experienced the end of a decade with a future that looks very positive. I'm very optimistic about the world tonight.' (That in itself was something of a change from the Jane of *They Shoot*

Horses, Don't They?) 'The dancing [in the film] wasn't the hard part. Getting under Gloria's skin was the real challenge. The character as written was completely without hope, not a ray of optimism. I had to draw out the pessimistic side of my nature.'

Neither her optimism nor her assertion that everything looked positive was to last. In fact, not even beyond the next paragraph. That was where the meat in the sandwich came. It was immediately after declaiming the optimism that the bombshell exploded. It reads like a cliché but that is precisely what it was – and what it was exploded.

'You don't mind if I turn on, do you?' she asked Reed, and as a result of that question the correspondence columns of the *New York Times* were to be filled by letters from people who did mind that she 'turned on' – which turned *out* to mean that she was about to get high on marijuana.

As Reed reported in his piece on 25 January 1970: 'Then her long fire-ice fingernails carefully rolled the tobacco out of a Winston, opened the cap on a dainty snuff box on her father's coffee table and replaced the ordinary old stuff that only causes cancer with fine grey pot she had just brought back from (where? India? Morocco? She couldn't remember; all she knew was it wasn't the tacky stuff they mix with hay in Tijuana, this was the real thing.)'

And, she declared, she was merely following a well-trodden path.

'Doctors, lawyers, politicians, I don't know anyone who doesn't turn on. Except maybe in the South. I guess the South is still fifty years behind.'

The paper's correspondence column was to prove that being 'behind' was not something with geographic restrictions.

'Arguing the Jane Fonda "Paradox" ' was how the correspondence page was headed.

Robert C. Katz condemned 'Miss Fonda's overt criminal act'. He went on to say: 'Monday's *Times* front-pages the arrest of New Jersey Governor Chaill's son for committing the same act. The Governor's son is quickly depicted as a troubled youth caught amid the veils of our society and is immediately assigned the role of a convicted criminal. And what of the illustrious Miss Fonda? She continues to inhale a lungful of dreams. Admittedly Rex Reed helps to sell papers, but does the *Times* have to go to pot?'

Another reader asked: 'Don't you believe, however, that any teen-ager reading about those very in-the-news glamorous people who smoke the stuff with impunity – and what's more, advertise it as though it were a revolutionary tartar-removing dental cream – must wonder why what's fun for some is a crime for them?'

Rex Reed himself was all for his interviewee. 'So Jane Fonda smokes pot. Big deal. So does just about everybody else I know. Yet the donnybrook that has resulted from her honest and candid revelation is both amusing and annoying. As an interviewer, I was merely fulfilling the obligation and responsibility of an objective observer. It had never been my purpose as a writer to conceal the realities of an interview and I do not intend to start now.... As for Miss Fonda, I don't think she needs any defence from me. She is a mature, intelligent, outspoken young woman who seems well equipped to deal with the Carrie Nations ... I think she can take care of herself.'

Nothing Jane Fonda had done before had created such a stir. But it was only a beginning. Soon, very soon, she was going to be at the centre of rows that made this one seem no more serious than a disputed point in a football game.

All Jane's actions indicated that there might be two sides to an argument, but hers was always the one on the left. There was a war in Vietnam and she was soon going to tell the world that it was killing and maiming innocent people and that America ought to get out. There were blacks in America who were being treated as sub-humans. Indians were being ignored – and were living below the subsistence line and were being deprived of their culture. All these were about to become Jane Fonda Causes.

Somehow, everything she had done before, all her old films, were just frivolous episodes leading up to what was about to come now. She was desperate to prove that she knew what was needed in this life. The world was a hard, cruel place and she believed it was her bounden duty to try to make it better.

She met various people, including the Marxist lawyer Mark Lane who had represented Lee Harvey Oswald as soon as he was charged with the murder of John F. Kennedy. There are those who say that Jane fell under his spell. That is not true. Jane was convinced that what Lane said was right. She would have been equally spellbound by anyone who said those things. The facts had got to her, not the man.

People were now beginning to take note of what *she* said and, as far as her career was concerned (to say nothing of her relationship with the sort of people who normally bought tickets for her movies) what they were taking note of didn't do her a great deal of good. For one, everything she did now was being monitored by the FBI.

J. Edgar Hoover was sufficiently concerned about her activities –

especially when she took part, in March 1970, in a march by Indians on an army base, Fort Lawton – to order a permanent watch kept on the activities of Miss Jane Fonda. The FBI were there watching at every demo which Jane presided, including the 'raid' she led on Fort Lawton.

The fort, near Seattle in Washington State, was claimed to be Indian territory. The Indian activists believed they were on to a good thing since the base was in the process of being abandoned by the United States Army and was about to be turned into a public park.

Jane's braves, as some newspapers described them, turned up for the occasion dressed in feathers and war paint and announced that they were going to establish an Indian university and cultural centre there. Jane then read a proclamation – addressed to 'The Great White Father', which was generally accepted as being President Nixon.

The party was not welcomed by the children of the Great White Father, however. In fact, for more than two hours they were held in custody before being set free with a warning none of them intended to heed.

To Jane, it all represented a huge challenge. She was *not* under any circumstances going to be put off what she believed was an essential part of the fight for human rights. From Fort Lawton, the braves moved on the nearby Fort Lewis – where again they tried to read their proclamation and where they were again rounded up.

Jane said that the Indians were her brothers and sisters. There were some, however, who were not quite so sure they valued Jane Fonda's sisterly affection. To a few of them, her sentiments had the smack of 'do-gooding white folks' about them.

In an article in the *New Yorker* magazine two years later, an Indian civil rights worker named Khan Tineta Horn was to write: 'The sooner she never mentions Indians again the better. She led Indians into Fort Lawton and when the TV and newspaper people came around ... she was protesting Vietnam. She forgot which crusade she was on. Do we need a White woman to lead us? She's just exploiting us.'

That was not sufficient to stop either Jane's activities on behalf of the Indians or the FBI's concerns over her. Mr Hoover, meanwhile, opened the Jane Fonda File.

14

To the straitlaced dictator of the Federal Bureau of Investigation – he had been in charge there since its establishment, when its officers were known as 'G-Men' – the raid on the base was tantamount to treason.

In years to come, it would emerge that part of Hoover's near-paranoiac concern about the activities of people in public life was as much because he saw them as a threat to his own position as a menace to America. He didn't mind how much he destroyed others if, in the process, he preserved his own role in the government of the nation.

On Hoover's instruction, the FBI's Jane Fonda file was scrupulously maintained. His agents attended every rally and demonstration that Jane attended and sent complete details to Hoover. Every press cutting about her was carefully filed. When she started making speeches, federal agents were there with tape recorders and shorthand pads to record all that she said.

For the moment, Hoover kept the file locked away. Jane didn't know she was being monitored in this way. But when she said that she was now going to dedicate herself to helping the Indians get their rights and was to travel from one end of the country to the other to do so, Mr Hoover was studying the notes and reacting with a smirk which was not unlike that on the face of Nero when he gave the thumbs-down signal at the Colosseum. The atmosphere of *They Shoot Horses, Don't They?* now was nothing compared to the conditions she saw for herself. She was disturbed that – as she saw it – kindly, inoffensive, peace-loving Indians were being treated as animals by healthy, big whites in positions of authority. She called for full rights for the Indians. 'I always thought that the Bill of Rights applied to all people,' she declared, 'but I've discovered differently.'

Henry, meanwhile, didn't really know which way to turn. He admired his daughter's feelings for less fortunate human beings but he wasn't prepared to take part in any demonstrations. He said he supported the 'peace' candidates involved in the plans for the next presidential election in 1972, but wasn't going to go any further than that. Nor would he attempt to get access to the White House. Henry Fonda was one of those privileged actors who, by virtue of their longevity in the business and their clean-cut looks, were considered to be almost equivalent to elder statesmen.

Jane still tried to convince him to go further. She took a couple of Vietnam veterans to meet Henry at the Bel Air house and to tell him about the horrors of the conflict. 'My father sat and listened very quietly, obviously moved,' Jane reported at the time, equally moved and grateful that he should react in that way. But she was exceedingly disappointed that he wouldn't do more than just appear moved.

Henry obviously knew that the influence of an elder-statesman actor was somewhat limited, but Jane didn't think so – and because she didn't, others in the movement didn't either.

Jane was beginning to make speeches that almost scorched the FBI agents' tape machines. She condemned Nixon, and praised the government of North Vietnam in Hanoi.

Years later, Jane admitted that her early work against the war had been expressed in a wrong way, particularly at the beginning in the late 1960s: 'There was a lot of unnecessary abrasiveness in the sixties, especially if you were inexperienced and somewhat naive, like I was. Because I lacked confidence in myself and experience in talking publicly as Jane Fonda, I would borrow other people's rhetoric – rhetoric that doesn't suit me.

'In many instances, I didn't even know what some of the words meant. There must have been something that seemed false about it, that I think turned people off and I can understand it. It's not that my emotions were false, but that I sometimes chose the wrong manner in which to express them. Maybe it's my fault for being the way I am – I *am* impetuous. I *am* an extremely emotional person.'

Jane had not yet revealed any details about the sort of thing that makes most women emotional – men, too, for that matter – like her marriage problems. It seemed perfectly reasonable for people to ask her what Vadim thought about her political activities. At about this time, he was saying: 'Speaking quite personally, I would prefer being married to someone soft and vulnerable than to an American Joan of Arc.'

He was to use the phrase again and again, and it bit deep, even though he usually said it with a chuckle. But it was plain that if Jane was at home – and she wasn't very often – she was the one who was now wearing the trousers, figuratively as well as literally.

Vadim plainly did not like that. 'Every man has his feminine side,' he said, 'and every woman her masculine side. Right now, I would say that my feminine side is taking over while the man in Jane is temporarily in the ascendant.'

He was also worried about his own future. 'Many times the telephone rings and when I answer, the people hang up. It could be they're friends who prefer, naturally, to talk to her instead of me. But it could also mean threats of physical violence – and that worries me, but not her.'

Indeed not. In fact, Jane was answering questions about Vadim's views that had also been put to her. As she said at the time: 'Well, he approves of what I'm doing, though he doesn't agree with it all. It's very difficult for a Frenchman.'

Apparently, it was also difficult for the wife of a Frenchman. She couldn't understand his attitude to her complaints that the Black Panthers – a black power group who seemed to want to consign the entire white race to oblivion and did what they could to achieve that aim – were never granted bail. As far as Vadim was concerned, that was nothing to grumble about. Nobody had bail in France once arrested; should alleged killers and traitors?

When they met – and they still did, with Jane continuing to 'nurse' her husband's unhappiness – they still argued over such matters. It didn't serve to improve their love, but all the evidence now was that Jane really didn't worry a great deal over that. She believed she was her own woman and anything that could demonstrate it was grist to her mill.

Her relationship with Vadim continued to puzzle journalists, but only from the strictly romantic point of view – how could people like them still be lovers? No one knew that they no longer were in love. She told the Hollywood writer Joyce Haber that one of her neighbours in Malibu kept shouting at them that they were living in sin. She thought that was very funny – until she remembered that that was precisely what they had been doing. Telling tittle-tattle like that was better for her image than any public confession that their marriage was now over. And better than all the political talk. That, too, was a Jane Fonda paradox. She revelled in the publicity for her causes, yet somehow knew that the other side of her life had to be preserved, too.

The suggestion was frequently made that she had merely been looking for causes that would prove that she thought for herself. That is patently untrue. Her causes were her own passions.

But it did leave the impression that she rejoiced in no longer needing a Svengali and wanted everyone to know about it.

And she used occasions that ostensibly had no political background as opportunities to demonstrate her positions on these campaigns. When she went to the Oscar ceremonies in 1970, not knowing whether she was going to get an Academy Award for *They Shoot Horses, Don't They?*, or not, she was greeted by the crowds not shouting or swooning or begging for autographs as usually happened, but by Black Panther-type salutes. She was the first star known to man- or womankind who ever stepped out of a long, long limousine wearing a gleaming Chanel gown under a mink wrap to clench her fist and give the same salute.

She didn't get an Oscar that night, but not because of her political views. The Academy of Motion Picture Arts and Sciences, which had experienced enough witch hunts of its own, was more intelligent than that. More intelligent, however, than she was prepared to give them credit for being. She was on record for years after that as thinking that she was a victim of her politics and that if she had not been so outspoken in favour of civil rights, the statuette would have been hers.

However, after that night, Jane Fonda entered the Richard Nixon Enemies List – and that of every Right-wing organization in America. J. Edgar Hoover smirked again and once more glanced at his Jane Fonda file. He swore that one day, and before very long, he would get her.

But what *was* the effect on her career?

'I keep calling my agents and asking if there is any effect,' she said at this time, 'and there isn't. As long as someone can make a buck off me, they're gonna do it. And as long as I can go into Hollywood and make a movie and make a lot of money which I can use to support the struggles I'm involved in, I will.'

Despite all that he had been saying, Jane was still claiming that at the root of her political beliefs was her father. 'I was brought up a liberal Democrat,' she said. 'You know, my father broke television sets during the McCarthy era. He campaigned for Stevenson. That meant I would sporadically involve myself with causes. If I discovered there were black people trying to get together a ghetto school for children, I would be involved in that. I was a white person rather paternalistically helping the poor people. It never changed my life.'

But things were different now – and Mr Hoover knew it as well as anyone. She provided him with a great deal of ammunition to further his aim.

Her own first target now was the Vietnam War. A cause was turning into another crusade. The world was getting to hear stories of villages razed to the ground by napalm – and when the casualties began to mount, Jane decided that for the moment this had to be her priority. A large section of the nation was behind her; but to the FBI and its director, what she was saying and what the young men who demonstrated by burning their draft cards were doing was close to high treason.

She got into an army camp in disguise, to protest at the arrest of troops held in the stockade. She tried to distribute literature. At Fort Hood in Texas, she was placed under arrest and read the equivalent of the Riot Act – a letter banning her for life from the camp. It was a punishment many of the inhabitants of the camp would have begged to have been given.

This was neither her first army camp visit nor her first arrest. Twice before the same thing had happened. Now she was going to sue the Secretary of Defence, Melvin Laird.

In April 1970, she went to Fort Carson, in Colorado, to talk to the GIs there. She found that three black soldiers were under arrest because, it was believed, of their connection with the Black Panther movement. She promised to address meetings on their behalf and said she would be back. She was.

On 20 April, she went to 'Homefront', an organization set up by the troops at Fort Carson at which they protested about the war. It was one of the ironies of the situation that such a group, no matter how unofficial, was allowed to exist. But it was just one of a whole group of 'coffee houses' set up by disenchanted troops all over the nation. Jane made it her aim to go and visit them all.

The coffee house represented both a labour union and a soldiers' opposition group – neither of which was normally tolerated in military services, particularly at time of war, declared or undeclared. In fact, it was not legal and the members were always conscious of what might happen if any of them were ever identified.

The least that *had* happened to any of them was to be 'harassed' and the men present given extra duties.

The Homefront coffee house was where Jane chose to speak. Its reputation as a radical meeting place was now established in the whole area of Colorado Springs, where Fort Carson was situated.

She decided to make herself at home – and the first thing she did was go to the kitchen at the back of the centre and make herself a cup of coffee. Then she moved into the main room and said she was going to 'rap'. (Using the right terminology was plainly the most important thing she had to learn to do.)

Between thirty and forty men gathered themselves in a circle. 'Is there anyone here who doesn't know about the movement?' she asked. None of the assembly put up a hand.

She suggested that the thing to do was to 'work from within'. One can only imagine J. Edgar Hoover's reaction when he read that. It was doubtless with a mixture of anger and delight. If he was going to nail the Commie Bitch, this was the way to do it.

'We've been going to Washington for a long time,' she told the GIs. 'But what is Washington?' As far as she was concerned, the whole of the capital city of the United States was only an extension of the Defence Department at the Pentagon, after all.

America had 'put in power in Vietnam a government and this government has nothing to do with the people. The people are against us,' she said.

The United States, she alleged, had $160 million in holdings in that part of Indo-China. The military was there 'to protect our interests'.

It is interesting that she used the word 'our'. It was an effective demonstration of irony; talking about 'our' as the country of both herself and of a group of men who were manifestly not accepting a government policy none of them would vote for, especially since they knew they might have to die for it. But it *was* rhetorically effective and she continued to use it.

'The mass of the population are fighting us,' she went on. 'Why? For the same reason we fought the English, for the same reasons the French underground fought the Nazis. There are people fighting to be free and we [the United States] are fighting against them.'

The 'coffee house' movement had been founded by Fred Gardner, and it was he who asked Jane to make her tours. Before long, she was doing so practically full time, going into cold and dismal buildings and raising the temperature with the kind of speeches which, had she been given them in a script, she would have decided were pretty powerful.

Her big ambition now was to make a political movie, although the right one had not yet come along. But it would, she was sure. Meanwhile, she was not just working for the cause in which she believed passionately, she was also very much getting the feel of the nebulous role to come.

The men were not unaware of the risk entailed in being at Homefront. Nor was Jane. 'I am sure there is a fink here right now who is going to go back and distort every word we say,' she said at one meeting. Several of the troops knew they were regarded as suspect. One man said that he was under investigation – for owning a picture of Lenin. Jane thought that was no more than might have been expected.

The support for their cause was bigger than the attendance at that meeting indicated. One man there told her he was against the war even though he had been decorated several times for his services at Vietnam. Others, though, were frightened of being harassed for speaking their minds, ending up in the stockade and then getting a dishonourable discharge. 'That would screw them up in civilian life,' one young soldier said. Another told her: 'There are people on restriction tonight. Apparently, the word got around that you were going to be here.'

To Jane, none of this made sense. As she had said, wasn't what they were doing no more than had been done in the American Revolution? 'Suppose the English had come over here and dropped chemicals on us and sprayed us with poisons, destroyed our cities and put us up in concentration camps?' These were very emotive words and, as always, Jane knew how to use them. 'The majority of the rural population of Vietnam are in concentration camps, and we put them there. They are tortured and killed.'

Soon, though, she was changing the use of that word 'we'. No longer was she referring to the United States and the government which, she said, only claimed to represent the nation. Now she was speaking for the dissidents. '*We* are the ones who are fighting at the risk of our lives for what this country stands for.' The troops like those at the Homefront were the ones who could end the war and change American society.

'It seems to me,' she said, 'that for anyone who knew the facts it would be more honorable to get a dishonorable discharge than go to Vietnam and kill people.' As she might have admitted later, that was a pious thought which was not always practicable for a young black soldier from Mississippi with a family to support.

The FBI regarded it as reasonably close to sedition and made furious, copious notes. A 'fink' was indeed there to record the proceedings.

The next night, Jane went again to Fort Carson. And, as the Colorado Springs *Sun* reported, 'with the exception of one brief "skirmish" with the MPs, failed to engage the enemy'.

She went first, with four other people, to Homefront again and then drove to the Fort itself. She was 'totally undetected', the paper reported, as she entered the post, driven by Private Lloyd Phillips in a Volks- wagen bus bearing a Fort Carson sticker on the bumper. They went to the religious coffee house, Inscape. It was a large room, dimly lit, more usually the scene of Bible classes and gatherings of which Army chaplains – who in other armies in the past would have seen their principal task as blessing banners to be carried in battle – approved.

Jane moved to the small stage at the top of the room and from this platform told her audience that she was not only with them, she would be taking further action for the cause. But, once more, she added: 'It's up to you guys to change things.'

Soldiers were supposedly – or so the government of the United States claimed – fighting for democracy and freedom. But she said they were being 'trained by a system that is most ...'

It seemed for a minute that she was unable to finish her sentence. She was searching for the right word. One member of the audience decided to help her out. 'Fascist,' he shouted, to a huge eruption of support. Such things had never been heard on an Army base before. During the two world wars, statements like that would have resulted in sessions before the firing squad.

Someone suggested a fund-raising dinner to help them fight their case. 'Do what you can to raise support, using my name, and I will come here for it,' she declared.

Soldiers, she said, were 'controlled slaves of the rich.'

There were others there who were more familiar with their sur- roundings than most people in the building. An Army chaplain was cynicism personified. Who was Jane to talk about 'controlled slaves of the rich?' he asked, not totally unreasonably. There were few people with more money who had ever set foot in that environment, and she better know it.

'Yes,' Jane admitted. 'I could be laying out in the sun in Beverly Hills. It is very beautiful in Beverly Hills right now. But when I get up in the morning, I can't look at myself in the mirror, knowing all the things that are going on right now that are wrong.'

The soldiers cheered; the chaplain said something else which was drowned by the noise from the GIs who had formed themselves in one of their rings around the stage. Jane then distributed leaflets, including

Bertrand Russell's article, 'Appeal To the American Conscience'.

Jane's own conscience meanwhile dictated that she continued the fight. A month later, she and Mark Lane were at Fort Meade, near Washington, DC. They announced they were going to open an anti-war office. 'We're going to raise funds,' she declared, 'by speaking to businessmen.'

She was accompanied much of the time by Elisabeth Vailland, widow of the French novelist Roger Vailland, a woman who said the only English she knew was 'Power to the People', 'Right on', 'jail', 'strike' and 'peace'.

At Fort Meade, Maryland, she and Elisabeth Vailland were arrested again – the fourth time. 'We are now being searched,' she called out to demonstrators from a partly-screened upper window. 'We're going to get them on a charge of brutality.'

The charges and the threats of further charges to come multiplied, but none of them amounted to very much in terms of pure legal satisfaction.

This time, she and her companions were kept in custody for four hours. Jane asked a colonel what offence she had committed. 'I do not know,' she later reported he told her.

That evening, a friend phoned the officer saying he was a reporter from the *New York Times*. The Colonel told him that Jane had been in the process of provoking a riot when arrested. The group were then handed writs which declared that they were banned from all military bases in future. Mark Lane had been given one, too.

That was when both Lane and Jane decided to sue. The writs, they said, contradicted the United States Constitution and violated the first and fifth amendments, 'freedom of speech, freedom to assemble and freedom to have a trial if accused of doing anything illegal. Before handing over a writ to a person, a trial is necessary.'

By 12 June, the anti-war fever had become an uncontrollable passion for her. At Fayetteville, North Carolina, she led 2,000 anti-war demonstrators in a march on Fort Fragg – to distribute leaflets and talk with servicemen.

And she carried on the fight outside of military institutions, too. At the University of Maryland, Jane turned up on schedule – well, fifteen minutes late, which as has already been established, was to her the height of punctuality – to address another 2,000. 'Who's getting rich off this war?' she demanded. 'When World War II ended, the Defense Department had $160 billion worth of property. It's doubled since then.' That statistic might have been open to question and she knew

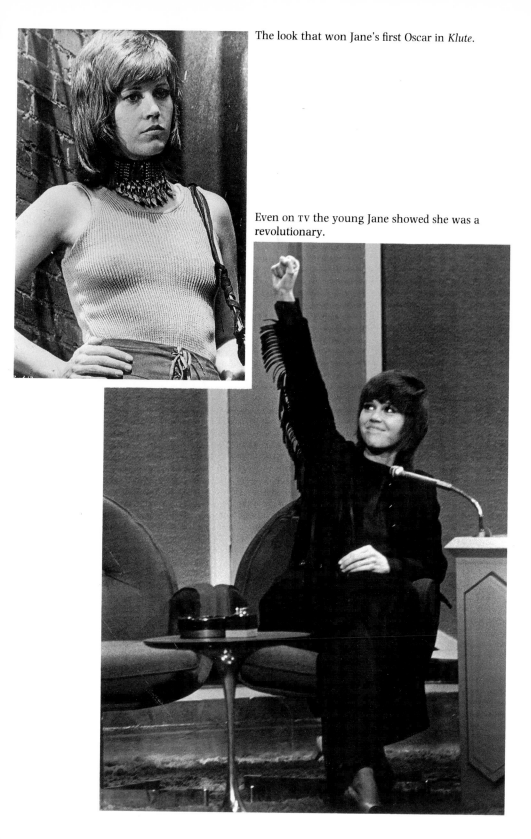

The look that won Jane's first Oscar in *Klute*.

Even on TV the young Jane showed she was a revolutionary.

Mr and Mrs Tom Hayden. Their marriage brought great changes to them both.

Tom Hayden's 1976 Primary campaign. He didn't win but Jane was his biggest asset.

Few political speakers ever looked as good as Jane Fonda.

Pensive: Jane and Vanessa Redgrave in *Julia*.

Two of a kind – Jane and Vanessa Redgrave.

Two Oscar winners – with Jon Voigt after both received their Academy awards for *Coming Home*.

The sophisticated-lady look – in 1981 in *Rollover*.

Office girl. Fighting with an elevator wasn't her only battle in *Nine to Five*.

Tom and Jane – protesting outside the White House against us nuclear policy.

Family reunion: Henry celebrates his seventy-fifth birthday with his fifth wife Shirlee, Peter and Jane in 1980.

Henry Fonda's final chapter –
with Jane his real and his
screen daughter and film wife
Katharine Hepburn.

Jane at forty-seven. Queen of
the workout – and plainly
without any blues of her own.

With Anne Bancroft in *Agnes of God*, their 1985 film.

By 1984 she was older and gaining much more respectability in the eyes of the Establishment she had once so estranged.

it, so she moved from figures to emotion. 'The Army,' she said, 'builds a tolerance for violence. I find that intolerable. They think it's normal to throw prisoners out of helicopters because "it's the only way you can make 'em talk". I find that tragic.'

Jane was about to start work on a new film, *Klute*, in which she would play one of the victims of society with whom she felt such sympathy. That was all part of her campaign to show that she was using her own particular talents to get through to society. Not everyone understood that.

At Maryland, a drama student asked why she was still part of the Establishment. Establishment? Yes, because she was still working as an actress. 'But,' he added, 'I'm not questioning your motives, of course.'

'Yes, you are,' Jane retorted like a politician dealing with a heckler at an election meeting, a situation she plainly enjoyed thoroughly. 'You think Jane, as an actress, is any more part of the Establishment than you are as a student. What about the soldiers?'

'What does your brother think of the war?' asked another student as Jane tried to fight her way to her car through the crowd. 'And your father?'

'They make their own protests their own way,' she replied.

There were harder things to answer. One man suggested it was all a publicity stunt. 'Publicity?' Jane asked, pretending to be shocked and not giving away the fact that she had been expecting the accusation for weeks. 'What do you mean? I don't get it.'

'Well,' the man replied, 'you must be getting something out of this.' A criticism that was being voiced by certain anti-Fonda forces in the country was finally being expressed to her face.

She told him: 'You think this is fun? Standing in this heat talking to a bunch of lethargic students! I could be lying by a pool in Beverly Hills getting a sun tan. You think this is for kicks?' Beverly Hills was plainly on her mind. Jane was very well aware of the suntan and the swimming pools she was missing.

She was taking the country by storm – in a way it was like the old circus performers going from town to town. This was a minstrel with a message, however.

Not all her visits to bases or college campuses were totally satisfactory – at least to observers who claimed to be impartial. When she spoke at Clemson University, South Carolina, in November 1970, the university's paper, *The Tiger*, noted: 'Jane Fonda's visit to the Clemson campus proved several things. First, that she is a better actress than orator than dialectician; second that the average Clemson student has not changed much during the last century....

'Miss Fonda handled herself very well through her speech, although she did lean quite heavily on emotionalism instead of logic, but during the question and answer session which followed, she frequently was not prepared for the questions which were asked. Thus her replies failed to satisfy many members of the audience and tarnished the effect of her speech, which had been given a very favourable reception.'

Jane did not presume to suggest that she was more effective than any other speaker. 'You don't change anybody's mind with a speech,' she declared at about this time. 'You just make them ask questions.'

But she was very worried about the immediate future. 'If Nixon wants to win the war,' she said, 'what are his alternatives? Tactical nuclear weapons – and that's a real danger. There is not a fascist regime that could survive without our financial support.'

And she had some damning things to say about every American cartoonist's favourite Aunt Sally, Vice President Spiro Agnew, shortly to lose his job in the midst of scandal. She called him 'the country's most unguided missile'.

Four thousand students heard Jane speak at Clemson, which was now about par for her course. She had become the most popular speaker on the university trail. 'The young people of today are an incredible threat to the opponents of change,' she said in one speech. 'More and more young people are rejecting the principles upon which the American way of life is based: racial superiority, male supremacy, private enterprise, opportunism, military success and the success-oriented "money is sacred" kind of principles.'

These speeches were arranged for her by an agency, who took their percentage of her own $1,750 fee. The rest of the money was divided between a soldiers' defence fund – to pay for legal representation of GIs accused of anti-war activities – and a Winter Soldiers rally to be held in Detroit the following January. An event which, as we shall see, would prove very important for Jane herself.

One of the people she greatly admired was Donald Duncan, a former Green Beret and a member of the American Special Forces who invaded Cambodia in 1963. Duncan entered the political scene, and Jane's life, when he refused to sign papers promising not to write or talk about the things he had seen on active service. Later he wrote a book about it. 'It is he,' she said in 1970, 'who explained to me that, for a soldier, it was more efficient to fight for his ideas within the armed forces than to be a deserter. For instance, a deserter can always be replaced. The movement of the GIs has been existing for the last three years and Duncan wants to help the mass of soldiers become conscious.'

The political connotations of all that were not lost on the FBI, who proceeded to record them in their dossier. They mentioned, too, that Jane was the daughter of Henry Fonda, whose films, they just happened to mention, included *The Grapes of Wrath*, *The Man with the Golden Arm* (this was not a Fonda film) and *Twelve Angry Men*, all of which they implied were left-wing. *Twelve Angry Men* was the story of a juror who wouldn't go along with the idea of convicting a boy who he wasn't sure had committed a murder. The film he hadn't made, *The Man with the Golden Arm*, was about the fight to rehabilitate a drug addict. Doubtless to Mr Hoover and his squad, these were dangerously subversive notions.

Vietnam may have become a crusade, but it was not the only one. All that Jane had put into the anti-war effort she also now devoted to what in the Kennedy years had been known as 'civil rights', but which had become a much more militant movement.

She was close to Angela Davis, the Black activist who had been jailed and was now the centre of one of America's most celebrated trials – on charges of supplying arms for a shootout in a Californian courtroom. Miss Davis, a college professor, denied the charges and Jane was with her every inch of the way of her fight.

'She is one of the most brilliant, extraordinary people I have ever had the pleasure to know,' Jane declared.

Before her eventual arrest, Miss Davis had disappeared. It was an opportunity for some typical Jane Fonda cynicism. 'The FBI seemed to think I knew where she was,' she said. 'I got quite a few calls. I was certain she had skipped the country and I can't understand why she didn't. She has no chance of having a fair trial.'

In June 1970, Jane gave an interview to the French Communist daily, *L'Humanité*, one of the leading papers in France. She thought it important to state her attitude to the sort of activities in which she was involved. 'We wish to do only legal things,' she told their reporter. 'What is more, we wish to compel the leaders who violate the laws to respect them.'

The paper headed its interview: 'Jane Fonda Is The Cry Of An

America Which Has Chosen Peace.' It went on to say about her: 'She has the wish and the will to fight against injustice somewhat in the fashion in which Don Quixote fought against windmills.'

They quoted her, contrasting her own political views with those of Henry. 'My father is a rather liberal democrat,' she said. 'I, too, was "liberal". But I used to live out of all those things because I had a privileged social position. I sympathized very much with emancipation movements; however, I could not identify myself with their problems. I was barely conscious of these problems. Then I started the discovery of what was done to the Indians in my country and the motives for this. The war in Vietnam and the horrors which were committed there under the cover of the American flag or under the cover of the defence of the "free world" led me to raise questions concerning our society.'

Soon after that, Jane's eyes filled with tears. 'I have seen people who are literally dying of hunger in a country which is so rich; that is unacceptable. I am still asking myself how I did not notice it before. Perhaps because I lived in France during the last six years.'

Again, she referred to the seeming contrast between what she did and her role as a film star. 'I will not discontinue my occupation,' she said. 'It bothers me a little bit; but, since my name is Jane Fonda, I can be useful. When I go to a coffee house near a base and when I can talk with GIs, they come to see me because I am an "actress"; however, this does not prevent the GIs from talking about their problems.'

If the coffee houses represented a radical movement within the armed services, the Black Panthers were that for the civil rights movement – multiplied a thousand times. In the course of what they did, they alienated moderate blacks as much as liberal whites. But Jane was with them as though she were Abraham Lincoln and they were the slaves. The severest criticism was heaped on her for that. About that time, Leonard Bernstein entertained a group of Black Panthers at his apartment. 'Radical chic' was the way one wit put it at the time. They were to say altogether less kind things about Jane Fonda.

Three Panthers leaders were being held at Soledad Prison at Soledad, California, on charges of murder. Jane addressed a rally in their support on 19 June 1970 at 217 West 1st Street, Los Angeles.

The document in the FBI archives – originally stamped 'Confidential' and with most of the first page blacked out – is headed: 'Jane Fonda Security Matters – Anarchist.' Jane Fonda an anarchist? Even her most ardent supporters would have queried that, but to J. Edgar Hoover it underlined his anger at what she was doing – the kind of anger that made the blood rush to his face and sweat engulf the back of his bull neck.

The document reports that 'a representative of the FBI was in attendance' and recorded the speech. Jane was not yet aware of how sinister that all was. But she saw other things that concerned her.

'Did you notice that lately, whenever people get together to demand their freedom,' she pointed out, 'there are new symbols of repression flying overhead – the helicopter, the symbol of 20th century repression?'

When in August 1970, one of the founders of the Panthers, Bobby George Seale, appeared in court at New Haven, Connecticut, Jane was there among a group of supporters – her new close friend, the actor Donald Sutherland and Mark Lane were on hand, too – to supply encouragement. She raised her fist in the Black Power salute when Seale's co-founder, Huey P. Newton, who had himself been serving a prison sentence and was currently out on bail, arrived at Kennedy Airport on his way to give evidence on his colleague's behalf.

Jane declared: 'We are right now, at this moment in history, locked in a struggle for survival against a monster which has been created and which we are perpetuating if we allow it to exist; and that monster is the American society.

'Put that on your television, you'll be arrested by Spiro Agnew for freedom of speech! If you strip away the facade and the false sense of freedom and social justice and comfort that lulls the white middle class into thinking they're safe, you can see what it is, racist, oppressive, totalitarian and monstrous. And the only way that that system is going to change, particularly the courtroom system, is if we, the people, throw our weight entirely against it. We must denounce the unjust laws, we must denounce the unjust justice, and we must bring the system to a halt until it is again working for the people to protect the people.'

Then she went on to a matter which had come very close to her heart: 'Rigged criminal trials for the purpose of wiping out anybody that the authorities don't want around, for the purpose of repressing political ideas and organizations by exterminating the leaders and by intimidation, is nothing new in this country. If we are silent this time, we are the enemy and eventually we are the victim.

'Can you really believe that you are safe? Do you really think that it is sufficient to say, "I am innocent, I have not done anything." This is not Los Angeles in 1970.... This is not Los Angeles in 1970. It is Berlin in 1936 and we are all Jews. The prisons of this country are overflowing with people who may be executed not because of what they have done but because of what they are.'

That was the sort of thing that particularly worried Mr Hoover and made Jane Fonda his – and that of his like-minded friends – favourite *bête noir*.

The following day, at an apartment rented by Jane, Newton promised to hold a rally outside the courthouse – this time to protest at what he called 'the legal lynching' of another Black Panther, Lonnie McLucas, who was on trial in connection with a murder.

Jane firmly believed there were good reasons for the stand she took. 'I'm willing to give my life, if it comes to that. That doesn't mean revolution. The Black Panthers are not violent. They're armed in self-defence.'

And she added: 'Are we going to be Germans and trust our leaders or are we going to act decisively and form ourselves into small political collectives of people who know and trust each other and who decide how we want to relate to the problems of America? Are we going to start making special demands on campus? These campuses belong to us.'

Then she added in an aside which must have caused the FBI man to fall off his seat – in anticipation, if nothing else. 'Some of the best people in America are behind bars – Angela Davis, Bobby Seale, the Rev Daniel Berrigan and, of course, there was Christ – the greatest revolutionary of all.'

She was full of strictures on people who didn't respond the way she believed that they should. 'If more of you don't applaud,' she told one university audience in Miami, 'it's because you believe what you read in the newspapers. You don't understand violence – the kind perpetuated on poor blacks by poverty and the police.'

The papers in the area had as much a field day as Mr Hoover. The *Miami Herald* described Jane as the actress 'who practices motherhood by long distance telephone'.

The Detroit *Free Press* told its readers: 'She's gone through a lot of changes within the last year. The girl who once played Cat Ballou is now infatuated with the Black Panthers. At 33, she is still stunning, eyes iridescent, shanks slim, the whole of her lit from within by that kind of luminosity that people call presence.'

Now that was the nicest thing she had read about herself for a long time. But the paper had to disillusion her. 'But she talks like a long-playing record, her words a socialist sermon. It is as though the Weatherman faction kidnapped Barbarella and then turned her loose again with a movement tape recording running in her throat.'

Jane's response to that sort of thing was to declare in a statement that would have brought as much joy to readers of *L'Humanité* as to J. Edgar Hoover's FBI: 'I would think that if you understood what Communism was, you would hope, you would pray on your knees that we would someday become Communist.'

The 2,000 students at Michigan State University who heard that were not quite sure how to take it. Nor her subsequent statement about 'good soldiers', which would have got the American Legion anxious to press immediate sedition charges. Speaking about Vietnam's GIs, she said: 'They're a new kind of soldier. They're not John Wayne freaks over there. No order goes unchallenged. When they're sent out on patrol, they just go out a little ways. They lie down on a little knoll and blow grass and stargaze.

'They're good soldiers. We should be proud of them. They're not only doing what they're supposed not to do, but they're not even performing the basic functions of soldiers.'

That was not the sort of thing Americans used to hearing how Bob Hope, Al Jolson and Marilyn Monroe had entertained the troops in Korea – and all the other stories of people going out to World War Two battle theatres – had come to expect. Was this not treason? Jane protested that she was more patriotic than any of her detractors.

In the midst of all this, how was Roger Vadim, the man who was still her husband and who had now been virtually forgotten by the papers? He was well, she believed, and indeed he said so. But he wasn't too happy with all the political shenanigans. 'I feel like I am baby-sitting for Lenin,' he declared – which made Jane, when she managed to take a moment off from her crusade, see a different kind of red from that claimed by the FBI.

'I love him,' Jane protested. But it was also a different kind of love – certainly from the sort usually spoken about in films, hers or anyone else's. 'He is my friend,' she said, and that, too, sounded like something out of the peace movement. 'But I am not in love with him.'

So there was a difference. Yes, of course, there was, Jane believed: 'But I care for him very much.' By telephone, the Detroit news-paperman may have concluded. They still spoke, but Vadim, when he picked up the receiver at the Malibu house, probably still felt as though he were in the Kremlin nursery.

None of this now really seemed to matter to Jane, which many of her friends believed was the principal tragedy in her life. The crusades had become an obsession; and in the process of that obsession, they felt they had begun to lose someone very precious to them. If Jane had heard that, she would doubtless have said that it was a question of priorities.

J. Edgar Hoover himself had much the same sort of thought. His priority in the summer of 1970 was simply to Get Fonda. His methods were questionable in the extreme – in fact, among the most questionable of a regime that had been full of charges of excesses, the kind to which no government agency would care to admit.

The FBI dirty-tricks brigade decided that it would be a good idea to 'plant' a letter in the showbusiness 'Bible', *Variety*. One that would bring Jane into disrepute.

There is an element of both the Alice in Wonderland of *Barbarella* and of *Nineteen Eighty-Four* in the letters that went by registered airmail between the FBI's Los Angeles office and Hoover himself on 17 June 1970. The sender, identified as 'SAC, Los Angeles' and later found to be one Wesley G. Grapp, suggested writing to the Hollywood-based *Daily Variety*'s columnist Army Archard – and headed his letter to Hoover: 'Re Los Angeles teletype to Bureau, 6/15/70, entitled 'Committee United For Political Prisoners (CUPP) IS-MISCELLANEOUS, THREAT AGAINST PRESIDENT NIXON', which sounded pretty daunting by itself. The letter, however, had about it a whiff of the kind of nastiness which would later figure in Senate investigations: 'Bureau authority is requested in sending the following letter from a fictitious person to Army Archard – who noted in his 6/11/70 column that Jane Fonda, noted film actress, was to be present at the 6/13/70 Black Panther Party fund raising function sponsored by CUPP in Los Angeles. It is felt that knowledge of Fonda's involvement would cause her embarrassment and detract from their status with the general public.'

The letter this official wanted to send read:

'Dear Army,

I saw your article about Jane Fonda in *Daily Variety* last Thursday and happened to be present for Vadim's [*there was clearly considered to be something damning in calling her by her married surname*] "Joan of Arc" performance for the Black Panthers Saturday night. I hadn't been confronted with this Panther phenomena [sic] before but we were searched upon entering Embassy Auditorium, encouraged in revival-like fashion to contribute to defend jailed Panther leaders and buy guns for "the coming revolution", and led by Jane and one of the Panther chaps in a "We will kill Richard Nixon and any other M...

F... who stands in our way" refrain (which was shocking to say the least). I think Jane has gotten in over her head as the whole atmosphere had the 1930s Munich beer hall aura.

I also think my curiosity about the Panthers has been satisfied.'

The letter to Hoover bore the footnote: 'If approved, appropriate precautions will be taken to preclude [sic] the identity of the Bureau as the source of this operation.'

Mr Hoover *did* approve. In a personal letter to his Los Angeles office, headed: 'Counter intelligence ... Black Nationalist – Hate Groups. Racial Intelligence. Black Panther Party', the Director wrote:

'You are authorized to prepare a letter as set forth ... to Army Archard, the Hollywood "gossip" columnist. Insure that mailing cannot be traced to the Bureau.'

The letter was never used. Archard later said that he did not remember ever receiving it and even if he had, he wouldn't have used it without first checking the authenticity of its source.

Jane Fonda, meanwhile, was proving to be an exceedingly authentic source for a great deal of the stories emanating from the anti-war movement – to say nothing of the anti-anti-war movement.

16

That November, Jane was arrested again – as she stepped into the arrivals lounge of Hopkins International Airport in Cleveland, Ohio. This time it wasn't any 'ordinary' arrest – or at least not as she might have used the term. She saw it as having connotations even she had not previously imagined. Once more, Jane Fonda was in the world headlines – and this time it appeared that Mr Hoover might just have bitten off a little more than he was comfortably able to chew.

It happened as she arrived from London, Ontario, to fulfil a speaking engagement the following day at the nearby Bowling Green State University.

It was alleged that when she arrived at the airport she kicked both a policeman and a customs agent. It was enough to land her at the Cuyahoga County Jail. But the offences were less prosaic. She was charged with drug smuggling. This time, not marijuana, but Dexedrine, Valium and Compazine. It seemed that Jane was once again taking diet pills followed by tranquillizers; an innocent enough pastime, but to the immigration officials at the airport it all seemed much more sinister.

The story was that the Canadian Mounties had warned the American customs authority about her after she had been lecturing to students at a college in Ontario. Jane insisted that there was a concerted campaign to 'get her'.

She denied she was drug smuggling or that she had kicked any officers of the law. Jane had merely been trying to get into a toilet when her way was blocked by a customs agent. 'I pushed him to try to get into the bathroom,' she declared. She was eventually bailed on a $5,000 personal bond and released on a $500 surety bond.

These were the bare bones of what happened. Putting the meat on those bones gives an idea both of the importance put on Jane Fonda the activist and of the paranoia of the times.

Jane saw what she alleged to be the fiendish proportions of it all, beginning with the first thing that they did: they took away her address book. To someone who was in the public eye in a controversial way, taking away an address book had *Nineteen Eighty-Four* connotations. Was this not like a resurgence of McCarthyism – with all the naming of names that that entailed? (The address book was arranged in states. 'When I got it back,' Jane later said, 'Canada was in Florida and Florida was in South Carolina.')

In an attempt to keep her mind cool, she sang to herself – French revolutionary songs. The customs agents and the FBI didn't enjoy them. In fact, she said, they 'set them off'.

Later, she spoke about the next thing that happened: the steps that got Jane Fonda labelled a drug addict. As she explained the matter, it was another event with tragi-comic associations. 'The second thing they did,' she said, 'was open a bag which contains the now infamous 102 plastic vials, organic health food and vitamin pills, which any wise person can buy at your corner health food store without a prescription.'

As she went on: 'On the top of each vial was written the letters in red nail polish, "B", "L" and "D".'

She told the story later at the University of Houston, Texas, and added by way of explanation: 'In case there are any agents in the audience [of course, there were – the FBI type] you can pass along to your superiors that the decoding of that is "breakfast, lunch and dinner". That'd really freak them out. The reason I had so many was because I have to keep up my energy because I was on the road for a month and a half. Those pills are now in Washington being analyzed. Maybe Agnew is getting healthy.'

It was now funny, the way that she recalled it, but it was a bitter irony and she was more even more bitter than she had been before.

She described being pushed into a chair by 'two husky FBI agents' and told to shut up. 'At the end of three hours, not having any superhuman powers over my body, I had to go to the bathroom. This was also denied me, rudely – and another agent blocked my way into the restroom.'

This was when the alleged assault took place. The agent 'joyfully said, "You're under arrest for assaulting an officer!" and slapped handcuffs on me. He was just waiting, waiting for an excuse to arrest me. I was then searched and in my purse they found a small bottle of personally-prescribed medicine which I purchase with a prescription from my doctor in this country and which I have been carrying around for a number of years in and out of this country – which no one has ever hassled me about.'

She was now saying that ever since she had started speaking out about the Vietnam war and human rights, every time she returned to the country from abroad, she was stripped and searched.

Her doctor claimed that the FBI had been in his office every day for three weeks. And, Jane added for good measure: 'They've searched all of my books, all of my tapes, all of my research material, notes of my speeches.'

The police officer she was alleged to have kicked decided to sue her for $100,000. 'He's the same police officer that drove me to the jail,' reported Jane. Then she added a choice bit of sarcasm which one of the various scriptwriters who had produced material for Jane Fonda over the years might have envied: 'He wasn't on crutches or in a wheelchair or anything like that.' And she added, relishing the irony: 'I don't know what's happened to the manhood of the FBI. I never did kick him and ah, well, anyway, I spent ten hours in jail. They didn't do anything because they knew I would be out in ten hours. They knew I could afford a lawyer, that I could afford my bond. So they couldn't beat me. But I'm probably the only woman that's been in that jail who's not been beaten.' That was an exceedingly blunt accusation, but she would say she had reason to make it.

When she *was* allowed out, the FBI gave her back all her belongings. She went through them with the proverbial fine-tooth comb, examining every item; checking the linings of all her bags and clothing to make sure nothing was being planted on her. She played through the tapes she was carrying to make sure they had not been erased. All the time, FBI members had to sit and listen. It was an experience they didn't enjoy any more than they had her impromptu performance of French revolutionary songs. Jane savoured their discomfort.

The case against her at the preliminary hearing was not helped when one witness described Jane as being 'dirty and filthy, wearing blue jeans'. Such things were supposed to matter.

At first, the United States Commissioner Clifford E. Bruce, who presided, insisted that Jane should be banned from leaving the country, but her attorneys promised that she would come back to Cleveland for her trial and the requirement was dropped.

Later, Mark Lane said that it all arose because the authorities were out to incriminate Jane. 'Her arrest was an act of terror, an act of violence. This is the Nixon-Agnew terror.'

And what about the 'assault' on the customs officer? Jane repeated that she had merely asked to go to the bathroom, but 'this big, burly federal agent wouldn't allow it,' so she put up a fuss.

Other people put up something of a fuss at the police station and courthouse, which had never in living memory been so crowded. One lawyer, a certain Fred Jurek, enjoyed the proceedings immensely, but with a degree of regret. 'I saw her in *Playboy* [this was not calculated to make him a friend] a couple of years ago and last night I took the magazine out again to check what she really looked like. She really looked like something. Now, she's mixing with all these hippies and she don't look so good any more.'

The Cleveland *Plain Dealer* headed its story: 'Court Needs SRO Sign for Jane Fonda's Fans' (SRO, Standing Room Only, is one of the hallowed words in showbusiness.)

Jane was arraigned in what was commonly known as 'Drunk Court'. Things were far from pleasant at the hearing. Patrolman Robert Peiper gave evidence to explain the kick. It happened, he said, after Jane shouted at him: 'Get the --- out of here, you pig.'

She, in return, condemned the conditions in the cells to which she was taken. This was going to be her testimony to justify the claim that she was the only woman who left a prison cell unharmed. Jane said in evidence: 'I spent my time in jail on the floor of a cell with Barbara Cahn. She told me she was repeatedly beaten on the arms and legs by guards. [Ms Kahn, an eighteen-year-old Cleveland girl who was usually referred to as a Maoist, had been jailed for breaking up a parade by the United Hard Hats of America.] 'She has the bruises to prove it. She is a political prisoner like thousands of others in this country.'

As for the jail itself, it was 'deplorable, criminal, violent. The inmates are assaulted physically as well as psychologically. They all told me to tell what it's like when I get out. If this can happen to me, you can imagine what happens to less visible people who are trying to do something in this country.'

Things were worse for her, she said, because she was in the midst of a period at the time – which was why she needed to get to the ladies room. 'A policewoman finally arrived with a sanitary pad,' she said. 'Then she stripped me and searched my handbag and found some tranquilizers plus an old bottle with a few Dexedrine pills. Dexedrine is not a drug: it's a medicine to help you stay awake when you haven't slept for two nights. I had bought it in the States with a prescription.'

Mark Lane defended her. In a statement at a press conference, he said: 'Her arrest was an act of terror, pure and simple! An act of violence.'

Jane herself believed that Nixon was trying to get at her – she didn't know much about Hoover at the time. As Mark Lane described it, 'This is the Nixon-Agnew terror.' Lane said that Jane was on a special list which decided that she would be stopped and charged with drug smuggling wherever she went.

As for Jane herself, 'I am a health food freak,' she said. She was not a smuggler. 'The pills they found in my luggage were vitamins you can buy in any health-food store . . . I was never hassled until I started talking against the war.' She said it was all a political arrest.

She was asked if she wanted to be tried there and then. She opted for trial by jury – when it was revealed that all she was carrying were her vitamins and tranquillizers.

The anti-appetite pills, she later said, she no longer used. She considered them dangerous and carried them only for use when she had not slept for two or three nights – she wanted nothing, especially hunger, to interrupt sleep when it finally came.

As if making a gesture of defiance, she, by return, sued for $100,000 for personal injuries.

Eventually, the hearing of United States of America, plaintiff, vs Jane Fonda, defendant, was settled in Jane's favour by Judge Edward F. Feighan at the Cleveland Municipal Court. Within days, the local police asked for the trial to be heard again, but later conceded that they had no new evidence to bring. Jane meanwhile decided she would no longer be pressing her personal injuries suit.

The proceedings did not endear her to all of Cleveland society. In an editorial, the city's *Observer* commented: 'W. C. Fields once quipped in one of his movies – "I like children – as long as they're well cooked." Fields's wisdom also applies to actresses like Jane Fonda who rally to political causes. Any woman who makes a name for herself as a sex-symbol and then enters into politics in one form or another should be viewed with a healthy measure of scepticism.'

Jane still worried about becoming a victim of the state again – and before very long. As she said: 'I'm afraid dope will be planted on me.'

Vadim wasn't so sure about it all – in fact, he was making his first statements in Jane's favour for a very long time. He was filming *Pretty Maids All in a Row* with Rock Hudson at the time. But living alone with Vanessa in their Malibu home gave him time for thought at the way his wife was being treated.

'It is difficult for me to make really any comment which involves myself, but I will do it anyhow,' he said. 'My position, not being an American, has always been not to get involved in politics, with Jane doing it. I have accepted that. But there's a difference between politics and police harassment.'

That was a subject which had always been close to his heart. 'I know about police harassment because I went through three years of the Nazi occupation of France. Jane tells me she was sent to jail and met this girl who was so badly beaten she couldn't stand up. I wasn't there. I can only assume Jane was telling the truth.

'Jane was detained for nearly three hours. When a woman's detained and gets ill as a woman can get ill and has to go to the bathroom and the police won't let her, I think those methods must be called Fascism. If you allow the police to go in this direction, there is no end and you will finish by suffering from the same conditions that France suffered under Germany or after the Algerian war.

'This is a democracy and we can still talk, at least. Nobody will stop the police but the journalists. Nothing can change things but public opinion. That's why I'm talking to you.'

Not that Vadim agreed totally with Jane's pills regimen. 'When this silly doctor tells her just to take vitamins and not eat varied foods, that is wrong. But that's a crazy doctor. That has nothing to do with the police or the law. Nobody had a gun. Nobody was rioting. It was just a lady with too many diet pills in her bag because she's afraid to eat.'

The winning of her case didn't do much to change Jane's views on the American political system. She didn't even intend to vote – because she had seen too many 'good guys turn bad. I've become cynical. The answer is revolution.'

To be fair to Jane, *that* at least was a view she would later modify. She wanted workers to share in the profits of their labours and American troops to be withdrawn from overseas countries, although there would be increased technical aid to the underdeveloped lands. 'This is not isolationism,' she declared, 'but internationalism.'

For the moment, she talked in speech after speech about the low morale of American troops – how officers who sent men out into danger zones were being 'fragged' by their men. 'Fragged'? It was a word that for a time would enter the lexicon of people who considered themselves revolutionaries.

'The first time I ever heard about fragging was about a year ago,' she said in one speech at Tallahassee Community College, Florida, in January 1971. 'A soldier had just come back from 'Nam and he told me that in his company if they had an officer that they didn't like because he was endangering the lives of the men, they would put a price on his head. Each soldier would contribute a dollar or two. The soldier who fragged him – which means rolling a hand grenade under in his tent flap in many cases – would collect the money.'

That sort of information was certainly not calculated to improve morale in the front line – which was precisely one of the reasons she was now being attacked. And it was bound to have an effect on her principal career as a film actress.

Jane plainly worried people who wanted to love her for her God-given talent. She herself hated the idea of being called a sex symbol.

She apologized for some of the things she had done to date. 'When we made *Barbarella*, I didn't know what male chauvinism was all about. I wouldn't make a movie like that now. There are many movies I wouldn't make now, movies I am not proud of.'

So was this just newly emergent Women's Lib? Jane now had no difficulty in expressing her views on equality. 'We don't want to be equal to men who are being sent to Vietnam when they don't want to go. Women's Liberation calls for restructuring of society so that everybody is liberated.' And she added: 'Women's liberation is men's liberation.'

But what was she now? An actress or a political activist? And if she were both, as it seemed she was, which came first?

'I see myself,' she declared at the end of 1970, 'as a renegade actress, a slob who doesn't fit into any Hollywood mould.'

And a slob who didn't need the money either. She had no thought of material possessions. That was news likely to please the Hollywood studios considerably. But not if she could help it. 'I'll try to rip them off for everything I can get,' she said.

And then she added, in a moment of apparent bitterness, 'They don't give Academy Awards to people like me.'

Was this now time for the fragile family unity of the Fondas to come unstuck? People were now waiting for Henry's damning comment. It wouldn't come. In an interview in the September 1970 issue of *McCalls* magazine, Fonda declared: 'Hers is not my way of life and hers is not too often my exact way of thinking.'

But he was not in a mood to disown or denounce her. As he said: 'I love her. I respect her right to say what she says and she and her husband are obviously deeply in love. That's the way I feel about my daughter.'

He did feel that way about his daughter. But, as we have seen, she wasn't deeply in love any more. At about this time, the Malibu beach home was ruined in a fire that swept through the area. It must have struck them as being peculiarly ominous.

Vadim probably thought that it wasn't nearly as important as her continuing campaign. The Texas Union Speakers Committee sponsored another Fonda speech in which she condemned 'oppression in the United States' and came out in favour of women's lib, gay lib, GI rights, black militancy and amnesty for political prisoners.

She continued her tour of American universities, making the same speeches – 'Nixon says he doesn't want to go down in history as the first American President to lose a war; how about the first to lose an Army?' – and raising money by so doing for her various causes. Occasionally, as at Fort Worth, Texas, she was told to postpone a Texas Christian University speaking appearance because she did not have 'sufficient administration approval'.

They were doubtless afraid of repeating what had happened at Atlanta, Georgia, where Jane predicted a revolt by American troops in Vietnam. GIs, she said, 'can no longer find a reason to die ... they no longer accept anything unchallenged and are quick to recognize hypocrisy.'

As for the Black Panthers, she said: 'They're beautiful, brave people.'

The 'American Way of Life' was her principal target. 'If you were good students, you'd be fitting the American mould, trying to join the ruling class,' she said at the Texas speech. 'The more opportunistic you are, the better you can make it. You will be elevated to a high level of society and be able to participate in high-level corruption.'

The people gathered in the Texas Union Main Ballroom were impressed as she told them: 'Establish a Socialist economic structure which will do away with profit-oriented control and do away with exploitation and will put technology to use for the people. These are the alternative conditions we are struggling for today. Whether the transformation is peaceful will be controlled by the people in power.' Then she added: 'We must live our politics.' Vadim had been given a similar message, he would have said.

The union speech was followed by another to students at the University of Texas's Arlington campus. Two and a half thousand young people heard her speak for an hour and ten minutes. This time she talked about terrorism.

'The Administration talks a lot about terrorism and violence. I think that terrorism on the part of law enforcement officials of this country against citizens of the United States is the most dangerous kind that exists,' she declared.

Then she added: 'If they isolate a political prisoner, that person is contained forever. I also realize that everyone in jail is a political prisoner.'

She didn't embellish that thought but decided to switch the attack to President Nixon: 'There is a law that states that if the President invades a foreign country without Congressional approval, he is to be impeached.'

And from the President to the students – who were complaining about military cadet training on the campus (the ROTC). 'The American institution is collapsing and the Administration is trying to disguise that collapse by using you as scapegoats. It is the antithesis of a learning institution that an officer should receive faculty status for learning how to kill. If the students don't want ROTC on campus, they shouldn't be there.'

From Arlington, she moved on to Houston, where she talked some more about everyone being a political prisoner. 'The murderers, the junkies, the thieves, all victims of this oppressive, dehumanizing, threatening society that we live in and very truly all of them political prisoners.' And she went on about her recent imprisonment. 'I became aware of two very important things during the time I was in jail,' she said. 'Up until then, my support of political prisoners had been rather theoretical. But I realized that for a political prisoner that the only hope, that the only hope, that they have is support from the people, from the community, on the street. If they can be isolated and shut off from the community, they are lost. That is something that we must all bear in mind.'

It was difficult for Vadim to bear much in mind – other than the effect it was all having on his marriage. In December 1970, he made the first public statement since the barbed comment about babysitting for Lenin.

At first, he confined himself to comments about her political activities. 'It is difficult enough to live with an actress,' he said. Then he added: 'But if the actress is also oriented toward politics, it becomes very difficult. When she talks only about politics all the time, there is no time to establish feelings.'

Before long, he was admitting: 'Jane has been gone, more or less, since the beginning of the year.'

So did this mean that it was all over? 'There's a vast difference between a difficult moment and an ocean,' he replied in one of those somewhat inscrutable statements for which he had become well known among Fonda watchers.

It wouldn't have pleased Henry to know much about that – and until then he didn't. In fact, while Jane's father was saying those loving things about Jane and Vadim, the couple were talking about divorce.

/ **17** /

T he sad thing for Vadim was that Jane didn't really appear to care very much about either staying married or getting divorced.

In fact, Jane said that she found it difficult to understand why her erstwhile lover and husband was so unable to accept the reality of their present situation. Finally and painfully, it dawned on him that Jane was not going to return from her political excursions to the kind of home he thought was theirs.

'I think he's beginning to understand now,' she said. 'He's an intelligent man, he respects people, but he wasn't prepared for what happened. He would better understand a woman who leaves him for another man.'

The problem was mainly that the 'other man' was the one marching with her to some university campus or other or an army base – or, probably more accurately, he was the demo itself: the Cause. She excluded Vanessa from that leaving. For her she felt a love which she had not previously understood existed.

The love she had for her father was still complicated – especially since Henry couldn't relate to her lifestyle now any more than he ever had before. The liberal actor, who made the Okies stand and cheer him when he made *The Grapes of Wrath* was extraordinarily revealing – and not in a particularly charming way – in the course of an interview with the *New York Times*.

He apologized to the *Times*'s writer Guy Flatley for being late. 'I was on a long-distance call to Washington,' he explained.

Washington? The President? The Vice President? His senator? At least a congressman? No, Henry was talking to his 'erstwhile … with my alleged daughter'.

Now that didn't read any nicer than the way Jane felt when she heard about it. But Henry didn't hold back. 'She asked me if she could go to my house in New York and bring her whole entourage with her – for a week.'

That was what bothered him. Not the numbers of people involved. But 'it's how unattractive they all are'. No, the Okies would not have been pleased. But they stayed just the same. As Henry explained: 'Gee, I would love to have been able to say, "I'm sorry but the house is all filled up," but I just couldn't do it.' Jane can't have been at all pleased at his reasoning – or the degree to which his conscience pricked.

When, in March 1971, Jane visited Angela Davis at the jail in Marin County, California, it was really no more than anyone would have expected. And it no longer caused any furore.

Much more of a fuss, however, came with the now somewhat rare appearance of the 'Other' Jane Fonda – Jane the actress. In June 1971, *Klute* opened at the Cinerama theatre on Broadway, her first film since *They Shoot Horses, Don't They?* – and the acclaim from both critics and public was palpable. It won her an Oscar.

Jane herself found it difficult to totally understand her acclaim, so different was it from the sort of response she received for her politics. 'Being a movie star is not a purpose,' she declared.

Her decision to take the studios for as much as she could had plainly paid off – for both sides that signed the contract. And it proved one thing: a strange thing for students of such matters, a phenomenon that was so very different from conditions at the time of the last Hollywood 'scare' during the McCarthy era. For now, despite all the vitriol that had been poured on Jane – and for all of the same substance with which she had deluged the American 'Establishment', she was still being hailed as an outstanding actress, probably the best in the country.

The publicity for the film didn't shy away from her connections with the movements that she had espoused: peace, the Blacks, the Indians and women's lib. Any story she made about the evil that is done to prostitutes must have been seen in the context of her political feelings and associations. Not only that, her co-star was her friend and fellow activist, Donald Sutherland – as the cop from out of town who goes to the big city in search of his missing best friend. His main contact is

Bree Daniel (Jane), the prostitute who is supposed to have received an obscene letter from the missing man – but at first she denies him any co-operation in the process of defending her calling and blaming the men who make it all financially worthwhile.

(But not everything was fine in other directions during the making of *Klute*. When she turned up on the set to start with, certain members of the crew refused to talk to her – and hung up an American flag to demonstrate their animosity. 'They viewed me as unpatriotic and as a traitor,' she recalled later.)

There was detailed research before she began filming. She spent time with a New York hooker who gave her sage advice – like: 'The first thing you do is get your money. You get it before, because you're not going to get as much afterwards. The thing you do is make sure the man thinks he is different and he really turns you on. You get more money that way.'

Jane used the information in her discussions with the psychiatrist in the movie. Actually, Bree, the girl she played, likes to 'trick', as she calls the work done in a profession which may be the oldest in the world but in which she finds new things to do every night. She is a bit mystified by it herself, as she constantly tells the analyst who plays a big part in the movie's proceedings. None of her talk to the psychiatrist was scripted. Jane herself ad-libbed it all – again taking the professional prostitute's guidance in the sort of things she should say.

The director, Alan Jo Pakula, said about her: 'I felt she could play a range of characters beyond that of any star of her generation ... Jane is one of those people who have a vivid, supreme star personality and also the capability of a superb character actress. That's very rare. She's so alive, so immediate, so interested, and she has genuine curiosity about other people and other ways of life.'

Another time, he said: 'There seems in her some vast emotional need to find the centre of life. Jane is the kind of lady who might have gone across the prairie in a covered wagon a hundred years ago. I don't think any actress expresses the complexities of her time and her generation, its whole quest for fulfilment and an identity in society as much as Jane.'

The *New York Times*'s reviewer, Roger Greenspun, noted: 'The acting in *Klute* seems semi-improvisatory, and in this Jane Fonda, who is good at confessing, is generally successful. Everybody else merely talks a lot.'

Time magazine was a little more generous. '*Klute* is a sharp, slick thriller about murder, perversion, paranoia, prostitution and a lot of other wonderful things about life in New York City,' wrote Jay Cocks.

He thought Alan Pakula 'still has a tendency to go soft on his characters, but his camera eye and his sense of the rhythm of a scene ... have improved considerably. His talent with actors seems now beyond contention and under his guidance Jane Fonda gives her best performance to date.

'A couple of years ago, in *They Shoot Horses, Don't They?*, she brought power to a part in which she was basically miscast. In *Klute* she is profoundly and perfectly Bree: she makes all the right choices, from the mechanics of her walk and her voice inflection to the penetration of the girl's raging psyche. It is a rare performance.'

A rare performance which the following spring earned her her first Oscar – notwithstanding her political activities and all they represented. She also won the New York Critics' Award again.

She wouldn't deny that there was a message there. She said soon afterwards: 'The question one should pose is why was she a call girl in the first place? Why does a college graduate in the US become a prostitute?' She wasn't sure that the film's answer was the right one. 'In order to deal with those problems, you don't go to a psychiatrist – a Freudian psychiatrist particularly. It is a problem of society. You have to deal with the whole relationship between men and women – why does it exist that way in the US? The film didn't even pose the question, much less touch upon solutions.'

But it did give her the bucks and did provide her with her prizes.

To Jane, though, perhaps yet again the most important award of all was the praise of her father. Henry saw the movie and declared: 'I've always been proud of her, but now I'm even prouder of her.' And he explained why: 'She can do things that I cannot do. Take that scene in *Klute* where she talks to the psychiatrist – the scene that probably won her the Academy Award. Her first one. Anyway, the scene was not written, there were no lines. It was Actors Studio stuff, improvisation. She was magnificent. Not in a million years could I do anything like that! I mean, they could drag me to the Actors Studio and put me in manacles and I couldn't do it. But there was Jane, improvising every word, and it was breathtaking.'

That seemed to be the way he thought of his daughter now – breathtaking. 'Another thing Jane has, that I don't, is her capacity for speaking out.' Now here was the first sign of approval for Jane's political activities. 'In her activism, she feels so strongly about things that she can get up in front of 5,000 people and talk for an hour without notes and she can be forceful and dynamic and eloquent. Well, I feel just as strongly about everything she believes in – despite what you may have read in the past – but I could just never do that.'

It was difficult to know whether that really was what he believed. In April 1972, he was back on his familiar kick of knocking his daughter and her causes.

'When she is working for the right causes,' he said, 'it is for most of the wrong reasons. I guess she won't be satisfied until they burn her like Joan of Arc.'

Vadim's phrase had stuck. Was Henry so ambivalent towards Jane that he was contradicting himself? More likely, he was telling the truth when he spoke of the way he saw her motives. Just occasionally, however, the pride that he also quite genuinely felt took the ascendancy. Occasionally, he was much, much more cynical.

'She probably went to a party and heard somebody talk about the American Indians and she came home and in the morning ... instant cause. I look out of the window and I see this guy taking books out of a Volkswagen. I mean not twelve books but eighty-four books. And all about Indians.'

What that did not demonstrate was just how real Jane's commitment was to her causes. Real – but natural? There were columnists at the time who said she was a phony. That was no more correct than was the assumption that everything she did, all those crusades that she mounted with such passion, were worked on simply because she believed in them so greatly. Sometimes one was left with the feeling that she was still trying to justify them all herself.

'You think, well, "I did it,"' she was to say. 'Then you begin to realize, so what? I'm not the actress I should have been. People whom I respect, don't respect me. My father was very loyal, but he didn't approve of some of the films I did. And suddenly, I'm thirty years old and what am I doing with my life anyway? ... One night I came back from some idiotic scene I was doing and Peter comes rolling in on his motorcycle. He was at the beginning of his counter-culture trip. He'd just finished a scene where there was this huge fight in a church and he had his guitar with him and he was writing songs. And I realized that at least he was relating to something that had to do with the American culture, while I was making this ridculous movie about a young mistress of a married executive.'

So that was how it all started. There were those – inside her campaigns as well as out – who might have preferred it if she had waged fights in which she believed, rather than simply those that made her feel better. On the other hand – and with Jane, there was *always* another hand – her contribution to those campaigns was immense. Many of them could not possibly have functioned without her assistance. As she moved from one crusade to another, she left her fellow workers with the profound belief that they were more important than anything else in her life.

And she did not, contrary to what some people said, forget old friends as she developed new ones. She called to see Angela Davis in jail. 'What we need,' she said afterwards, 'is civil disobedience. What we need is laying our lives, our bodies on the line in massive protests.'

Jane did have time to think of more work, – like, for instance, another film to be made in France.

Tout va bien (*Everything Is Fine* is the English translation) was made in French with some English dialogue by Jean-Luc Godard, a man a number of Americans were quick to point out shared Jane's political views, and Jean-Pierre Gorin. Jane played an American radio journalist married to Yves Montand, a French film director who makes commercials.

It was more significant than merely teaming Jane with one of France's most prestigious and attractive actors. It was the most political film she had yet made and was replete with references to both Vietnam and the pill.

The film is little known, although it was one of the finest in which Jane has ever been involved. The story was controversial – focusing on the aftermath of the student revolts of 1968 in Paris – and so was her relationship with the director, who she decided was not quite her idea of a radical.

'To be a revolutionary, you have to be a human being,' she said. 'You have to care about people who have no power. Godard had contempt for people, contempt for extras. I'd rather work with someone ideologically very different from me if they have concern and humanity toward their crew.'

Of all the complaints levelled against Jane, lack in this regard has never been one of them.

Jane's next professional engagement was in a somewhat different show, although again Donald Sutherland was co-starring. This was a semi-variety stage production called *FTA* or *Free the Army* (it was also suggested that what it really stood for was *Fuck the Army*). Officially, the letters were meant to represent 'Free Theatre Associates'.

In fact, what it was intended to be was the antithesis of all the USO-type junketings that Jane had started opposing when her father became a participant in one. No protests that they were merely set up to provide entertainment for the men she cared about so passionately would assuage her concerns.

In a way they were a throwback to a previous generation; a throwback and a throw-out, an antidote to all-soldier variety shows like Irving Berlin's *This Is the Army*. What Jane was saying was 'This Should Not Be the Army'. But, like the Irving Berlin production, she and Sutherland took it literally round the world – in areas where American troops were stationed.

They tried to put the shows on totally legally. A request went in to the Pentagon asking for permission to perform on military bases on the same terms as the USO. Surprisingly, the Pentagon did not immediately say no. Instead, the Defence Department said that Jane and her colleagues should go to the commanding officers of the individual bases.

The first stop was Fort Bragg – because it had a reputation for being more liberal than other installations. The commanding officer, General Tolsen, said no. He thought it would be detrimental to the morale and discipline of the soldiers.

A 1,800-signature petition was presented to the general by men at the base, but to no avail.

Naturally enough, Jane took full advantage of that sort of backing. 'I don't want Bob Hope to have a monopoly on glorifying the war,' she said, perhaps unfortunately. She wasn't in the business of glorifying the war, although she couldn't deny that freedom to put on an anti-government show at all (even if off-base) was unlikely to be given in North Vietnam.

Next the group tried to use a public auditorium in North Carolina. That was turned down, Jane suggested, because of military influence. In the end, they put on *FTA* at one of the sort of coffee houses where she had made her own debut, talking to servicemen. Later, it was also performed for the crew of the USS *Constellation* when it docked at San Diego. Occasionally the show played to civilian audiences, like one at New York's Philharmonic Hall at a benefit paid for by a group called the United States Servicemen's Fund.

Jane put on US Army fatigues – and looked beautiful in them – in one sketch, and in another she imitated, somewhat unkindly, the First Lady, Pat Nixon. Donald Sutherland provided a radio-type commentary on a battle as though he were covering a football match. Sutherland, in another scene, imagined he was Nixon's TV adviser and suggested that the President brighten up his Press conferences by tooting a horn or 'wearing' a rubber chicken on his head.

Black comedian Dick Gregory – who had been on a 'fast for peace' – occasionally performed, too.

When the company arrived in Japan, there were noises from the immigration authorities that they would not be allowed to perform. The following day, however, the Japanese Ministry of Justice ruled that the show should go on – for three days. It did.

So did her relationship with her co-star. She and Sutherland were in love and in the midst of a short affair. Because it was being conducted so many miles from home, it escaped the notice of most people who normally charted the affairs (in the broadest sense) of the two Jane Fondas.

In May 1972, the show won a special citation at the annual Off-Broadway awards. Before long, *FTA* was filmed, as a combination documentary and 'live' variety show. Soldiers were interviewed and said what they thought about the war and fighting it. Others complained about military discipline and said simply and movingly, 'They just won't let you be an individual.'

Contrary to some of the stories circulating at the time, Jane did not advocate revolution in the movie. She did, however, call for as much 'radical' thinking in middle America as was evident on the East and West coasts of the nation. If it was preaching revolution, that was the extent of it.

Roger Greenspun in the *New York Times* commented about that: 'So much time is given to the audience, whose insights, though real, are neither original nor profound, that the actual performance comes across in scattered bits and pieces.... But as presented in the movie, most of the show doesn't seem very funny, except inadvertently – as when Donald Sutherland seriously recites the prose of Dalton Trumbo with a straight-from-the-shoulder solemnity that happens to be perfectly in keeping with his phony-preacher characterization in Jules Feiffer's *Little Murders* ... For all its agility and pressing close-ups [the critic mentioned 'an occasional glimpse of deep happiness in the eyes of Miss Fonda'] the film doesn't capture the spirit – or even adequately show the kind of experience that might have let it grow.'

By the time, they were home again, the romance between Jane and Sutherland was all over.

Vadim might have been glad that it was, although he no longer really fitted into Jane's life in any noticeable way. She said of him: 'The fear that threatened Vadim the most was that we would no longer be friends, and that I would take Vanessa away from him. But now he knows I would never do that.'

Nothing, though, would have surprised certain sections of America. When the Hollywood Women's Press Club awarded her their Sour Apple prize – for presenting the worst image of Hollywood to the world – it was no more than she would have expected.

Her third 1972 film, *Steelyard Blues*, seemed to confirm that view. Once more she and Donald Sutherland were teamed together. Once more she played a call-girl and he a customer, an ex-con.

But the combination did little to enhance either the film or the relationship. It made a few attacks on Establishment morality but on the whole deserved to be quickly forgotten.

There were some who believed that she would take her campaign into Vietnam itself. She did – but to North Vietnam. In 1972, she went to Hanoi, Ho Chi Minh's capital, and met government officials including the Vice-Premier Nguyen Duy Trinh. It seemed to put a stamp of officialdom on what she might otherwise have claimed was an unimportant personal visit.

While there, she broadcast on Hanoi's radio station – an action that set more hackles rising. Remembering the effects of 'broadcasting for the enemy' during World War Two, it was not an event calculated to win friends or influence uncommitted strangers back home.

One newspaper cartoonist showed Jane with a North Vietnamese officer and a gun crew behind her and a microphone in her hand, from which spouted the words: 'Enemy – Propaganda – Broadcasts – To – Demoralize – Americans – Still Serving – In Vietnam'. The cartoon was headed: 'Mighty Like a (Tokyo) Rose'. (Tokyo Rose was the name GIs in the Far East gave to the owner of the woman's voice which broadcast Japanese propaganda to them – telling them of revolution at home, starvation, and how a Japanese victory was always just around the corner.)

Jane denied that in her broadcasts she had urged American troops to disobey orders. 'I would no more tell the soldiers to defect and fight on the side of North Vietnam than . . .' She couldn't finish her sentence. 'The North Vietnamese don't need American soldiers to fight for them. They're doing just fine.'

The CIA later issued verbatim statements attributed to her. Among them were these:

'Tonight, when you are alone, ask yourselves: What are you doing? Accept no ready answers fed to you by rote from basic training . . . I know that if you saw and you knew the Vietnamese under peaceful conditions, you would hate the men who are sending you on bombing missions.'

'Have you any idea what your bombs are doing when you pull the levers and push the buttons?'

'Should you allow these same people and same liars to define for you who your enemy is?'

She was appalled by the effects of American bombing that she had seen. She believed 'profoundly that dikes are being bombed on purpose' to cause flooding.

She denied she was anything but an American patriot. 'I will fight to the death against any country trying to harm my country.' But that was not the case with North Vietnam, she said. 'They have done me no harm.'

She came back more keen on her campaign than ever, although there were those (inevitably) who said that she was shown only what the Communists wanted her to see.

Not true, she riposted. 'There have been approximately 600 POWs released. Of these only twenty-five said they were tortured and at least an equal number say they were not. I believe most were treated amazingly humanely. Have you ever seen any other group of returning POWs who look like football players.'

Commenting on the Government's 'Operation Homecoming' celebrations for returning prisoners, she said: 'Operation Homecoming has been a carefully orchestrated public relations operation on behalf of the Pentagon and the American people have no reason to believe them. The Pentagon has been lying to us for years about our involvement in Indo-China.'

No one could believe that the hawks in Washington or Hollywood would be particularly pleased to read that. Nor another statement in which she said: 'We have no reason to believe that US Air Force officers tell the truth. They are professional killers.'

She spoke of Vietnamese children who were victims of chemical warfare, children 'born with fins instead of hands, with no feet, with no tear ducts, with soft craniums resembling what we call, being a racist country, Mongoloid idiots . . .

'We are turning Southeast Asia into an automated murder machine. Yes, there are fewer American casualties, but is that all it takes to pacify the American conscience?'

That was just the beginning. She told reporters: 'I have no reason to feel the Vietnamese people are my enemy.' As for the American bombing of the country, this was 'all the more awful when you can see the little faces, see the women say, "Thank you. Thank the American people for speaking out against the war." '

In speech after speech she told similar stories. Thousands of youngsters sang 'Give Peace A Chance'. Kids shouted, 'Are you listening, Nixon?' And Jane, in her element, told them: 'I spent two weeks in the Democratic Republic of Vietnam. While I was there I saw four residences razed to the ground, not just bombing of residential areas. I saw schools bombed ... In Vietnam there is a saying that if you go out of your house you will meet a heroine, and I witnessed it. Everyone is a soldier. Everyone, as I sat at the hotel eating my meals, the men and women who brought me the meals, when the alarms and air raids would begin, within three minutes were in uniform with their helmets and guns...'

Some Americans did not like hearing stories about *their* air raids and what it felt like to be in one – from the other side; on the ground. It was the year of the presidential elections. Jane was doing her bit for Senator George McGovern in his hopeless fight against Richard Nixon's bid for a second term in the White House – Nixon was to win by a landslide.

Before voting took place, however, she said that American prisoners of war she had met in North Vietnam was begging their parents, wives, sweethearts and friends to vote for a McGovern victory.

The stirrings in Washington were considerable – although, once more, not nearly as much as might have been the case in the McCarthy era less than twenty-years earlier.

An attempt was made to subpoena her to testify about her trip before the House Internal Security Committee. The committee decided it might be 'premature'.

A petition circulated among some of the delegations at the Republican National Convention in 1972, calling for the indictment of Jane. But, like many things at national conventions, it fizzled away to nothing before anything could be done. That did not mean that people were not very angry about her.

In the House of Representatives, Congressman Richard H. Ichord introduced a bill to restrict overseas travel – brought on, he admitted, by his antipathy to Jane's Hanoi trip. There would be penalties of up to ten years in prison and $10,000 in fines for anyone who made trips to countries with which the United States was at war – unless authorized by the President. It was, said the Democratic chairman of the House Internal Security Committee, 'designed to inhibit the travel of people like Jane Fonda and others whose visits to the enemy camp and utterances over the enemy's broadcast facilities, tend to undermine the morale of American Servicemen, while rendering propaganda encouragement to North Vietnam.'

Mr Ichord said: 'At most her actions and statements are criminal; at the very least, a distorted sense of values. She has been used by North Vietnamese propaganda experts.'

In a letter to the Attorney General, Richard Kleindienst – later to resign because of his contacts with those involved in the Watergate hearings – Mr Ichord wrote: 'I am sure that you recognize the pernicious nature of Miss Fonda's statement to our servicemen and the seriousness with which nearly all members of Congress view her conduct. Although it might be fairly said that public support for American involvement in the Vietnam conflict is steadily declining, such aid and comfort to a nation with which we are engaged in hostilities is nevertheless condemned by the public.'

The Attorney General decided to take no further action.

Congressman Fletcher Thompson was more emphatic. 'I am a patriot,' he said, 'and in my opinion Jane Fonda is guilty of treason – undeclared war or not. I've sent my evidence of her behaviour in Hanoi over to the Justice Department and I've asked Justice to investigate.'

Jane, in response, said that she welcomed an investigation into her activities – and she would base her defence on the Nuremberg war crimes doctrine. 'Nuremberg rules define President Nixon's actions in Vietnam as war crimes and give every American citizen a legal basis and a moral right to resist what is being done in our names.'

She said much the same thing when she appeared on the David Frost and Dick Cavett TV shows – another indication of the paradox in which Jane was involved. On the one hand she was being excoriated by an important section of the American public. On the other, she was being given some of the most valuable publicity platforms in America.

The matter came before the Maryland legislature where a member of the House, Del. William Burhead called for her to be put on trial. He said he wouldn't go as far as having her executed. 'But I think we should cut her tongue off to keep her mouth quiet.'

Meanwhile, the US Justice Department's Internal Security Division said it was 'looking into' Jane's statements in Hanoi to see if she had violated the 1940 Sedition Act. Assistant Attorney General William Olson denied that she was actually being investigated, because, he said, 'Treason is not involved in the technical sense.' What his division was doing was holding an inquiry rather than an investigation. A nice point, but it meant that no investigation would be held and no charges would result.

By this time, even Henry had changed his views on the war. He made a TV commercial condemning the fighting. Jane couldn't have been more delighted. 'My father represents a lot of people,' she declared. 'He's made a wonderful thing for TV. A very large Church organisation financed sixty-second spots and he did four. They are just wonderful ... In the beginning when they asked him to do it – one of them was all about napalm and the escalation of the war – he said, "I don't believe this. We are not doing that." They kept coming back offering proof. By the end of it he said, "It is not enough to do a sixty-second commercial, I want to do more" .'

Not that any of that was enough for the younger, female Fonda. 'He always stops there,' Jane said, thinking about Henry's suggestion of doing more. It remained just a suggestion. 'He doesn't understand,' she said, 'that in fact he *could* do a lot more.'

Saying that, she wasn't merely condemning her father. She was expressing the same old heartfelt desire that he really be a lot more like she was herself. She wanted that affinity with him as much as she ever had before. There was something about her that was still a little girl who yearned to put her arms around her daddy's neck. Why didn't he give her more of a chance to do just that?

There were plenty of others who by now would not have minded putting a rope around Jane's. They were ready to believe practically *anything* about Jane Fonda. In April 1973, Republican Congressman Robert Steele nominated her for the title of 'the rottenest, most miserable performance by an individual American in the history of our country'.

Strong stuff. So was the decision of a Democratic Southern Senator to give her a special prize – of a one-way ticket to Hanoi.

Opposition was being expressed at lower levels, too. The state of Maryland's General Assembly had a resolution put to it, declaring Jane 'persona non grata' and urging a boycott of her movies in the state. And Jane's reply? Much more muted than before. 'I want to eradicate the emotionalism, to make people understand, to help them see the truth of all this.'

Another time, she added: 'The Nixon Administration has declared war on the American people.' Certainly, J. Edgar Hoover was continuing his war on Jane Fonda. The FBI, she said in June 1973, had obtained copies of her bank statements.

By then, in the midst of the Watergate scandal, no one was disposed to disbelieve her.

Other things at home were difficult to understand. She still thought about the Sharon Tate murder by the Charles Manson 'family'. The victim, she kept thinking over and over again, could have been her. That made her think about the values of American society. California was spending billions on consumer goods while a pregnant, beautiful film star was murdered.

One writer reported her living in a barely-furnished house in a 'run-down neighbourhood'. There were mattresses on the floor of the living room and anti-war posters were on the wall. 'As you can see,' she told him, 'this is nothing. Everything I have goes for my various causes.'

She needed to put things into perspective. That was why she didn't bother to repair the roof of her Malibu home, which was falling rapidly into disrepair, and why she used her Oscar for its most practical function – as a doorstop. As she said: 'Two pairs of jeans and two sweaters. That's all I need.' No mention of being down to her last mink.

Then she was found to have sold some jewellery. The inference was that she had put so much money of her own into the 'peace' campaign that she was now broke. Jane dismissed the suggestion in much the same way as she had thrown out any idea of supporting the war. The jewellery had all been inherited and she hadn't liked it very much. In fact, Jane rarely wore sparklers of any kind. 'I'm not broke or anything like that,' she emphasized.

The war was still, especially until the US withdrawal in March 1973, cause number one. With some good reason, she described why she was so keen on getting to the troops, particularly those in trouble: 'Most of the guys are poor and from working-class backgrounds. They couldn't afford fancy lawyers and psychiatrists to keep them out. They went over believing in the war, and they risked their lives. When they came back, they said, "This is crazy."'

Jane's problem was getting some degree of respect from the kind of people who could help influence the Establishment. Too many of them seemed to be saying to Jane, '*You* are crazy.'

Not much was now heard of her activities for the Black Panthers – although the FBI still stayed on her tail in this direction. They claimed it was she who led them to a group of Panther activists they had been seeking for some time – because they were found in a car that had not been stolen. As an FBI agent said: 'We knew Jane Fonda was in town. We called Hertz-Rent-A-Car, got the licence number of the car she rented and picked it up immediately. She doesn't know she helped us. We thank her.' Such irony was not calculated to make Jane Fonda smile.

But things were now beginning to change for her. Despite prognostications that her political work would put her on some grey list, she was still getting a tremendous number of offers of work, most of which she rejected. She didn't, for instance, want to play the Faye Dunaway role in *Chinatown* because she didn't think it good enough; and she rejected, too, the chance to make *Oklahoma Crude* and to have the Lee Remick part in *The Exorcist*. Neither of them she considered sufficiently 'meaningful'. But she did take another role which she considered right down her women's lib street – Nora in director Joseph Losey's new version of Ibsen's 1879 play, *A Doll's House*.

There was, however, a much more important move on the way. She was finally divorcing Vadim.

And then she was getting married again. Her new husband would be a fellow political activist, Tom Hayden, head of the Students For A Democratic Society group. Almost immediately, he was thrust in the midst of a couple of problems which manifested themselves during the course of filming *A Doll's House*.

One of these difficulties was of her making; the other was not. The one for which she bore no responsibility was that she was in the midst of The Battle of the Doll's Houses. The one for which she was held to be partly to blame was The Battle of the Dolls – Versus the Guys.

The first was the simple one of two people having the same idea at the same time. Just as Losey was getting under way with his larger, more expanded (by David Mercer) version of the play, Patrick Garland was directing his own more theatrical version with – Jane apart – a more conventionally impressive cast: Claire Bloom, Dame Edith Evans, Anthony Hopkins, Anna Massey and Ralph Richardson. This more stagy attempt was generally held by easily overawed reviewers to be the superior one. No one knew that when Jane started work on her film. In any case, it was clear to see that she was more concerned with her own personal happiness.

The engagement – before anyone said anything officially about a divorce – was announced in a house in Röros, the town in northern Norway where the movie was being shot, while a blizzard was in full force outside. Tom, as far as everyone else was concerned – since none of them had yet any inkling that a divorce from Vadim was on the cards – was there just to be with her.

Despite all their activism, neither of them, it appeared, had any difficulty in adapting to their chosen careers when it came to it. Hayden now announced he was going into full-time politics, and local Democratic groups were lining up to have him as their front man. Jane, meanwhile, got on with starring in *A Doll's House* and yet again, no one suggested that politics should have anything to do with her ability to take the role of Nora. As A. H. Weiler wrote in the *New York Times*, 'We have always thought Jane Fonda was a real live doll.' It was not the sort of comment usually directed towards a young woman branded variously as a traitor or an anarchist.

Joseph Losey shared the sentiments. As he said, 'I've thought for some time that this drama of a meek, middle-class wife who finally asserts herself would make an excellent vehicle for Jane.'

David Warner – playing Jane's husband – Delphine Seyrig, Trevor Howard and Edward Fox were her co-stars. The film cost less than a million dollars to make, which even in the early 1970s was regarded as 'low budget'.

That didn't worry Jane, who said that the role was just made for her. 'I think Nora is very intelligent. This may come as a surprise to some people who think of her as being flighty, superficial and a silly woman who suddenly changes. People don't become something that they never were before. You evolve. But you are always essentially the same person. Nora is intelligent. She is free like a bird. She has a very large, open generous spirit, far more than her husband's, but like a lot of women, in order to hold her man, she has had to reduce herself to the lowest common denominator, which in this case is her husband.'

Tom Hayden was not supposed to read anything into that, although more than a few who knew her plans were asking why Jane, with her views on women's and all the other kinds of lib, was again contemplating chaining herself to such an archaic institution as marriage. Perhaps she was speaking through Nora to explain her position.

Not that she was totally happy with the way the movie was being made. 'Ideally,' she said, '*A Doll's House* should be written by, filmed by, photographed by women and some day that will happen.' And she said: 'Usually if you see two women, it is two women competing with each other for a man, two women who have been talking about whom they love, talking about who has left them – relating to each other only in the context of men. Why? Because men write films, men direct films, because men photograph films and because men don't have any idea how women speak.'

Not long before that, she had told a meeting: 'What women's liberation is talking about is restructuring our country from the ground up so that everyone is liberated. Everyone. So there won't have to be any more role playing. Nobody's gonna have to go anywhere now and prove that they're men. Women aren't going to have to be docile sex objects and men are not going to have to be great heroes, bread earners. I would be so happy if I were a man in America today, to know that women are beginning to say "Give me some of the burden, I can shoulder it. I am capable".'

Joseph Losey would before long wonder whether it was a good idea that *this* woman was shouldering his new burden. 'Jane Fonda is hardly the easiest actress with whom to work,' was how he put it to me and that about summed up their relationship. 'We didn't get on. I found her selfish, difficult and often thoroughly unpleasant.' It was his assessment of a woman about whom, when work started on the project, he had declared: 'She has energy, honesty and passion.'

Twelve months after making that statement, he was telling the London *Daily Mail*'s David Lewin that he now felt somewhat differently about her and confirming the opinion he had expressed to me: 'She is confused, she wastes time and money on too many causes and she is unaware of other people, cruel to them even, to a degree I wouldn't have thought possible.'

He knew it was not going to be an easy movie to make when they first settled in at Röros. 'I knew this is a male society with male laws which are enforced by men,' he told Lewin. 'And I was certainly sympathetic to women's lib when I started making this film with Jane, whom I am still prepared to like. But after my experiences . . . I have become a bit anti.'

Losey wasn't a 'bit anti'. He was prepared to climb on to soap-boxes to shout his antipathy towards her. He was ready to organize fund-raising rallies in his battle against her. If anyone had suggested an *FTA* aimed at fighting Jane Fonda, he would have agreed to direct, produce and finance it all on his own.

It became a women's lib war from the start – particularly after Jane had unburdened herself of her statement that the movie should have been made by women alone. The men stayed in one hotel, while the women hired their own houses where they lived with their assistants.

'Jane Fonda seemed totally unaware of my existence, the existence of the crew or the male members of the cast including David Warner and Trevor Howard, who felt totally isolated. For the first week when I should have been rehearsing, they spent their time in their houses, sending in pages of notes on what should be done with the film.' That was not his only complaint. 'And Jane Fonda was spending most of her time working on her political speeches and making innumerable phone calls about her political activities. With a week wasted and no work done, I knew it had to stop.'

For one thing, he saw his minus-a-million budget flowing down the drain with all the phone calls. So he called a meeting, banned the women's assistants – he had by then realized that Delphine Seyrig was France's own Jane Fonda and women's-lib organizer – and the drinking of hard liquor. If the members of the party wouldn't agree that they could all work together, he was packing up and going home. In the end, an agreement was reached and the film was completed in only four and a half weeks.

There were other emotional problems for Jane, who took Vanessa with her while working on the movie and then wondered how she was going to be able to look after her. Vadim came to Norway, too – but just so that he could be with his daughter. There was no question of his trying to change his wife's mind about divorce. He didn't stay in Jane's house, naturally, but in the men's hotel.

When Jane was first called to start filming – on the Sunday – she said she wouldn't be able to show up, because her nanny was off duty. Then she agreed that Losey's wife would look after Vanessa. Fine. But then she told the director: 'I'd forgotten Vadim is here. He can look after Vanessa.' End of problem.

Or was it? Not really. The venom that Joseph Losey felt for Jane stayed in his system. He didn't like her and didn't like the way she reacted to the work. 'Jane Fonda has encased herself from being hurt by men,' he said, and added: 'And for a woman to encase herself like that is not an easy way to live. In a love scene on set, she will kiss energetically, but off-set she did not speak to any of the men and she shrinks from anyone touching her.'

The exception, he noted, was when she was with Tom Hayden. That at least did bode well for the future.

/18/

Jane first saw Tom Hayden on television – at the 1968 Democratic convention in Chicago which, with Vadim, she watched at the American Embassy in Paris. He was in the process of being arrested.

Later, he was one of seven men convicted of conspiracy (a verdict later overturned) in connection with disturbances in Chicago – the so-called Chicago Seven. Before long, he would prove to be, as far as she was concerned, one of the most positive of all the aspects to come out of her crusade.

He and Jane eventually met at the Winter Soldier investigation, sponsored by 2,000 veterans belonging to the Vietnam Veterans Against The War. They were all prepared to tell their stories about America's conduct in what they called 'Nam, demonstrating that the one admitted American atrocity, the My Lai massacre of 1968, was not an isolated incident.

Jane was one of the most active participants in the affair. Tom was another. But there were also off-duty moments and it was in one of these that the two realized that in the midst of the misery being discussed, they themselves had a great deal going for them.

She said that she admired his brain as well as his good looks – at this time he resembled Dustin Hoffman in, appropriately enough, the future film of *All the President's Men*. She had read all the five books he had written on politics, but most of all, she loved the way he laughed. As she said, it was unusual for a man so brilliant to be so good humoured. It would be a fact she would recall again before long.

On 16 January 1973, the marriage of Jane Fonda and Roger Vadim ended officially in divorce. She no longer called him 'Vadim'. Rather unkindly, when Jane did refer to him at all, he was usually 'the Crazy Russian'. Vadim has never said anything on the record – or off it to friends who would have remembered such things – similarly disparagingly about Jane.

Three days later, Jane and Tom were married in Los Angeles. The ceremony, described as 'free form', was held at the new home Jane had taken in Laurel Canyon. It included the singing of Vietnamese folk songs by a group of students from that country and the dancing of Irish jigs. By all accounts, a good time was had by all, including Henry, Peter and Vanessa – who at four years old was just about old enough to appreciate a party when she saw one. About a hundred friends of the couple were there, too. Jane wore trousers, Tom a sweater.

The ceremony was performed by an Episcopalian priest, the Rev. Richard York. He asked the bride: 'Will you, Jane, marry Tom and will you try in this marriage to grow together, to be honest, to share responsibility for your children and to maintain a sense of humour?' Jane wanted her husband to keep laughing.

'Yes,' she vowed, 'I will.'

The singing and the dancing were ready to begin, but the minister added: 'Although clapping is sufficient, one more thing has to be said, sisters and brothers. You have heard what Jane and Tom have promised. I declare they are married.'

Two months later, Jane announced that she would have a baby 'sometime next fall'. They admitted that wanting a child was the principal reason for marrying. They decided it would be more sensible to do things officially 'rather than hassle with criticism that would drain our energies from our real work'.

Hayden had a reputation for being a 'leftie' – a troublemaker in his way no less difficult than was Jane. Yet he was a glamorous figure, dark, good looking, with hair almost as long as his wife's – which she, like a number of women at the time, plainly found very attractive.

Jane, although never more mature as an actress and totally committed in her politics, was, in a way, like a little girl who had just made a conquest at a tea party (the kid she used to hate) when she was with Hayden. Even when they were on political demonstrations together, it was as though she were showing him off – and feeling very proud to do so.

When Tom planned a 'cook out' – it was also called a 'starve out' –

outside the 'Western White House', Nixon's California home at San Clemente, Jane was by his side, anxiously planning arrangements for a demo against the South Vietnamese leader Nguyen Van Thieu's visit to the President. Then Jane led the singing of the Viet Cong peace song, 'Twenty-Seven Years'. She also proudly played a tape sent from North Vietnam, paying tribute to 'My American Comrades'.

Later, when Hollywood paid tribute to veteran film director John Ford, who received the American Film Institute's first Life Achievement Award at the Beverly Hilton Hotel (Nixon was there, too; so was Henry), Jane and Tom were at the head of the 300 people demonstrating outside and shouting, 'Five, four, three, two – down with Nixon, down with Thieu.'

Sometimes, it was difficult for Jane to believe that life was not just perfect. If she had any problem herself it was still the familiar one of trying to reconcile her political beliefs with her theatrical and professional obligations.

'The problem with this profession is that you get famous and rich quickly and that tends to create insecurities. You can lose it all overnight and that makes for conservative thinking.' Conservative thinking was not a term that usually came to mind when discussing Jane Fonda.

'It brings out self-centredness in stars and it isolates them from reality,' she affirmed. 'Most people who become movie stars live in large Beverly Hills houses and don't have to face the everyday crises that most people have to face. So, generally speaking, while their hearts may be in the right place, their bodies don't tend to follow, except in the most minimal way.' She would get to become an expert in the bodies of the beautiful people of Beverly Hills, but for the moment that is another story.

Jane's own 'minimal way' was to be a good mother as well as a good actress and a good 'political animal'. In July 1973, she gave birth to her second child and her first with Hayden – a son they called Troy; in full Troy O'Donovan Garrity – names belonging respectively to a South Vietnamese patriot, an Irish revolutionary and Hayden's mother before she married.

Like many another new mother, Jane worried about the future for her offspring – particularly whether the family business would be good for them. She concluded it would not.

'Show business isn't for them,' she said in words that might one day be eaten. 'It's not a happy business, very competitive and not too intellectually stimulating. You have to fight to stay human and it brings out the worst qualities in people.'

Many people still thought that Jane frequently brought out the worst in herself. But now, slowly, the Establishment was starting to come round to her way of thinking.

In mid 1974, Jane decided to take action about what she now knew the FBI was doing against her. She took out a $2.8 million suit against the federal government. It was a propitious time. The word Watergate was on everybody's lips in America.

There were other things on *her* mind, however. The Arab-Israeli Yom Kippur War of 1973 had thrust the world into the midst of an energy crisis. She and Tom – who headed an organization known as the Campaign for Economic Democracy – now decided that finding alternatives to oil was vital for the nation's wellbeing. Both were scared stiff of the risks involved in nuclear power, the most frequently talked-of form of energy to eventually replace the viscous black liquid. That was why they thought, in California at least, there was an energy source just ready to be harnessed – the sun.

For Tom, and with Jane backing him every way she knew, solar energy had to be the next priority. Once, that is, Jane had got a few other things off her chest.

She and Vanessa Redgrave were now talking about a new film based on events in the life of the author Lillian Hellman – or, at least, they were then believed to be based on Hellman's life; more recently, much of her 'autobiographical' writing has been shown to be largely fictitious. Before the film was more than an idea, she and Vanessa spent hours discussing politics.

Ms Redgrave was decidedly more radical than Jane had ever been. Her principal crusade at that time was a Palestine state. Jane thought there was merit in that case and decided that the state of Israel was merely an American vassal that needed to be expunged. It was not a sentiment that endeared her to America's Jewish community – who not only formed a considerable part of the Hollywood Establishment but who had been some of the most fervent campaigners over the years for civil rights.

She dismissed American Jewry's support of Israel as simply a 'knee-jerk reflex'. The studio bosses, most of whom were Jewish, didn't like her any the more for that.

It was not a help to her career, but she continued her fights just the same. Once more, it was J. Edgar Hoover and his friends close to Nixon that represented her principal target.

She asked a federal judge to order a former White House aide to name names – and the judge agreed. The man she was aiming for was

Tom Charles Huston, who had suggested that President Nixon start wiretapping and similar intelligence operations against people on a list. Judge Malcolm M. Lucas accepted Jane's demand that Huston be ordered to name the people who were on that target schedule. She knew, of course, that she would be one of them.

In November 1974, Jane went back to campaigning in her more usual way. She did it via a film about the still-continuing war, *Introduction to the Enemy*, a movie she and Tom had co-directed with cameraman Haskell Wexler during a visit to North Vietnam and the newly captured northernmost province of South Vietnam in April. The movie began with a totally dark screen, black – until one realizes a lantern is swinging. It is a tunnel. A woman's voice asks: 'Is this where they lived during the bombing?'

From then on, the film swung like the lantern did. It was critically well received, exceedingly so. That in itself was indicative of the changing climate in the United States since US troops had left Vietnam early in 1973. What public uproar there was, was somewhat more muted than it had ever been before.

Nora Sayre wrote in the *New York Times*: 'The film seethes with small children; it seems quite amazing that there are so many Vietnamese children left alive or that smiles of all ages should be turned toward the camera. Miss Fonda and Mr Hayden function as unobtrusive guides. They journey from Hanoi to the south, crossing the Demilitarized Zone to the Quang Tri province.

'Miss Fonda interviews people about their work, asking why one chose to become an actress or a translator or a member of the resistance. The answers are thoughtful, decisive – as much personal as political.'

It was one of the nicest things said about her political activity to date and that too was indicative of changing attitudes.

And Jerry Oster wrote in the New York *Daily News*: 'At its best, it is an interesting look at, as a newspaper editor interviewed in the film says, "a small undeveloped country that history has placed at the centre of the world's contradictions" ... At its worst, it is an elaborate home movie.'

But an elaborate home movie would have looked too easy. Jane was never satisfied with the easy option. In fact, her press agent was constantly complaining of how with all the things he was having to record – an arrest here; a statement in Congress there – he was constantly having to change her official biography in a way that never happened with most film actresses.

Her next picture was slightly more bizarre. She played a cameo role in an Elizabeth Taylor movie shot by veteran director George Cukor in the Soviet Union – based on Maurice Maeterlinck's 1908 play *The Blue Bird*. The less said about that the better, which was most people's diagnosis. A more interesting idea seemed to be the picture about the American Revolution she was planning to make with Henry and Peter. Alas, it was never to happen.

What did happen, however, and it was slow and not always easily detected, was that Jane was changing her mind about a new kind of revolution.

19

Nixon finally resigned in August 1974 and the Vietnam War eventually became history. There were still causes worth fighting for: Jane still wanted to see more rights for Indians, and felt there was need for the women's lib movement. But it wasn't terribly difficult to detect a change in her approach.

Somehow, she was more keen to demonstrate the side of her that defined Jane Fonda more as a mother and housewife than as an activist; even more than as an actress.

The Haydens lived in the somewhat rickety second floor of a house in Santa Monica, just outside LA on the California coast, but not in one of the fashionable ocean-fronting streets. The walls were decorated in what writer Martin Kasindorf described in the *New York Times Magazine* as 1969 psychedelic. According to Mr Kasindorf, Mrs Hayden was blissfully happy and wanted nothing more of life than driving Vanessa to her 'experimental' public kindergarten in a battered stationwagon and pushing a trolley up and down the aisles of the local supermarket.

That was not quite true. She still, until the war ended, ran the switchboard at the Indo-China Peace Campaign offices.

But Henry noticed the change in his daughter. 'She has other commitments now,' he said in 1974. 'How long, they will remain priority commitments, I don't know.'

Yet she *had* changed and Tom Hayden had changed, too. Now the young activist was donning shirt and tie and announcing he was running for the US Senate in the 1976 elections. He didn't get further than the primary campaign that time; but it was one of the most impressive fights experts in that field of sport could remember, and Jane worked for him as though she were still waging a one-woman battle with Richard Nixon.

Hollywood rallied to his aid. Groucho Marx spoke at meetings and even though his old, shaky voice was barely heard, Hayden had the benefit of a telegram from the showman that brought him considerable comfort. 'Dear Tom,' he wrote, 'you can bet your life that you have all my support, including my arch support for your walk through California.'

Jane came out $300,000 poorer after the campaign, but a great deal richer in many ways. Fighting what some would call a more legitimate political campaign than any she had engaged in before, she evidently enjoyed the experience as much as Tom did. It did her no harm at all to show that, despite what her detractors had long been saying, she was not spurning the more conventional democratic roads to power. Jane Fonda espousing democracy was heartening.

Even Henry took part in the campaign. Tom Hayden was apparently the first man in his daughter's life of whom he totally approved. That, however, made her anger over what had happened in the previous few years only more acute.

By 1975, the extent of the involvement of the FBI in trying to frame Jane had already become known. That was when she and Tom decided to launch their massive 'breach-of-privacy' suit against the Government, demanding 2.8 million in compensation. A whole list of defendants was named, headed by former President Nixon.

Four years later, the matter was finally settled. The Government – by this time under President Jimmy Carter, in his last year of office before giving way to Ronald Reagan – admitted wrongdoing and would now adhere to surveillance guidelines established after the case began.

And the money? Nothing more was heard of it. The Haydens decided to drop their demands. As Jane said: 'Money is not really what we are going after. We were trying to illustrate a principle.'

It was a principle that was illustrated with all the colour and fervour Jane had been using for her fight against the Vietnam War and for equal rights for American Indians and Black Panthers. It was another crusade.

Every time a judge, as it went from one court to another, ruled that the evidence was classified and could not be revealed (and so, by refusing to allow the Haydens to see the files building up against them, seemingly destroyed their case), they made speeches, organized petitions and went on lobbying missions.

They were plainly right to do so. If Jane had said nine years before that she was representing the poor and the inarticulate, she was doing much more of the same now. Both she and Tom maintained that there were thousands who were victims as they were, but could not afford to do anything about it. Their case was costing hundreds of thousands of dollars, and was being handled by the American Civil Liberties Union.

The FBI and the CIA – it had moved beyond the FBI by now and the favourite federal *bête noir* of American liberals had taken its place in the story – were charged with violating Jane's civil rights, harassing her with 'overt and physical surveillance, burglaries . . .'

But slowly the information leaked out, the most damning of which was that the CIA had intercepted personal overseas mail addressed to Jane. (Even worse was to come: an agent revealed later on that he had bugged Jane's bed.)

A 'protective order' had been imposed in July 1975 by US District Judge Malcolm M. Lucas. Representatives of the Justice Department had begged that it should be instituted because 'persons not party to the suit might be harmed by prejudicial publicity'. It banned anyone from disclosing any information gathered in connection with the case.

Jane immediately dubbed it a 'gag order'. 'If this gag order had been issued earlier, the American public would not have known that the CIA was opening mail,' said Jane. The CIA did not attempt to deny that charge.

It was not news to Jane. 'To tell you the truth,' she said, 'at the time we were so sure that it was going on that it was something that was almost laughable.'

And she kept banging away at her theme, just as she had before, making statements about it when she addressed gatherings big and small which she still did. (She had recently been on a tour of Europe.)

When an 'Assembly to Implement the Paris Peace Agreement' was held in Seattle, Jane stood on the platform and demanded her rights. 'We are no longer a protest movement,' she declared. 'We are developing into a people's movement that intends to change the policies of our Government.'

When, in 1974, a rally was held in New York's Madison Square

Garden calling for an end of 'brutal' colonial exploitation of the Puerto Ricans, Jane was one of the speakers.

Meanwhile her own affairs took new twists and novel turns. The Internal Revenue Service decided that Jane's anti-war charity should no longer count for tax exemption. Almost immediately afterwards, they reversed their decision – after learning that otherwise they would have to tell Jane the methods they used to spy on her.

On the whole, she was becoming more and more pleased with the way things were going, and so was Hayden. 'Watergate,' he said, 'has given us legitimacy. The people who wanted to put the Chicago Seven in jail are going to jail themselves.'

People had even stopped calling Jane 'Hanoi Hannah'.

The magic of Fonda persisted, even though her hair was often long and lank and her slacks no longer showed signs of costing $200 a pair. Tom for sure had in public circles a certain respectability he had not enjoyed before. When he announced he would conduct a three-week school on Capitol Hill on the Vietnam War, hundreds enrolled to attend.

He said he believed it was important to work within the established 'grass-roots Democrats' rather than a third party which would have been impractical. He said that he had 'redefined' his political approach rather than abandoned his principles.

Columnist Roy McHugh had seen the writing on the wall quite a time before. 'When was the last time a politician, a general, an admiral or the state commander of a veterans' organization publicly denounced Jane Fonda?' he asked. 'Is anybody boycotting her movies these days?'

They were questions worth asking – for the answer was no. Jane cared passionately still, but somehow she no longer disturbed people. Normally that would have been cause for complaint on Jane's behalf. Now she had reason to be grateful for it.

/20/

T his was a more relaxed Jane Fonda than anyone had noticed for years. There were grounds for claiming that Watergate had proved correct all the things she had been preaching for so long. Undoubtedly the smiles and cheers with which the Haydens greeted the end of the Nixon era had had an effect on her outlook on life.

When she appeared on a network television interview programme with Geraldo Riera, the host said that it was obvious that a 'mellowing process' had occurred. Jane was 'still committed but not reckless any more'. She wouldn't go along with that, but she did say, 'I feel my life has meaning.'

She even allowed that some of the things she had said were 'inhuman and alienating'. There are members of Congress alive and well today who never believed they would live to hear her say anything like it. Henry felt much the same way. Even so, she did say: 'I would rather be sticking up for something I believe in and be a thorn in people's sides than go back to the way I was before.'

She even accepted that there was importance in Vanessa joining the Girl Scouts. She had herself dropped out from the Scouts long before she might have described the movement as pretty reactionary. Now she said she approved thoroughly. It was a 'socializing experience that is very important'.

Not everyone was so impressed. The American Legion's 55th annual New York State convention called for a boycott of her films after her 'preference for a Viet Cong victory in Vietnam'.

That did not seem to worry her either; and even if it had, she no longer thought of using the abrasive ways of saying so that had previously been her common currency. Even if she still believed in the things for which she used to say she lived, there was less of an intensity in it all. Tom's laughter had proved fairly infectious.

She even started making films that made people laugh again. She wouldn't do another *Barbarella*, but if she were ten years younger one now had the feeling that she would have loved to remake *Sunday in New York*.

Fun with Dick and Jane may have been conceived with that thought in mind. It had a few political overtones – an executive in the aerospace industry is fired and resorts to crime – but it was mainly intended to be fast-moving farce, involving another married couple who looked good together, even if their methods of remedying a parlous economic situation too familiar to many were not to be generally recommended.

Jane and her new screen husband, George Segal, were very attractive and, if it had been a better movie, one would have hoped for a reprise before long. As it was, the *New Yorker* described it as 'a nitwit mixture of counterculture politics, madcap comedy and toilet humour'.

The toilet humour referred to the conversation Jane conducted while sitting on the lavatory. The sequence was later removed from the movie, a fate that might reasonably have been applied to the remaining 100 minutes. In fact, the film was reasonably cheap – Jane's fee was reputedly $100,000 – and all concerned, including the stars, did very well from the box office.

Part of the profits – half a million dollars' worth of them – went to finance a ranch at Santa Barbara, California, which was going to be used as a headquarters for Tom's Campaign for Economic Democracy. (A year later, the Haydens were in the embarrassing situation of having to evict a dozen tenants who had set up home in the property. One of them reported Tom as saying that he could sympathize with them 'because he was a renter all his life and could never afford to own his own home until he married Jane'.)

Even if it did make her a lot of money, this was not its only virtue in Jane's eyes. She said she saw it as a comment on 'a false American dream'. Maybe. She was lucky that not too many also saw the picture itself as the kind of nightmare that would prevent her making another film.

It was, however, very much a time for self-assessment on Jane's part. In December 1977, she was forty years old. Was life going to begin at forty? She gave every impression that it was.

'I'm not afraid of growing old,' she said at the time. 'But that's not to say I'm in love with my wrinkles.' It was a terribly natural, feminine thing to say and there were not a few people who detected that and welcomed it.

As she added, 'I'm happier now than I was at twenty and if I can live another twenty years with all the wisdom and maturity of my forty years, that would be really wonderful.'

'I am an extremely happy and lucky person,' she said at the time. 'I have a good home life. My political life is focused in a direction that I know is right and I'm making movies that I believe in.'

That was a worthy sentiment. Even so, she could have been forgiven for still wanting to prove something. As she achieved – finally – respectability along with her maturity, she was concerned about the stinging nature of the response from those whom she would previously have regarded as her natural allies.

Jean-Luc Godard, who had seen her as such perfect casting for his *Tout va bien*, was totally disenchanted with her. So much so that he and Gorin produced a documentary, *Letter to Jane*, in which they said that she was naive and did no good for the peace cause at all.

What ought to have endeared Jane to some people was her obvious concern for people who considered themselves to be victims, yet didn't have the benefit of a big campaign behind them – like the time in 1977 when she was smuggled into a textile plant at Roanoke Rapids, North Carolina.

Workers at the J.P. Stevens factory had been complaining about conditions there to the point of organizing a boycott of their products, ranging from bedroom slippers to billiard table covers.

'I stepped through the door of the plant,' she said. 'The sound of the machinery – wall-to-wall looms towering over the workers – was deafening. The noise and the working of the machinery made the entire floor shake violently. I screamed just to see if I could hear and I couldn't hear my own voice. It was like being inside a tremendous machine. There was dust flying through the air, clinging to everyone and everything. It looked like a snowstorm ... I couldn't understand how men and women could work in such medieval conditions for eight hours or more every day, having to eat their lunches out of brown paper bags while standing by their looms. Even if you have a lunch hour, there's no place to go....'

Later, Jane posed with posters reading: 'Boycott J.P. Stevens.' Not long before, that would have been precisely what would have happened to her films. Now, though, it wasn't.

Her next major movie was to prove much the same sort of experience. She and Vanessa Redgrave were finally able to make the picture they had planned for so long, *Julia*, in which Jane played Lillian Hellman herself and Vanessa an American woman living in Austria and then Berlin, who in 1938 is murdered for her anti-Nazi beliefs.

The story was based on one episode in Hellman's set of semi-autobiographical sketches, *Pentimento*, and was expected to be the harbinger of a new era in films; new 'women's pictures' like *The Turning Point* with Anne Bancroft and Shirley MacLaine.

It was controversial from the start, particularly because of the line, 'I love you, Julia,' delivered by Jane, as a budding playwright who gets involved with anti-Nazi politics.

Jane spent hours with the real Lillian Hellman and found her a sensuous woman, passionate in many ways. She recalled seeing the way she sat – legs wide open so that Jane couldn't avoid seeing her 'satin underwear'. But she decided to play her much more straight.

Ms Redgrave won an Oscar for her role as Julia. She did not, however, totally win Jane's friendship. People working on the set say that Jane – of all people – complained about the amount of time Vanessa spent on her political activities, distributing leaflets and supporting the PLO. That was the moment when Jane herself finally decided to curb her activities, knowing when and where to practise them. To some, though, she gave every impression of being just as politically involved as the British actress.

Rosemary Murphy, who played the writer Dorothy Parker, was having her second experience of working with Jane – she was the great success, as the deceived wife of *Any Wednesday*. She told me it was 'like working with two totally different people'.

As she explained: 'In *Any Wednesday* she had been terribly, almost frighteningly strong. She felt she had to be vulnerable and you have to be strong to be vulnerable.'

In *Julia* it was totally different. 'It was all rather scary,' she remembered for me. 'I didn't agree with her, but I didn't want to argue with her because she was now so opinionated.

'Before, she had been sweet – even allowing for that wish I had that I had some of her chutzpah. Now, though, it was much harder to be buddies. I knew that she had boxed me in as a conservative – I was not, I was very much a liberal – and I didn't work with her long enough to succeed in straightening her out on that point. I found that interesting, because I had known her better – and her better side – before.'

Rosemary was impressed with one thing – the style of democracy that Jane practised. While shooting the film on location, Jane shared her apartment with her make-up woman and others in her entourage. She didn't eat a lot while making the picture – in fact, the director Fred Zinnemann suggested that she was fasting. Old ideas died hard. So did slightly newer ones. After a hard day's filming, Jane would go off to an exercise class.

Vanessa Redgrave was not the only Oscar winner on the picture. The Best Actor Award went to Jason Robards Jnr – he played Dashiell Hammett, Lillian's common-law husband. Jane, like the film itself, Fred Zinnemann, Maximillian Schell and Georges Delerue had to be content with nominations.

The critic Pauline Kael wrote of the production: 'After a while, it becomes apparent that Zinnemann and Sargent [the scriptwriter Alvin Sargent] are trafficking in too many quotations and flashbacks because they can't find the core of the material.'

Newsweek said of it: 'Fonda and Redgrave are close to perfection and the pathos and power of friendship they create is the movie's great virtue ... The film has its faults, some of which are legacies from Hellman's seductively graceful but sometimes ambiguous original ... but *Julia* is moving in its glowing commitment to the power of friendship.'

Jane herself was able to bask in just that power of friendship and was seemingly forgiven for the past when that year she was invited to preside at the ceremonies when Bette Davis received the American Film Institute's Life Achievement Award.

Jane was rightly generous to the star of a previous generation – who had a reputation for being something of a Fonda-type spitfire on her own account forty years earlier. Jane said that Miss Davis had 'redefined the words actress and star'.

People, meanwhile, were continuing to redefine Jane Fonda – and finding her surprisingly acceptable.

Most surprisingly of all, she was gaining acceptance in what so recently had been regarded as the enemy camp. After years of wanting to take other people's money and run, Jane was now going into business herself, with her own moviemaking production company.

It was true that by now virtually every star who was a star had done just that: made their own films and allowed one of the big studios who had scooped up all the profits in the past – and borne the losses –

to distribute them. But with Jane it represented the opportunity she had long wanted – the ability to stand up to those who had sneered at her and show that she was easily their equal.

Jane said of her decision: 'Nixon was President and I couldn't get a job. I can't say I was blacklisted, but I was greylisted. I was disillusioned by the exploitive quality of the few offers I was getting and by the cowardice of people who didn't disagree with my stand against the Vietnam War but who didn't dare give me a job. I was seriously toying with leaving the business. Instead, I decided to make one last stab.'

It was not something she could do on her own. She needed a partner, someone whose knowledge of the industry, particularly on the business side, was the equal of hers. A year or so earlier, there could be no doubt that she would, on principle, have chosen a woman. Now, though, the priority was making the enterprise work. She wanted someone who only had the business at heart. She found him in Bruce Gilbert, who had been active in the peace movement with her. They believed they had a great deal in common, mainly the idea of putting together films with a relatively simple theme of which they both approved. The result was IPC Films, Inc. IPC stood for – no one was ever sure. Jane said it was the 'Indo-China Peace Campaign'. Bruce said they were just a set of initials. They could have simply stood for 'Independent Production Company'. The simplicity of the name would be reproduced in the films they made. Or would it? If the plots were to be relatively simple to understand, that did not mean that the movies would not have messages or make people think. That became evident the moment they announced their first venture.

It was the result of a series of meetings Jane had had with wives and girlfriends of Vietnam veterans.

'I wanted to make a movie about those women, I knew I couldn't do it alone. I can't do anything by myself. I'm not a good business woman and I'm not good at strategies.'

But her first project she knew was going to be right.

In fact, it was precisely the sort of thing that would have been expected of her just a couple of years before. In *Coming Home* she played Sally, the bored wife of a United States Marine Captain; to while away the hours, she goes to work in an ex-servicemen's hospital. There she meets and falls for a crippled Vietnam veteran (Jon Voight), a man who tries to make life as normal as possible in the midst of all the medical and emotional torments. She tries to show him how much she loves him, even though he is paralysed from the waist down and she can demonstrate it only by helping him along, as in one of the most explicit of Fonda love scenes – she said she wouldn't do another of these after the *Barbarella* experience, but this was important.

The original story by Nancy Dowd dealt with the relationship between two women in the wake of the Vietnam War. There were hints of lesbianism as the wife of the Marine officer (to be played by Bruce Dern) is more and more disgusted with his obsession with Vietnam. Surprisingly – it might not have been the case a short time before – Jane did not think that was the message that had to be got across. Instead, she and Gilbert commissioned Waldo Salt and Robert C. Jones to play down the women's friendship and write another – 'heterosexual' – kind of love story.

Jane felt it equally important to state that this wasn't a conventional story of heroism – as though any Jane Fonda movie could be. 'No heroes ever came home from Vietnam. Men were killed and wounded while we watched that war on television, from the comfort and safety of our armchairs.' Both her director, Hal Ashby, and the producer, Jerome Hellman, apparently thought the same way.

Sally's friend, Vi, no longer a central but still an important part, was played by Penelope Milford. She told me: 'Jane always allowed everyone around her to work creatively. I always had the feeling from her that we were helping each other. She didn't socialize off the set, but she didn't change the moment the director said "Cut" either. She was always the same person privately as she was a working colleague. And I'm not interested in politics. There was no need to discuss it with her. I just enjoyed knowing what sort of a person she was. She just loved working and was working all the time.'

Most people thought that work showed. There were, however, others who thought differently. Movie expert Leslie Halliwell described the picture as a 'self-pitying romantic wallow'.

But Jane's acting was superb, and so was Voight's. They won the 1978 Best Actress and Best Actor Oscars for *Coming Home* and no one could deny that they deserved them. They were among the least controversial Academy Award winners in recent history. Another anti-Vietnam picture, *The Deer Hunter*, was Best Picture of the year; and Jane now had a new doorstop. (With two of them, she was contemplating using them as bookends; which showed somewhat greater respect.)

Jane might have been thought none too delighted with the choice of celebrity presenting the Best Picture award, John Wayne, who was making his last public appearance before his death from cancer. But she was unperturbed.

Just a few months before, Wayne had presented her with the award of the Hollywood Women's Press Club, who were making up for their previous gift of the Sour Apple. Wayne told her: 'I'm surprised to find you at the right of me.' She said, 'I'm glad to receive it from you, Mr Wayne.'

Others involved in the peace movement and political change at the time wondered about *Coming Home*. One of them who met the Haydens soon after the film's completion in 1978 told me these activists regarded it as 'too soft'. But she believed it had achieved what everyone concerned with the picture wanted – an awakening to the continuing legacy of Vietnam.

The sense of conflict she had for so long felt between her principles and her work seemed now to be part of the past. She was working harder at her career than she had for years. 'I'm making a conscious effort to be in as many films as I can – as a kind of good example to others. I want to show that you can go out on a limb for what you believe in and still go on working – and that the quality of your work won't suffer. There's a cliché that, when you get involved with left politics, your work becomes doctrinaire. That's just not true.'

Well, in Jane's case, perhaps only partly true. In fact, she would have a difficult job sustaining that argument. If you looked for political values in what she did – and it became a national sport to do so – you found them. That was one of the things she had to think about when deciding to do so much screen work.

'My friends helped persuade me that there was value in acting,' she said, 'and particularly that I could contribute through my film work. That's when I decided not to be so passive any more.' The man who helped her feel that way was Bruce Gilbert. Between them, they had a crop of new ideas that would both be sensible as projects for films and fit in with her principles.

Just occasionally she merely looked pretty – like the time she and Helen Reddy sang a duet together in an hour-long TV variety show. In between, there were still the Causes, although there were people who wished that there weren't. The *New York Post* in April 1979 headed an article with the cryptic instruction: 'Jane, you're terrific. But please get off the soapbox.' Jane, however, stayed firmly on it – although she got off to walk.

When New York tenants marched in 1979 to try to draw attention to their fights against greedy landlords, Jane joined them for a Tenants Unity Day.

Jane used to sit in at Hayden's political offices at the Broadway

Building in Los Angeles. 'She had this enormous energy: could start at six o'clock in the morning in the studio; raise a family and work in politics at the same time,' said a volunteer. 'She was a quick learner. She would see papers and read them and before long be able to speak on them. Tom was a tremendous influence on Jane. She respected him; someone who had done his homework, who didn't make a stand on an issue until he had it pretty well mapped out.'

Jane was to agree: 'I have inordinate energy and can't stand to waste time. That's why I get a lot accomplished.' So much that she was to admit: 'I've lived three different lives.'

She also said: 'I couldn't possibly balance my lives as actress, political activist and mother if I weren't married to Tom.' The impression now was that Hayden had stabilized his wife, and not just politically. It was noticed. At this time the *New York Sunday News* headed a feature, 'They've Stopped Hating Jane Fonda – Time Passes, Doesn't it?'

Indo-China continued to occupy the Haydens' thoughts. In 1978, they called on Jimmy Carter to intervene and stop widespread executions being conducted by the Communist Khmer Rouge government in Cambodia. That was an answer of sorts to the people who had called Jane a communist.

Just as the Haydens had changed, so had their political machine. They were now regrouping with the aim of establishing more progressive thinking in the Democratic Party, endeavouring to make the people who held the power think of not just solar energy, but also the disposal of toxic waste and the need for more low-income housing. They started 'chapters' all over the state of California.

Their aim was to let the people know how their elected representatives looked after their interests. Jane believed that the day when the country had to be run just by 'big business and big labour' and by elected representatives who were always far away, was over. The CED was there, both she and Tom declared, to keep those representatives on their toes, 'to have public pressure to keep them honest and a spotlight on what else was going on in the public arena. More people in charge of their own destiny.'

'Jane was very instrumental in going to various grassroots chapters events, auctions, raffles. Anything they had she would try to visit them, and help get them off the ground,' recalled the volunteer. 'She would get involved in all the strategy. She would appear at steering committees and Tom would be there and Jane would always put her two cents' worth in. She was never arrogant in how much she knew as far as politics were concerned. You always felt that she wanted to learn. She was quite humble. She never thought she was an expert in political science. She just had strong views on these issues and was there to learn and take part in the give-and-take.'

And she still believed in putting her political aims into her work. 'I take movies a lot more seriously than I used to,' she said. 'I refuse to do cynical films. The movies I make will have something to say.

'I'll be as far removed as you can get from a liberated woman, but I think it's important to show the conflicts and complications that develop when two completely different human beings meet.'

Life would have been easier, she believed, if only there were more good parts written for good actresses. Most people thought that there were as many good parts for women as for men – weren't there as many women in films as there were men? Not so, apparently. 'I believe parts for women aren't being written because the women's movement has grown to such an extent. The consciousness of women has changed in the last five years and old stereotypes are no longer valid.'

Politically, she believed that the issues to take up were the ones on which she could have an impact as well as being in her view part of the 'progressive political agenda'. She wasn't interested any more in simply emotional issues, she wanted ones that could be built upon.

It was never totally straightforward for her, though. In July 1979, she was rejected by the Californian State Senate as a proposed member of the California Arts Council. Governor Jerry Brown said the senators behaved 'like a bunch of little kids' – a bunch of little kids, nevertheless, who brought Jane to tears by their decision. The governor said: 'The fact that she holds political beliefs that make it difficult for some senators to be re-elected would only indicate that art must transcend politics.'

The Screen Actors Guild joined her fight. The Guild expressed its 'concern and dismay' and called for a censure on the twenty-eight members of the State Senate 'for a blatant negative abuse of power and [we] demand an investigation of the facts and a public apology to Screen Actors Guild member Ms Jane Fonda.'

As the Guild President Kathleen Nolan asked: 'If Fonda is first, who will be the second? Twenty-five years ago we were gutless. In the '50s we witnessed the carnage of careers. Actor testified against actor, writer against writer. We will be forever daunted by what we did not do.'

Jane expressed her gratitude to SAG. In a telegram, she said: 'I believe your action critical of the Senate's rejection proves that actors and actresses will not allow red-baiting to go unanswered. Politics should have played no part in the decision. Thank you not only for sticking up for me, but also for showing a lot of people that the fighting spirit is alive and kicking out there.'

Tom was still trying to decide what his own political future was going to be. His real aim was to defeat the Republican Senator S.I. Hayakawa, his target in 1976, when he didn't get beyond the primary. Now he wasn't sure if he would try it again, although at heart that was what both he and Jane wanted most. 'The radical or reformer sets a climate. The politician then comes along and inherits the constituency that the reformer created. My problem is to be both.'

As for Jane herself, she declared that her barring from the arts organization was 'Shocking' – 'shocking that a majority of the Senate voted to inject politics in what should have been a discussion of my merits as an artist to represent the arts community of California. These senators appeared to have forgotten the meaning of democracy.'

Two hundred fellow entertainers signed a petition which was featured in newspapers up and down the state, declaring that the decision was 'all too reminiscent of the 1950s'.

Sammy Davis Jnr said: 'What happened to Jane smacks of McCarthyism – no individual should be penalized for political beliefs.'

In the meantime, the Haydens concentrated on what they considered to be their immediate responsibilities and the work that had to be done as a first priority. And that was the coming US presidential election of 1980.

Tom said they agreed totally about the need to get Jerry Brown into the White House – ultimately, Jimmy Carter lost to Ronald Reagan – and added: 'We want to affect the politics and platform of the next President. We represent a stronger force than the pundits perceive. They'll ignore us at their peril.'

The only thing the two disagreed about was Jane's efforts to get Tom to be neat – which presumably pleased the people who complained about her own sloppy appearance just a few short years earlier. That, too, was a symptom of the change in Jane.

Not that she would have recognized it as such. 'I know people say I go off in a lot of different directions with a host of different causes. But my underlying strategy is consistent. My work towards ending the war in Vietnam was to stop American military imperialism. What I have been fighting in California is another kind of imperialism, the power of the US multinational corporations over one of our fundamental natural resources, namely food.'

But even as late as this, when there was a need to fight the FBI she screamed from the highest proverbial lamp post. The latest thing that bugged her was that news of being 'bugged' herself. Former FBI Agent Wesley Swearinger reported the news about the microphone that had been planted in the headboard of her bed. The Bureau denied it; Jane complained; but the matter died away quicker than might have been thought.

She still protested that wealth meant nothing to her and told anyone who asked that the house where she lived in Santa Monica cost $40,000 – although she wouldn't say whether or not she owned it.

'I couldn't care less about money. I've had my taste of wealth and all the material things. They don't mean a thing. There's a psychiatrist that goes with every swimming pool out here, not to mention divorces and children who hate their parents.' But she agreed: 'It's easy for me to say that I don't want anything because I have had it all.'

She admitted that perhaps things weren't quite as spick-and-span as they might be. 'Our house is not as clean as one run by some bourgeois lady who has a maid. But it's clean enough. Our children are very healthy. They eat regularly. And they get to school on time.' She applied much the same sort of logic to her work. 'I never took films seriously until I became politically conscious. Now I take out any lines I consider offensive to women or ethnic groups.' Besides, she didn't really have to work at all. By then, she was considered one of America's richest women – worth something like $2 million a year, it was reckoned. And she added – which was no surprise to anyone who had seen the Santa Monica house – 'We don't have the big overheads of many people and so I need only work when something interests me. I'm not interested in going to parties and hearing how much weight someone has lost.' She would change that last view before long, but that was another matter. Basically, she and Tom were trying to live as 'normal' a life as possible with their children – whether Jane was helping Vanessa with her schoolwork or Tom was teaching Troy karate or making the family dinner.

'Yes,' she agreed, 'I have a very happy marriage, but it's one of the few I know.'

Before 1979 Jane was making speeches, warning of another oil crisis in the light of the coming revolution in Iran. She was right. And Tom was right in teaching her about it.

What she did in her movies was, and had been for a very long time, much more her own thing. (She said that these days the industry was pursuing her 75 per cent of the time and she was pursuing it 25 per cent – which could be regarded as something of a comeback.)

That year's Fonda film, *California Suite*, has not had a good reputation – and her sequence as the successful woman executive battling
with her husband for custody of their daughter has been condemned
as the most boring episode of a portmanteau film about the various
people booking into the Beverly Hills Hotel. But this does a disservice
to both Jane and the man who now played her screen husband, Alan
Alda, to say nothing of the writer Neil Simon.

Jane says she took the part for that old showbiz reason, a challenge.
The character was so different from herself. But was it? She had known
the conflicts between family and profession (ignoring the causes and
all the torments that brought) and she had a daughter whose father
was no longer married to herself. One can't help thinking that perhaps
this was the most real Fonda of them all. That could, of course, be put
down to good acting. Her performance was nothing less than superbly
convincing.

It was what one would have expected of a Jane Fonda appearance.
All that she did was precisely that. In *Comes a Horseman* she made
a Western, as different from *Cat Ballou* as *Coming Home* was from
Barbarella.

The main problem with the movie was the title – it sounded even
worse in its full incarnation, *Comes a Horseman, Wild and Free*. The
picture was set in 1945 but its message was the kind that she and
Tom were still preaching as they stomped the country appealing for
justice for agricultural workers. In this case, the message was that
ranchers in Montana were coming under the heel of wicked landlords.

Jane had no difficulty in discussing the relevance of the film. 'It's
about a man and woman who want nothing more than to own a piece
of land and be left alone. But they end up fighting large landholders
and oil companies.' It sounded like a line from one of her speeches on
the big tour. To some critics, it might have been more appreciated in
that context than as part of a film.

Pauline Kael wrote: 'It's a film of few words (and about a quarter of
them mangled by the sound recording). The melodrama is smothered
under sullen, overcast skies.'

But Jane's performance, nevertheless, was not.

She had other ideas in mind. One of them was as far removed from
politics as the thought that Jane once used to spend her summers
sunbathing at St Tropez. The forty-year-old Jane Fonda was going to
find a way of telling other women that they could have bodies like
hers. But in case this seemed terribly frivolous – Jane would say that
women had a right to the kind of health that her plans would bring

them – she had a new movie lined up that would be anything but that.

Once more, the question of solar energy came up and once more the risks of nuclear energy were apparent. That was precisely when *The China Syndrome* was born.

21

By now, Jane Fonda was the best public relations organizer in the United States. Madison Avenue PR outfits spent millions on organizing prestigious campaigns to flood newspapers and TV stations with details about personalities or products that needed selling. Jane simply made movies that made money – and in the process got across messages that were more effective than all the tub-thumping in which she had been engaged for the past decade.

She had put the cases for the victims of the Vietnam War and the wicked landowners. Now she was dealing with the matter that was currently closest to the Haydens' joint hearts. But even she could have had no idea of how relevant *The China Syndrome* was going to be.

On 28 March 1979, a matter of days after the film went on release, Three Mile Island erupted. Until Chernobyl seven years later, it would be the worst accident in history at a nuclear power station. Radioactive steam burst from the towers of the station at Harrisburg, Pennsylvania, and people, especially pregnant women, were evacuated from the area.

At first, the power station managers thought only that a warning light was malfunctioning.

That was precisely what happened in Mike Gray's script for *The China Syndrome* – except that the outcome was not nearly as severe as it would turn out to be in real life at Three Mile Island and not one iota as catastrophic as at Chernobyl. Even so, the idea of a nuclear breakout from a power station that *might*, just *might*, have had disastrous results was enough to encourage not just IPC but Columbia, too, to take the plunge. They had no idea just how topical it was going to be.

Jane won no Oscars for her part as the TV reporter who, on a routine visit to the showplace plant, happens to feel the place rock – and stays with the story until the actual breakdown occurs. But it was perhaps the most effective thing she ever did.

This was as much a joy to watch as it was a jolt to one's natural complacency. She was the reporter who prided herself on drawing out the facts, yet faced the problem of having to deal with the problems of a kindly, fairly inarticulate production manager whose pride and joy this is – but who now accepts it is also a potentially lethal weapon. Jack Lemmon played the manager and gave a performance as moving as was Jane's own. Michael Douglas was also brilliant as her equally crusading cameraman, working in the face of opposition from both the electric company and their own TV bosses, who will not accept the reality of the situation.

Yet for all that, the star was the film itself; its plot encapsulated the anti-nuclear campaign much more tightly than the power station was able to contain its nuclear reactor.

Early on it seemed that the title of the picture would be as much a turn-off as *Comes a Horseman* had been. Except that with the events at Three Mile Island, the phrase entered the encyclopaedias. As Jack Brodsky, a Columbia Vice-President, put it: 'The minute someone says, "What does the title mean?" they're halfway to buying a ticket.'

What it meant was that if the core of a nuclear reactor melted, it could go so deep into the earth, the effect – in theory – would be felt at the other end; in China.

The studio's advertising campaign cashed in on that: 'Today, only a handful of people know what it means – and they're scared.'

It was a matter that had been concerning people in the industry for more than a decade. Indeed, it was early in 1972 that one nuclear scientist had expressed his fears to Michael Gray. 'If that were to happen,' he told the writer, 'it would be what we know as the China Syndrome.'

Gray had a title and a magnificent film idea.

He told me that he had tried for years to keep it *out* of Jane's hands. He knew she would be interested in doing it – but he wanted to direct the picture and he realized she wouldn't want him because he was an unknown quantity. It was on the basis of himself directing that he had sold the idea to Michael Douglas, who was going to produce.

'The woman's part was somewhat less in the foreground,' he told me. 'The two male parts were the dominant ones in my original story.'

Michael Douglas cast himself and Richard Dreyfuss in the leads. 'We expected an unknown to play the female part,' he said.

The deal was actually signed in 1977 – on the day that Richard Dreyfuss pulled out. He didn't believe that nuclear power was an important enough issue. So he doubled his price – which in Hollywood is known as a deal-breaker.

'That same day, Jane Fonda was at Columbia Pictures – with her own project.'

It is at this point that Jane's own idea for a film about nuclear power came into contact with Gray's. Jane had for years been trying to sell the idea of a move based on Karen Silkwood – a fictionalized version of the true-life story of a woman working at a nuclear plant in Oklahoma who had been killed in a car crash. The belief among her associates was that Karen had been murdered because she was about to break the story of the inherent dangers at the plant and the lack of safety precautions implemented there.

Columbia had put up some money for the Silkwood project but then decided they didn't want to make it. (The 1983 Meryl Streep version was backed by Twentieth Century-Fox.) The day Jane heard Columbia's decision was when *The China Syndrome* went 'on the rocks', as Michael Gray put it.

Someone got word to a Columbia executive that there was another anti-nuclear project being hawked about. Douglas heard of Jane's interest in nuclear power and, with Columbia acting as matchmaker, they met and immediately hit it off.

As Gray told me: 'She liked the script very much, but wanted it rewritten so that the female part became much larger, with some of the things planned for Richard Dreyfuss turned in her direction.'

A few weeks later, a dinner was held at the El Coyote restaurant on Melrose Avenue, Los Angeles. Michael Douglas, Jane and Michael Gray were there, enjoying a Mexican meal. Gray had done several black-and-white documentaries but had never directed a Hollywood feature before. He knew this was going to be his problem. Now he has to agree that 'it would have been insane for a woman of her standing to be directed by me'. At the end of the dinner he knew Jane was vetoing his directing role – although buying his script.

It was a touching moment. 'After the last enchilada, she put her hand on my arm, looked me in the eye and said, "Michael, I'm forty years old and hard to like."'

As Gray said, 'I knew at that time I was out of the picture. I was enormously disappointed. I had been working on that project for six years.'

But it was his story, with James Bridges as director. Bridges adapted the script to enlarge the reporter's role, to encompass most of what had been written for Dreyfuss. The remainder was given to the man played by Hector Salas, a sound recordist involved in smuggling out details of the nuclear leak, a character who – echoes of Silkwood – is himself run off the road as he is transporting incriminating X-rays. Jane insisted that the part be played by a member of a Hispanic minority group.

'I found Jane very pleasant,' Gray told me. 'She made the only intelligent decision she could have made.'

'Intelligent' is the word that seems to typify Jane at this time. 'She was amazingly professional.' Peter Donat, who played the TV station boss, told me. 'She was able to accomplish a shot with a minimum degree of fuss. Not only that, she knew precisely what the lighting had to be and how the camera had to work. Not many actresses know that sort of thing.'

Even so, she didn't lose touch with her other responsibilities at this time. 'She was always on the phone,' Donat remembered, 'talking about what time the children had to be picked up. And I didn't have the feeling that she was always playing the boss. She didn't swing that on any of us – and if anyone else had tried that, she would have spotted it. Similarly, I'm sure that if someone was sloppy she would have spotted that, too.'

Sloppy was not a word used in connection with *The China Syndrome*. In the *New York Times*, Vincent Canby wrote: '*The China Syndrome* is good and clever enough to work on several levels simultaneously: (1) as a first-rate melodrama; (2) as a story of big business, including the television news industry in which the people who present the news become more important than the news itself; and (3) as an ageless morality play about greed and vanity.'

Canby's newspaper questioned people about whether they thought a 'meltdown' could possibly happen. None of them really did, although the suggestion was made that a minor accident could set off a much more serious one.

Three Mile Island put an end to that sort of speculation.

Jack Lemmon and Columbia decided to stop their publicity campaigns for the film – they didn't want to be seen as attempting to cash in on the disaster for the picture's benefit. They need not have been concerned. Immediately, the film was a box-office smash. A picture that cost $4.2 million made $6 million in days. Columbia's shares jumped from $22.1 to $24.745.

The people who didn't like it were the corporate giants of the nuclear power industry. When Jane was invited to plug *The China Syndrome* on a Barbara Walters special TV show, the General Electric company withdrew its sponsorship of the show. GE said it would be 'inappropriate' to have anything to do with a programme that contained 'material that could cause undue public concern about nuclear power.'

As Jane was unfortunately able to prove, the public concern was anything but undue. So was any concern about Jane herself. As she said: 'When I was regarded as a pain and shrill, my phone was being tapped. I was being followed. It was not an easy time to be polite if you cared about what was going on. Plus I was new at it. My politics haven't changed, but I learned that change is preparing for the long haul and you have to learn to have patience and compassion.' And to know when things are working for you.

Jane had no compunction about cashing in for all she was worth – not as publicity for the film but to use the opportunities that were now being thrust in front of her for the fight she and Hayden had been waging so long against nuclear fuels. It would be too cynical to say that they now had a heaven-sent opportunity. What Three Mile Island did was enable Jane and Tom to tell everyone: 'We told you so.' They had been right over Vietnam. Now, their fears on nuclear energy were proved all too correct.

Jane immediately sent off a personal letter to Jimmy Carter. She demanded that he fire his Energy Secretary, James R. Schlesinger Jnr.

Never had the media wanted to publicize a Jane Fonda crusade quite so enthusiastically.

Nor to offer Jane Fonda more work. She was offered the part of Fania Fenelon, the half-Jewish woman who wrote the story of the Musicians of Auschwitz, the group who played Mozart – at risk of death for disobedience – as victims lined up for the gas chambers. She was too busy to take the role and it went instead – amid huge Jewish protests, because of her support for the Palestinians – to Vanessa Redgrave.

An easier decision was to accept *The Electric Horseman* (the similarity with the previous title related not at all to the storyline). This was about a man who gets fed up with being a salesman of breakfast cereals and decides to head for the wilderness. The cowboy was Robert Redford. It was Jane's second consecutive part as a newscaster. The two meet at a Las Vegas convention.

Vincent Canby said in the *New York Times*: 'Miss Fonda, in addition to being a fine dramatic actress, is a first-rate comedian, whether she's stumbling over a Utah mountain in her chic, spike-heeled patent-leather boots or suddenly becoming shy after a night well spent in the cowboy's sleeping bag.'

Nicholas Coster, who played in the film, told me he greatly respected her 'meticulousness – in her personal life as well as her professional'.

She didn't terribly like the 'neon jungle' of Las Vegas. 'Yet without compromising her integrity, the cohesiveness of the company meant so much to her that we ended up going to a club together as her guest.' It was a 'kind of big fun party – a circus, but it was a very wholesome evening'. Later, she shared Thanksgiving Day with the rest of the company.

'She was very down-to-earth about everything,' he said. 'She's a professional – and a very generous woman.'

Not that her generosity was noticeable when they first met. Things were very formal 'and not very friendly,' Coster told me. 'The night before we started work, my wife and I went to *Comes a Horseman*. I thought it was the best performance she had ever given. The next day I came to the set and saw the formal attitude with her. I just burst in and said, "I saw you last night in *Comes a Horseman* and I thought it was one of the goddamnest best things I've ever seen." Suddenly, the quizzical expression went and she said, "Oh, I ought to see it again!" '

She never needed to think anything of the kind about her politics. When Jerry Brown announced his candidacy for the US presidency that year, Jane and Tom determined to work for him. Tom became his energy spokesman and Jane was arts adviser. One local politician commented: 'Hayden and Fonda tell Brown to jump and he asks – "How high?" '

They undertook a thirty-two day, fifty-two city tour of America, stomping the country on Brown's behalf and calling for a new agriculture policy. Tom carried placards reading 'Support Farm Workers' and Jane another declaring 'Boycott Lettuce'. At least, it sounded a lot more peaceful than all the things she had been saying about Vietnam.

They addressed the biggest antinuclear demonstration in American history at Battery Park, New York City, in October 1979. It was organized by MUSE (Musicians United For Safe Energy) and among those taking part were such prophets of the seventies as Bonnie Raitt, Jackson Browne and Pete Seeger.

The Haydens said they had one target, 'unbridled corporate power'. And Jane put it even more basically: 'We have to think of ourselves as Paul Reveres and Pauline Reveres, going through our country town by town, city by city, warning people about the dangers.'

After New York, they were photographed outside the nuclear plant at Three Mile Island. They were not going to allow that to go away – even without a *China Syndrome* to plug.

But she did allow herself other thoughts. She was interested in new business ventures. And since she was telling everyone that at forty-two she felt twice as good as she had when she was 21, perhaps she ought to look in the direction of doing the same sort of favour to other women.

She felt that she wanted to 'invest in something watertight'. The result was the purchase of a gymnasium in Beverly Hills. She decided to call it Jane Fonda's Workout.

22

This really did seem totally in conflict with all her political views, but suddenly a Jane Campaign was putting the emphasis – to almost quote a film title – on Fun With Jane. But she wouldn't accept that there was anything out of character with what she had done. The Jane Fonda Workout would help women to improve their bodies. If they had better bodies, they would be more healthy. If they were more healthy, they would be able to ensure their place in modern American society.

There was nothing unfeminist about Jane's encouraging other forty-year-olds to wear leotards or pose in bikinis – both of which she was doing. On the contrary, this was carrying women's lib to what was only its natural outcome.

What was more, although it was situated in Beverly Hills, it wasn't in the swimming pool belt. The neighbourhood was about as rundown as was possible in Beverly Hills; and she decided that although she was going to make some money out of it, she wasn't going to charge outrageous fees for the regimen of dancing and exercises she planned.

As Jane said: 'Every woman owes it to herself to keep fit. You can't be liberated when you remain a slave to bad physical and nutritional habits.' And then came the point she hoped no one would overlook: 'Getting fit is a political act. You are taking charge of your life.'

She hadn't totally converted Tom to her way of thinking. 'My husband is a real Irish meat-and-potatoes man,' she said. 'But we're trying to eat more vegetables and grain. But I don't make any big deal about it.' No, not with Tom, or with the children. As she said: 'I sneak bran or wheat into their scrambled eggs or raw egg into their orange juice.'

As for her own exercise scheme, she said: 'The fastest, healthiest, most effective, interesting and rewarding way to lose weight is by combining vigorous exercise with a healthy diet. But you must exercise at least half an hour a day, three times a week, for it to have any effect.'

And, she said, 'You have to sweat. If I've got time, you've got time. I work long erratic hours, have a husband, children and a house to run – the works. I exercise as if my life depended on it, which in a way it does.'

She says that it wasn't until she was pregnant and thirty that she decided to change her way of living and start exercising. 'My body was literally telling me things. Sleep more. Eat better. I found myself drinking a lot of milk – something I hadn't done before. I no longer wanted coffee or cigarettes. I bought my first books on nutrition.'

In late 1979 when the Workout was planned and in 1980 when it was fully under way, neither Jane nor the top physical fitness experts she employed could have any idea just how far it would take her.

It also brought riches to a number of unauthorized imitators. Jane was asked to franchise her Workout to other centres. She always declined, because she said the ideas were her own and definitely not for sale. Unfortunately for her, other people then started copying her methods – stealing them, she would have said – without paying her a cent.

She was conscious of the effects of age. 'My pal Redford gets furrows and character lines, I get wrinkles and crow's-feet. It ain't fair.'

She met the same sort of cynicism about her next film, *Nine to Five*. In this she starred with Dolly Parton – not at all her normal type of companion – and Lily Tomlin in a picture about secretaries. True, the boss ends up being tied up and there's a lot of talk about sexual harassment. But was this a political statement, too? Did Ms Parton's extensive mammary development really help women's lib?

As far as Jane was concerned, it certainly did.

The story was by Patricia Resnick. She told me: 'Jane wanted to make a political statement about the problems faced by clerical women. She thought this was the answer.'

The critics were not quite so sure. 'The three actresses make an attractive team,' wrote Vincent Canby, 'but neither the screenplay by Colin Higgins and Patricia Resnick nor the director (Colin Higgins) uses them very effectively. It is clearly a movie that began as someone's bright idea, which then went into production before anyone had time to give it a well-defined personality ... Miss Fonda is an expert comedienne but the character of Judy Bernly is much too capable to seem especially comic.'

In the *New Yorker* Pauline Kael wrote: 'The picture is shaped as a feminist revenge fantasy.'

But there was worse to come: 'It's easy to forget that Jane Fonda is around; this must be the first time she has ever got lost in the woodwork.' That, as Miss Kael pointed out, was despite the fact that it was an IPC production.

For all the comments, the film was a huge box-office success ($59.1 million US rentals alone). Two years later, Jane was to produce a major TV series spin off from the movie.

Meanwhile, she was continuing to fight other people's battles – that of teachers, for instance. As she said in July 1980: 'I just can't understand how a movie actor can be paid a million dollars while teachers can barely pay their bills.' Her statement to *Forum* magazine was not the sort of thing most stars would make. But then Jane was never really conventional.

There were still the cynics. Gail Sheehy wrote in the *New York Times*: 'She is an actress always in search of a script for her life.'

And when she found one, people still criticized. In a letter to the newspaper, Carleton Sarver wrote: '... *The China Syndrome* is nothing more than a cheap shot. If Jane Fonda is to be "at the elbow of the writer" for future films so that "she can put across her message," then God help us all. She has amply demonstrated herself to be nothing more than a cheap opportunist, searching out the worst fears of the public for exploitation rather than for illumination.'

She was not fazed by that any more than she was by some of the other things said about her. If previously she had been accused of being pro-Palestinian, going to Israel in June 1980 was not to be seen as a political balancing statement.

She went to the Jewish state on what she emphasized was a 'non-political visit' in the summer of 1980 – and broke her left foot for her trouble. She was fitted with a plaster cast at the Hadassah Hospital and then hobbled on to visit the Western Wall.

Jane had slipped at the house in the resort of Herzlia where she and Hayden were staying while Jane was in the country to raise money for the Haifa Municipal Theatre. Despite the plaster cast, she appeared at the benefit shows for the theatre just the same.

Did this indicate a new as well as a more mature Jane Fonda? There were those who believed they had grounds for thinking it did.

(Two years later, she left quietly when the militant Jewish Defence League shouted and waved signs while she was taking part in a march marking the thirty-fourth anniversary of Israel's establishment. One of the signs read: 'Fonda is a knife in Israel's back'. Hecklers referred to her friendship with Vanessa Redgrave and the things she had previously said defending the PLO. Tom, then a candidate for office, stayed in the parade.)

In March 1981, she was saying the sort of thing most people would not have dared at one time to expect of her. That was when she made her statement about there being 'a lot of unnecessary abrasiveness and shrillness in the '60s, especially if you were inexperienced and somewhat naive, like I was. Because I lacked confidence in myself and experience in talking publicly as Jane Fonda, I would borrow other people's rhetoric – rhetoric that doesn't suit me.'

She was, however, still concerned with her principles, and still thinking about the energy crisis that a lot of people believed had now passed.

'Did you know,' she asked, 'and this to me is a staggering statistic – that if you weatherized 37,000 homes, you'd be saving more fuel than will be found on the entire North Slope of Alaska.'

That was not the usual sort of party chitchat. But it was Jane at her best when she was taking a break during a party scene shot for her next movie, *Rollover*. The film itself turned out to be no more inspiring than the mimed hubbub of the extras at the party.

There was the usual political message, this one about big business; but it seemed to get lost in an impossibly complicated plot in which Jane played the widow of a murdered banker. Her principal co-star was Kris Kristofferson.

'*Rollover*,' wrote Janet Maslin in the *New York Times* 'works neither as a love story nor as satire, and it isn't even the thriller it sets out to be.... Miss Fonda, lounging in gown after glamorous gown, makes Lee Winters' elegance an absurdly exaggerated trait, but her performance is otherwise so lifeless that the point gets lost.'

This was one to try to forget.

She wouldn't think of herself now any more as a revolutionary than the woman she played in the movie. She was a democrat – and emphasized that this was with a small 'd'. If she had made any mistakes when fighting her part of the Vietnam War, it was with a style that she yet again admitted was perhaps too abrasive. 'My only regret is that people still don't understand the war.'

But did Jane Fonda always understand ... Jane Fonda? When the *New York Times* asked her about Vietnam in the early 1980s, she replied: 'It's a country that was totally devastated by war and I'm sure that harsh measures have been taken to try to rally people around the cause of rebuilding and that means taking intellectuals and urban people and saying you've got to go into the country and work in the fields and they don't want to and they're forced to. Well, from our perspective, that's rotten but I don't know enough about what's going on out there to criticize.'

The words stuck in her throat as they found difficulty in registering in writer Michiko Kakutani's mind. She didn't know enough?

'Oh, Lord,' she added, 'why did I say that? No matter what I say I come off like an apologist and I'm not. I don't care one way or the other. I know what I know well and I feel what I feel strongly, but I'm not an organizer, I'm not a politician, I'm not a diplomat and shouldn't be.'

That was where she was wrong. She had been all those things. And, for all the abrasiveness, all the mistakes, all the difficulties, she had been effective, too.

That was why she was still given invitations that went usually to politicians and diplomats – to say nothing of political activists. And sometimes they still made her angry. That was an understatement concerning her reaction to an invitation from a South African student to come and visit him in his home country.

When the South African Government heard of young Sammy Adelman's invitation to Jane and Tom, they immediately put him on a five-year ban that prevented him from ever meeting more than one person at a time, and forbade him to contribute to publications or to attend political meetings. At the same time, newspapers were ordered not to quote him. Jane said she was 'outraged' and vowed to campaign on his behalf. It was to have slightly less effect than her outraged campaigns to end the Vietnam War or make people acquainted with the dangers of nuclear power.

At least her family relationships were now distinctly more healthy. Not just with Tom, which to anyone's eyes was idyllic; not with their children who seemed to be enjoying a much more normal life than those of most international celebrities. But with Peter and, most important of all, with Henry.

Peter became outraged when he dropped into Denver's Stapleton International Airport in Colorado and saw a poster declaring: 'Feed

Jane Fonda to the Whales.' The sign was pasted on a booth operated by the Fulson Energy Foundation, which promotes nuclear energy. He was so angry that he ripped down the poster and was immediately arrested for disturbing the peace and destroying private property.

Two important witnesses failed to show up at the hearing and the charges were dropped. Peter said: 'She's my sister and in my neck of the woods, you don't get away with saying anything bad about someone's sister, mother or grandmother.'

When Jane heard about the hearing, she told Peter: 'Go get 'em.' There was, however, a still bigger priority on the family front. She and Henry were going to go get 'emselves together – in a picture.

I t was an opportunity both would admit they had resisted. Henry, the now crusty, sick old actor, and Jane, the still attractive middle-aged daughter as set in her ways as a piece of cement. The idea of actually working together was a daunting prospect, a frightening idea.

There had been too many confrontations in the past. Too many times had Henry criticized his daughter and too often Jane had craved the love and approval of the father who couldn't begin to understand her and all that she needed.

Yet now, finally, they were agreeing to make a movie called *On Golden Pond* in which Henry played a crusty, sick old man and Jane his attractive, middle-aged daughter as set in her ways...

It was Jane's idea to get them together – she had been scheming for the means of a Fonda twosome for years. When she read the script by Ernest Thompson (it was originally a Broadway play), she said that she could hear the words of the difficult, retired college professor Norman Thayer coming out of Henry's mouth. It needed the force of a steam-roller to do it, yet what turned the tables was a joint conclusion that remained unspoken: both Henry and Jane knew it was going to be their last opportunity.

On Golden Pond was the story of an elderly couple – he approaching his eightieth birthday, she close to her seventieth – who every summer move to their house in New England on the shores of Golden Pond, where the loons scream.

This year was going to be special. They were to be joined by their forty-two-year-old daughter, Chelsea, whose main problem in life was not that she was divorced, living with a man who had a nice young son, but that she had never felt her father understood her.

Jane's company was co-producing the picture, but her own part was smaller than that of her screen parents. Yet Ernest Thompson's script made it to measure for her. A bespoke part.

The two Fondas had to agree that this first chance of working together since summer stock in Omaha could not be bypassed.

There was another problem: a mutual suspicion between Jane and the woman who was to play her mother, Katharine Hepburn. But for a time that seemed to be submerged under the bigger issue of how father and daughter would react to the notion, let alone the practice, of acting out their real lives. Except that it wasn't really their real lives – or if so, it was the screen life becoming reality. Not since Jane had been a little girl begging to have the name 'Lady' removed from her clothes tabs had father and daughter been together so much.

The setting was Squam Lake in New Hampshire, which was pretty well as far away from Bel Air and Santa Monica as one could get.

The unfamiliarity of the surroundings didn't help things along. Jane was amazed at her father's acting. 'Nothing seems to faze him,' she said admiringly – but, of course, the question to be asked was simply, 'Is this really acting?' She believed it was, and found the whole thing 'scary'. So scary that not a day passed in the early stages of filming without her throwing up. A worse symptom still was that she knew that she herself was overacting.

Henry, though, wasn't. As Jane said: 'The grouchiness is real and the difficulty in seeing that one can cause suffering for someone else – that's true of my dad. He doesn't always know when he's hurt somebody.'

Even when they were working, she had the feeling that her old dad was being impossibly selfish. Jane needed to look the old man in the eye when they had a close-up – even when only one of them was actually being photographed. Henry did not. In fact, he couldn't have been less impressed. 'I don't need to *see* you,' he bawled. 'I'm not one of *those* actors.'

Jane said that she felt like crying when he said that. On the other hand, she was having to remind herself, 'Great! These are the emotions Chelsea is feeling.' Both the real she and the imaginary Chelsea felt the same way. The real-life Jane Fonda felt herself saying: 'He can reduce me to feeling abject helplessness.'

She could forgive neither Henry nor herself for that.

As she told writer Lois Armstrong, the hardest line in the script was the one when she asked her father to also be her friend. 'I knew that for it to work, we had to be naked, as it were, prepared to reveal ourselves. That is never easy. We would read scenes at the dining-room table at the house. The moment I opened my mouth the tears came – so much emotion I could hardly control it.'

Henry also cried.

In one scene, totally unscripted, Jane reached out to her father and touched him. He was taken aback. 'Dad is the kind of actor who searches for the character and gets a lock on it – there aren't many surprises. But I knew this would take him by surprise. I could see his body start to shake as he fought to control his emotions.'

That was no more than the director, Mark Rydell, could have asked.

In the midst of this family reunion was the redoubtable matriarchal (although she has never in fact had children) figure of Katharine Hepburn, who simply by virtue of her prestige in the industry seemed extraordinarily intimidating to the younger woman. Jane's father was uneasy himself – at first.

Hepburn and Henry had never worked together before. But after the first polite greetings, that ceased to be a problem. Everyone knew that they were getting on superbly well when she looked Henry in the eye, said, 'Well, it's about time,' and then gave him a battered old hat that had once belonged to her lover Spencer Tracy. Fonda wore it throughout the movie.

Getting the two women together and to *like* being together was a different matter entirely.

Mark Rydell told me of the stalking exercises in which both seemed to be indulging as they sized each other up.

'I was worried about it,' he recalled for me. 'Here were these two immensely powerful women encircling each other like tigresses. Kate saw Jane as what she had been herself years before. Jane was concerned about Kate's authority and strength. In fact, it took time for Kate to realize that Jane actually revered her.'

He remembered the younger woman confessed that her main problem was that she feared she simply wouldn't be good enough. That was not something she had said frequently before.

'I was like a student around Hepburn,' said Jane. 'I was totally terrified. But then in rehearsal for our first scene together, I saw she was more nervous than I was. I paid close attention to everything she told me – and she told me even more about life than acting. She likes to test people. She likes to know exactly where you stand, how strong you are. And one of her ways of doing it is to come like a tornado to see if you stand up to it.'

But she admitted she treated Hepburn with kid gloves at all times, although she put it like this: 'I treated her with the respect she is due and I desperately wanted her to like me.'

And she did. When Henry's style upset his daughter, Hepburn was able to console her. That was a strange thing about Katharine Hepburn; she is so strong, so powerful, so important that many a young actress has been scared out of her mind at the prospect of working with her. Yet when other people are there to intimidate younger performers, it is Kate who comes to their aid. The British actress Toyah Willcox told me of the time she worked in *The Corn Is Green* with Hepburn: 'She saw I was frightened and that the director George Cukor was coming on strong. She told him not to bully me.' That was the sort of help Hepburn was now giving Jane Fonda.

'She put her arm on me,' Jane recalled, 'and said: "Don't be upset. Spence used to do that to me all the time." '

As Mark Rydell told me, 'They began trusting each other and became firm friends.'

There was another plus to it all. Tom was on the set a lot of the time with the children and Shirlee Fonda was there with her husband Henry, providing the gentleness and care that he needed. It was the first occasion that the family in that combination had spent any length of time together and all of them seemed to appreciate it.

'One day, I saw Shirlee standing behind his chair,' Jane recalled, 'and it suddenly struck me why they love each other. They're basically both simple, frugal Midwestern people.'

On the whole, the critics found nothing frugal about this distinctly Eastern story. *Time* magazine, which did a cover feature on the movie, said of it: 'In any season, *On Golden Pond* would be welcome.' It was a picture that 'addresses itself seriously and intelligently without sermon or sociology to an inescapable human issue: in this case finding a decent ending for a life'.

The *New York Times*'s Vincent Canby said it was very similar to the stage play: 'The movie . . . is still American cheese, but its stars . . . add more than colour to this pasteurized product. *On Golden Pond* now has the bite of a good old cheddar.'

He added: 'Miss Fonda, a brisk comedienne when her lines are good and a no-nonsense actress even when they aren't, survives her not-great role in *On Golden Pond*, even the kind of awful family reconciliation scene that happens with far more frequency in second-rate domestic dramas than in life.'

He concluded: '*On Golden Pond* is a mixed blessing, but it offers one performance of rare quality and three others that are very good. That's not half bad.' The best performance was that of Henry, 'one of the great performances of his long, truly distinguished career. Here is film acting of the highest order, the kind that is not discovered overnight in the laboratory, but seems to be the distillation of hundreds of performances.'

Pauline Kael in the *New Yorker* was not so impressed by it all. 'This isn't material for actors, no matter what their age,' she wrote. 'It's material for milking tears from an audience. Hepburn and Fonda are playing America's aged sweethearts – A Married Couple for All Seasons.'

She also said: 'Surely the only way to show respect for elderly performers is to hold them to the same standards that they were held to when they were younger, and it's almost impossible for Hepburn and Fonda to do anything resembling a creditable job of acting in a vehicle like *On Golden Pond*. It comes out of the Theatre of Safety.'

So what about the younger actress and her part? 'Chelsea is a terrible role and Jane Fonda plays it so tensely that she's like an actress in a soap opera telegraphing her psychiatric miseries. (In a lakeside scene, in a bikini, she looks spectacular, yet she keeps her body held in so tight that you can't believe she's breathing.)'

Fortunately, the Academy of Motion Picture Arts and Sciences took a more charitable – and a more accurate – view. Both Henry and Hepburn received Oscars. For Kate, it was her fourth. For Henry – apart from a special Award the year before – his first. But he wasn't well enough to attend the ceremonies himself. He had only just left hospital where he had been treated for a severe heart condition.

Jane received the Oscar for her father and then brought it to his home – she in her exquisite evening gown, Henry sitting in his chair wrapped in blankets.

Five months on, in the late summer of 1982, he was dead.

24

Jane's sadness at her father's death was compounded by the inevitable thought: at just the moment she had proved to them both that she had his approval, he was no longer around to bask in that joy.

Now she was doing all that she could to perpetuate his memory in a way he would have liked and which had some meaning: she headed a family plan to establish a memorial – a Henry Fonda Theatre Centre in Omaha, Nebraska. She was convinced that the place where it had all started was where it would do most good. Jane, Peter and Henry had all had their first roles there.

Henry had known of the plan to set up the theatre before it became his memorial. He actually wrote the first cheque. Now, it was up to Jane, her brother and stepmother – and Henry's sister Harriet Warren – to do the rest. The money poured in and Jane was happiest of all that it did.

As she has said so many times, she is an emotional woman – and all the emotion poured from her that one would expect. But she had the future to think of, too – and it had never looked more beautiful. Nor had she.

The Jane Fonda Workout had blossomed from its Beverly Hills gym to become a veritable movement. There were similar establishments in San Francisco and in Encino, not far from Los Angeles. Her *Workout* book, which followed as naturally as rain after black clouds, became the nation's number-one best seller.

She was speaking more frankly than before about the reasons for it all. Her mother's suicide, she now revealed, had come at a time when the woman had feared getting older. As for Jane herself, working with Henry had 'made me confront my own mortality'.

Apparently, millions of other American women were feeling the same way. Other actresses, from Sophia Loren to Linda Evans, brought out their own diet plans and their unique ideas on beauty – particularly for what was no longer being called the middle-aged. But Jane's was the most successful and the one to which everyone referred. They wrote articles about it, made jokes about it, even wrote songs about it for musical shows. It may all have stemmed in the first place from anxiety, but there was a happier side to the coin for Jane.

Those fears brought her almost as many dollars as her work in the movies.

She had good use for those profits, which were estimated to be at least $30,000 a month: before long, there were Jane Fonda Workout leotards, Jane Fonda Workout T-shirts, Jane Fonda Workout videos and the Jane Fonda Workout Record. By now her income from all sides was averaging about $2 million a year.

Workout classes were replacing Weight Watchers as the most fashionable thing for women to talk about at coffee mornings and around the dinner table – and without feeling guilty.

(Although by 1984 the bubble had partly burst; both the San Francisco and Encino centres were losing money and had to close. Jane's books and other items continued to sell like hot diet biscuits, however, and the original salon still made a profit.)

Jane didn't merely go home and count the figures on her bank statements. She was investing it in Tom Hayden's political future.

In 1982 he was back on the electoral stump again – running for the Californian 44th State Assembly District. This time, he won.

It was as much thanks to his volunteers in the Campaign for Economic Democracy as to Jane's money, but both were essential. Tom denied that he was a socialist. 'There are some people on the right and on the left who think economic democracy equates with socialism. But in my view, and I speak for both myself and CED, there is a vast difference...' He hoped that labour and consumers would be given what they needed most – a say in 'corporate decisions that effect them'.

When the election results came in, Jane was cheering loudest of all. As she was at the other big success in her life, IPC.

The company was basically still Jane herself and the man with whom she said she was involved in a professional marriage, Bruce Gilbert, with a secretary thrown in, and using office space that they rented when they needed it.

Gilbert came up with a new method of commissioning work. Journalists approached them with ideas for magazine or newspaper pieces and they optioned the movie rights – before the pieces were written. It may have seemed foolhardy but it gave them a great deal of potential.

Jane's next work for the outfit was a TV film which she said was 'as far from what I am as anything I'll ever play'. In *The Dollmaker* she played the pitifully poor wife of a Kentucky sharecropper, for whom the one redeeming feature of her life was her ability to carve small wooden dolls. It was a powerful document and the message, as usual, was there – about the wickedness of landowners to their defenceless tenants, forced to move to strange new pastures. It was based on a 1954 novel by Harriette Arnow which Jane had read in 1971 and vowed then to turn into a movie of some kind. Now she was able to play the heroine of the book, Gertie Nevels.

'I loved Gertie's courage in the face of bone-and-soul-crushing experience,' Jane said. 'I also loved her humility and her capacity for mothering.'

It was Jane's TV film debut; a beginning that was warmly welcomed.

'She is quite simply wonderful in *The Dollmaker*,' wrote John Leonard in *New York* magazine.

When Jane tells her screen husband Levon Helm, 'All my life I been doing what I was told ... you never asked,' Connor said, it may have sounded like a cliché. 'What ought to have clunked cliché-like counterfeit, is newly minted, true coin, rich.'

In the *New York Times*, John J. O'Connor wrote of the three-hour film: 'Miss Fonda may not, at first glance, be most people's idea of a plain and gritty mountain woman. But Miss Fonda is indeed an actress and, as has been demonstrated in films ranging from *Klute* to *On Golden Pond*, a good one. She has clearly prepared strenuously for the role of Gertie and the result is a performance that is nearly always spellbinding, even when the film becomes a bit too reverential about Gertie.'

Certainly, it was effective as a movie and women's lib didn't do too badly out of it either.

There were those who wondered whether the next IPC idea would be involved with America's space endeavours. Would she say the sort of nasty things about rockets as she had about nuclear energy – or, worse, about Vietnam? The White House rocked when, in June 1983, Jane attended the launching of the Challenger space shuttle.

President Reagan worried that an ex-activist like Miss Fonda was not the sort of person to be involved in his cherished space programme. No, she said, space was for everyone and should be bipartisan. Four months later, Robert Duff, the NASA public affairs director, left his job. He agreed that criticism over inviting Jane was responsible.

Others were equally critical – and Vietnam wouldn't die down either. A group of about a hundred war veterans gathered outside the UN building in New York, and cheered when an effigy of Jane was ceremonially burned. It was labelled 'Hanoi Jane'.

It didn't bother her any more. After all, she said in 1984: 'I've mellowed. But I'm still passionate about many things. It's so easy to lose your edge, to want everyone to like you. That's both human and dangerous. I'm trying to find a line between being human and being passionate – because the people I really admire are those who continue to feel passionate about things until they die.' And she told columnist Roderick Mann: 'I've spent a large chunk of my life doing very little that I'm proud of. I wouldn't want to go back to that. Helping to make this country a better place is important to me. Any change I can help bring about makes me feel good.'

Apparently she made other people feel good, too. In 1984 she was named by the World Almanac as the 'third most influential woman in the country'. To Jane this was a somewhat backhanded compliment, since Nancy Reagan was second. A Gallup poll the year later named her as 'the fourth most admired woman in America'. That was not at all the sort of thing they were saying about her when she went to Hanoi.

Even religion, which in her more activist days she was inclined to look at with all the benevolence of Josef Stalin, had new meaning for her. She said she made the 1985 film Agnes of God as 'a believer'.

In this she played Dr Martha Livingston, a psychiatrist who has to deal with the problem of Sister Agnes (Meg Tilly), a novice nun who claims she is visited by angels, has a baby without ever being with a man and then kills the child without knowing she has done it. A powerful performance – matched, it must be said, by Anne Bancroft as the mother superior who finds the dead baby in the girl's cell.

The film was shot in Montreal, a city in which it has not been unknown for Catholics to accept miracles of one sort or another – in the same way as Miss Bancroft's mother superior did.

'Agnes is about the conflict between faith and logic,' Jane said, and now she understood it perfectly – the conflict if not the logic. The faith was a little easier to comprehend. 'I have returned recently to a sense of the importance of a Greater Power in my own life,' she said when the film opened the 1985 Montreal Film Festival. 'I believe in a benevolent, loving God and I believe in the power of prayer.'

She only wished she had learnt that when she was a child – instead of being called a hypocrite by Henry when he heard she had gone into a Presbyterian church 'just to feel the peace and beauty of it'.

'I wish I had given my children what I didn't have,' she said, 'because I think being brought up with a formal religion gives a structure and ritual to our beliefs – a way to think about the real issues of life, such as what is its purpose and what are our responsibilities as human beings. And just sitting in a church, you feel a lesson in love.'

Her son was a believer, too. At the Academy Award ceremonies three years earlier, he had bowed his head and prayed for Katharine Hepburn to win an Oscar. When she did, he shouted, 'Mommy! I prayed for her to win and she did.'

Her own prayers had been answered in several ways – mainly, she would say, in regard to her marriage. 'My husband is very much an anchor for me,' she declared at this time – which wasn't at all a women's-lib thing to say.

'I think it's important that we have more movies that make audiences think, that challenge them,' said Jane. 'I think *Agnes* does that.' She was also fascinated by the character she played. 'She's a very professional woman, very sure of herself. But she needs a daughter and she finds it in Agnes. We all need daughters. We all have mothers and we all are trying to be mothers.'

And she added: 'I think there are just a lot of subterranean things going on that are beyond verbalization, a kind of texture and a resonance that very few movies have.'

Norman Jewison, himself a Canadian by origin, directed the picture and most people were glad that he did.

There was, of course, still time for more *Workouts* and their spinoffs. In January 1985, came the sequel, her book, *Women Coming of Age*. It discussed everything from the menopause and sex – women have more multiple orgasms as they get older, while men's sexual arousement decreases – to using teabags for removing puffs around the eyes.

The following year came *Jane Fonda's New Workout and Weight-Loss Programme*.

And there were still the Causes. That year, it was the turn of the farmers again. The *New York Post* was as sceptical as ever. 'It doesn't matter that Miss Fonda hardly knows a heifer from a hayrick or a silo from a sycamore. If there's a cause out there that attracts her fancy, she jumps aboard quicker than a conductor **working Amtrak.**'

There was even the Republican candidate who got into the agricultural row – by claiming that Jane's advice in her books to avoid red meat was endangering the prospects of America's farmers. Jane's response was that she herself did occasionally eat red meat – and pulled up at a hamburger joint to prove it. She devoured two Big Macs.

There were more personal causes – like the legal battle with her former lawyer Richard Rosenthal, who claimed he was due something like $2 million as his share from a number of Fonda projects. The matter dragged through the courts.

They were saying similar things about Jane's 1986 picture, *The Morning After*, in which she played an ageing alcoholic film actress involved in a murder mystery – hardly surprising, since when she wakes one morning to find a dead body lying next to her, she is the kind of woman who has nothing in her refrigerator other than a Mexican taco and a gallon of red wine.

Sidney Lumet was the director, with Jeff Bridges playing opposite her.

The part frightened her more than anything else she had done. She actually did drink while planning the film – as part of her inevitable research, like getting to know the hooker before she made *Klute*. It was a very dangerous form of research indeed. The drinking did not become addictive but the thought that it was numbing her mind did.

'I am not a drinker. I drink moderately. The trouble with my research was, I discovered early on, that when you're drunk you have no idea what you're doing. So you do the research and you learn absolutely nothing.'

She drank to the point of having a total blackout. 'Total. I know it can be total. To be honest, if I worked at it, I could easily become a drunk. One of the things Sidney had to keep telling me was to underplay the drunk bit a little, to modulate my performance.'

That wasn't easy. 'I wanted it to be totally realistic,' she said, 'but this movie isn't supposed to be the definitive view of alcoholism, it's a thriller.'

Vincent Canby thought it was also a winner; as he said: 'Miss Fonda and Mr Bridges are a winning, very funny pair of unlikely lovers.' As for the film itself, he wrote: '*The Morning After* becomes the kind of enjoyable, sophisticated comedy-mystery that requires much more talent to pull off successfully than is usually acknowledged.'

When she digested the reviews, Jane once more assessed her priorities. Her family, as before, seemed to be at the top of the list. When

Vanessa went to college at Brown University in far-off Providence, Rhode Island, 1986, Jane admitted she wept buckets. Troy revelled in the increased independence his sister's departure meant for him in his first year in junior high school.

Jane gave Tom every encouragement he needed – although she dismissed any suggestion that she was looking forward to one day being First Lady of the United States, a thought that would make J. Edgar Hoover turn in his grave as often as he had thumbed through the pages of the Fonda File. Nevertheless, Tom was being spoken of as a Democratic outsider for the 1988 elections. In November 1986 they were seen to embrace warmly when Tom was re-elected to the California State Assembly.

Certainly, they were changing. In February 1987, both Jane and Tom went to Poland – to offer their support of the Solidarity movement. Showing opposition to a Communist government would not have been their 'bag' at all a decade earlier. Jane had gone to the Soviet Union, too – to visit the long-term 'Refnsenik', Ida Nudel, in forced exile. Then, in October 1987, she flew to Tel Aviv to be at the airport when Miss Nudel arrived in Israel, a free woman. Jane hugged and kissed her at the airport. 'I can't tell you what a marvellous encouragement Jane was to me,' Ida told me.

Even relations with Vadim were better than they had been. 'We are very good friends,' the 'first Mr Fonda' told me in the Santa Monica house he bought so that he could be near to Vanessa.

When he wrote his book about the women in his life, Jane said she understood, asked him to take a few things out of the book and helped him with others. Deneuve and Bardot were less understanding. They said they would sue.

Then, in December 1987, came the big mark on the calendar. The girl who was once Barbarella was fifty.

Jane greeted the prospect enthusiastically, as became a woman who wrote a book on the subject: 'There is so much more when you are older,' she declared. 'There's a richer inner life, a wider circle of friends.'

The judgement of a remarkable woman. An actress who was a movie mogul, who was still a passionate believer in her Causes.

'There are days when I feel confident,' she said, 'and there are days when I feel I should pack it in, that I'm a complete fraud, that I don't deserve any of the accolades I have received.'

Fortunately, there are more days when others sit down and give the matter very considerable thought. Most of them come to a rather different conclusion. Jane is a very remarkable lady.

INDEX